DECIPHERED EMOTIONS

Emotional literacy is postmodern

© James Reynolds

Published by

ISBN 9780957306042

Typesetting by lifechariot

Printed and bound in Great Britain by
TJ International Ltd, Padstow, Cornwall

Deciphered Emotions

James Reynolds

CONTENTS

CONTENTS

Preface

Emotions! No one is free from them, and no one would want to be free of them. As an example in the chapter on anger points out, to be severed from emotion is a tragic loss of a system that's taken millions of years to evolve behaviour.

Deciphered Emotions is a comprehensive description of the core emotions that govern humanity. State of the art evidence-based knowledge is presented in a down to earth manner.

Distilled from thousands of hours of research, the article-length descriptions of individual emotions are drawn from current knowledge in the affective realm – everything to do with emotion. The chapters are underpinned by Charles Darwin's evolutionary perspective of emotion and updated with contemporary knowledge of neuro-biology, psychology and psychotherapy.

Guided by the author's two decades (over 20,000 hours) of studying perceptual philosophy, the straight-forward, everyday language delivers the punches of academic tomes in a relaxed air of common knowledge. The glossary gives concise, uncomplicated descriptions of the few terms the reader might like clarifying, and the notes pages list all the sources of evidence.

Deciphered Emotions appropriately refers to attachment theory, passive-aggressive behaviour and excess nervous system reactions accumulating into serious health complications. Throughout the book complex cognitive processes are simply laid bare and associated with neuro-biological functioning. The reader finds out which emotions are interconnected with other emotions and how and why this happens.

Introduction

Deciphered Emotions defines automated responses to perception: emotions! Contemporary research in affective science has made it possible to present unique and compelling evidence-based reading. Neuro-biological implications of emotions are explicitly drawn to show the link between perceptions and actions. Emotions are at the heart of evolution, for they are psycho-neuro-biological processes that have been bundled together to best adapt a person to act in specific earthly environments. Proven through aeons, emotions evolve to serve perception. Stagnant, they are not! Evolving, they are! As long as perception exists, there will be emotion.

Each emotion evolves to tackle a specific aspect of perception. As perceptions deepen, problems are more puzzling, for there is more data to interpret. A result of the accumulating knowledge from complex perceptions is emotions become more numerous. Each one tackles a specific set of events. The following pages describe over sixty of those reactions.

Throughout the book the depiction of physiological responses, such as facial expressions and body posture, are typically portrayed in their most intense form for the emotion in question. Less intense perceptions will cause the same expressions to be less pronounced. Any emotion can be felt at different strengths, and by describing the most intensely expressed features of an emotion the reader can easily imagine a milder form. The reverse is not so true.

Spread in chapters throughout the book are important philosophical insights about emotions in general – points that have consequence for more than one emotion. Chapters with a 'Key' beside them in the table of contents are considered to have such significance, for they contain information that allows the reader to make the affective realm more than the sum of its parts. Key chapters are principal chapters, for they're considered important emotions to understand in themselves, but they also contain insights that set the stage for the reader to appreciate the larger mind-body architecture that emotions animate.

Words marked with an * are described in the glossary. Words marked with superscript numbers, [10], refer to the sources of evidence given in the notes pages.

Admiration

Admiration is the emotion of marvelling at the characteristics of others. It is reached through astonishment at a positive thing. When a person is astonished, the instinctual reaction is preparation for another emotion. The eyebrows are raised, as the eyes open, letting more light onto the pupils. The posture becomes more erect as the lungs take a deep breath, and the body is poised to move away from the object of astonishment in the eventuality that danger is present.[1]

If the astonishing event turns out to be positive, the expression morphs into admiration or amazement. The eyebrows lower, the eyes softly reduce in size, while the open mouth closes and widens into a smile. Both admiration and amazement have a core element of wonder: pondering how something has happened. The mind settles, in the admiring process, on the appreciation of another's characteristics. Amazement is similar, but the appreciation would be placed on impersonal, external events. The duration of these instinctual reactions is linked to the intensity of the perceived event. Usually the first reaction of astonishment is measured in milliseconds and, less often, seconds. Nonetheless, the conviction placed in the wondrous event may last a lifetime and stay in memory for vivid visual recall for just as long. In an evolutionary sense, this suggests admiration has played an important role in human accumulation of personal information. Interest in developing and imitating skills observed in others is prolonged with admiration.

A broad smile with bright, positively charged eyes of wonder are the hallmarks of admiration and amazement. When people look at rolling plumes of thunderous clouds and see the ignition of forked lightning, it elicits an expression of amazement. In admiration the object of wonder is an impressive person rather than an impressive impersonal event. For example, when people meet someone who has achieved a confounding depth of knowledge in an activity they're interested in, admiration is the result. Also, if people witness a brave person who intervenes into a situation to stop a stronger, cruel person causing another to cower in terror, a normal response is admiration. Rather than live in a world where abusive actions are tolerated, some people put themselves at risk and succeed, and they receive admirable expressions. They possess something that enables them to succeed in the face of danger.

A spellbound quality is created by astonishment. Wonder migrates from astonishment to admiration as one emotion morphs into the other. Astonishment is a reaction to an event that is impressive enough to elicit immediate curiosity. When a person's character is first looked at through this neutral inquisitiveness, then deemed positive, wonder morphs into marvel. The eyes are free to move softly in any direction and be placed on any delightful feature. Warm respect and positive wonder create the smiling face of admiration.

Admiration is mistaken for envy and vice versa, yet envy has a negative sense of wanting the possessions of another (see Envy). Admiration, on the other hand, is expressed in relation to what people reckon to be positive characteristics. It relates to talents and aspiring appreciation. It has a positive moral overtone. Because envy is used in a negative light and has selfish and destructive overtones, it's often considered the opposite of admiration. Envy desires possessions whereas admiration appreciates talents.

Aspirations and hopes are included in this outlook towards others. The significant tone of this emotion is to appreciate and marvel at people's characteristics; we think they're marvellous! Admired people have a quality that others think has value, therefore admiration can hint at an admirer's potential directions in life. Admiration fits, like a jigsaw piece, into the subjectivity of whoever possesses it. It can be used to understand the structure of a person's personality.

The thoughts people have about the admirable traits of others can significantly change over time and are not set in stone. Yet, the process of astonishment which created the admiration places considerable conviction and respect in the admirable quality. Admirations are conviction encapsulated snapshots of wonder.

The characteristics that people admire will usually relate, somehow, to the overall positive outlook of a society and the memes* that are present in that society. Admirations create and follow paths of evolution as they motivate the development of skill-sets. One such meme is equal opportunities in the work force, and it's relevant to any industrialising country. Admirations evolve from generation to generation in terms of liking the specific talents and abilities of others in the present.

Nevertheless, admiration, in reality, endlessly supports the amount of appreciation that people have for a person's strength of conviction, or passion, when placed under adverse pressure. This seems to suggest that discernment that's coupled with courage is inherently marvellous. People will always admire the courage of others, and courage is probably the most universally admired emotion.

Admiration

Latin. *Admirari* = to wonder at.

1.   Respect and warm approval.

2.   An object of wonder, esteem; a marvel.

Amazement

Amazement is the emotion of overwhelming wonder at an impersonal, external event. It happens when people comprehend impressive things they're unable to understand – especially new experiences.

Amazement is reached through astonishment at a positive thing. When a person is astonished, the instinctual reaction, which usually takes milliseconds, is a preparation for another emotion. The eyebrows are raised, as the eyes open, letting more light onto the pupils to improve vision. The posture becomes more erect as the lungs take a deep breath, and the body is poised to move away if danger is present.[1]

If the astonishing event is deemed positive, the astonished expression morphs into amazement or admiration. Both are filled with positive wonder. The eyebrows lower, the eyes softly reduce in size, while the open mouth closes and widens into a smile. Amazement differs from admiration. The defining point that separates the two is that amazement is associated with impersonal events rather than the appreciation of personal characteristics.

The duration of this instinctual reaction is linked to the intensity of the perceived event. Most often, the initial astonishing reaction is measured in milliseconds and occasionally seconds, yet the conviction placed in the wondrous event may last a lifetime and stay in memory for vivid, visual recall for just as long. In an evolutionary sense, this suggests that amazement has played an important role in humans' accumulative knowledge of environmental events. The wonder of amazement helps sustain interests in external events.

Standing on the stone bank of a waterfall in the middle of a forest, a man realises the bulging torrent of water is caused by fresh rain water draining off the slopes of nearby mountains. He feels its violent motion vibrating the mass of rock beneath his feet. It rattles his bones. While trying to comprehend how drops of rain could be responsible for such powerful forces, he instinctively takes a step back. An enormous oak tree is speeding down river towards where he stands. While grazing the opposite bank, it rips bushes and branches from their majestic riverside residences before dumping them in its turbulent wake. The man stands fixed to the spot in astonishment. Then he watches in amazement as the oak tree roars past and over the waterfall.

'Rain drops did that!' he thinks to himself.

The origin of the word amazement comes from a maze or labyrinth. It describes the overwhelming wonder that such an intricate arrangement creates. As the depth and complexity of the event is first appreciated, milliseconds (longer with more dramatic events) of astonishment can be seen before the expression arrives at wide-eyed, smiling amazement.

Amazement

Latin. *A*+*Maze*+*Ment* = overwhelming wonder.

1. A feeling of great surprise or wonder.

Amusement

Amusement is the expression of finding something entertaining, pleasurable or funny.

Amusement is reached through surprise at a positive thing. When a person is surprised, the instinctual reaction is a preparation for another emotion. The eyes and mouth moderately open in coordination with each other in a fluid motion. The heart rate increases a few beats a minute as a little gasp of air is drawn and then held.[1]

When the surprising event turns out to be positive, the expression morphs into amusement. The eyebrows lower, the eyes softly reduce in size, and the moderately open mouth widens into a faint smile. This is often accompanied with a barely perceptible exhalation, a sigh of relief or a chuckle. When no harm befalls the persons concerned, people often find the mistakes that others make through inexperience amusing.

A mother watches as her toddler waddles by a wall mirror for the first time and shrieks in astonishment at his reflection. He freezes when the little person in the mirror shrieks too. Cautiously moving forward to greet the boy in the mirror, the toddler puts his hand up to the stranger's face. The little boy in the mirror does the same, and it startles him. Slowly the index finger is near the boy's in the mirror and their fingers meet. Puzzlement ripples through the toddler's mind as he finds the sensation solid and cold – not like a finger at all. While having the notion that the toddler in the mirror is not real, he slaps the mirror and shrieks once again. There's no reaction, only a strange symmetry. Chuckling with amusement, the mum watches as her toddler waddles to the corner of the wall mirror, peeks behind it, and then looks back at her with a wide-eyed smile of amazement.

A brief expression of surprise can be seen milliseconds before the faint smile of amusement adorns the mother's face. The word comes from muse, which means a diversion to think upon.

Amusement

Middle French. *Amuser* = divert, cause to muse.

1. The state of being entertained, or pleased.

2. Finding something funny.

Anger

Anger is created by perception of injustice. It's motivation to stop unjust things from happening to one's self or others. Anger is an under-appreciated *moral emotion*.[1] This under-appreciation of anger is partially attributed to people's fear of rage (see Rage), which is similar to anger but uncontrollable. Psychologists have documented that perception of deliberate and malicious injustice results in anger and aggression towards the offender.[2]

The initial instinctual reactions usually take milliseconds to appear and often go unnoticed. How long they stay, and to what degree the expressions are exhibited, is a reliable way to gauge how angry a person is truly feeling.

Inner eyebrows tighten inwards and down. The forehead follows the eyebrows, being stretched down and inwards, wrinkling towards the centre. Eyebrows contort, often rising on the edges with increasing escalation. Heart rate increases to a fast and steady pace. Breathing is heavy to oxygenate the bloodstream and muscles. The mouth is closed as the jaw muscles tense, and the nostrils flare to improve airflow to and from the lungs. The mind focuses with the eyes onto the object of anger.[3]

Blood flow to the hands and face is increased, often turning them red, while the nervous system releases endogenous analgesia – natural painkillers.[4] As a supplementary consideration, this may be the reason people immediately become angry when accidently hurting themselves – such as stubbing a toe or hitting a hand with a hammer. Nevertheless, the main evolutionary reason for anger's physical adaptations is to prepare the body for defence. It enables people to fight an aggressor or rescue a child from a dangerous situation.

The shoulder, chest, spine, and hip muscles all contract in varying degrees, lifting the torso, to create a firm posture from which to strike or evade a blow.[5] Hormones and neurotransmitters are released to prepare people for intense physical action. This influx of nerve stimulation and twitching muscle fibres often makes the hands shake. An aspect of this priming process shuts down access to unnecessary intellectual networks to increase reaction times by decluttering thought processes and relying more on instinct.[6] Cognitive abilities will be more inclined to focus on the silhouetted body language of offending persons – the physical parameters of a situation – to make continuous risk assessments that will aid overcoming an immediate threat, rather than focusing on the details of clothing or the time of day. A less intense version of *weapon focus** assumes control of thought processes (see Terror). Eye-tracking will follow the assessment of threats according to their perceived intensity – gesticulation of the arms, the movement and positioning of bodies et cetera.

Anger triggers the fight element in a fight-or-flight* scenario. It biasses decision making towards taking risks, and this mentality will affect all decisions that are processed whilst angry. These reactions, that vary from mild to extreme depending on the intensity of the emotion, characterise the subconscious, neuro-biologically processed, expressions that people are so often unaware of.

These hypertensive* (showing elevated blood pressure) biological reactions prepare people to tackle abusive behaviour. The closing of outer capillaries is proper when people face malicious actions as they're primed to stop and deal with physical danger. Be that as it may, these reactions are set into motion by perception alone. If people believe a misperception, they will become angry inappropriately and experience the same biological responses.

Anger is an appropriate adaptation for offences that are happening or are ongoing. It relates to the present. If anger is felt for a past offence, maybe the transgression is being thought about in the present tense. The biological responses of anger function to tackle offences in the here and now. To become very angry about a past event is maladaptive because it creates unnecessary neuro-biological load. Historical events cannot be stopped.

Inappropriate angry reactions can happen because of learnt, habitual ways of responding to others' behaviour. If the biological turning on and shutting off of defensive dispositions happens continuously, it will have adverse effects on health. Accumulation of such inappropriate defensive stresses over decades significantly contributes to serious health complications, including primary hypertension, cardiovascular disease, decline in physical functioning, and even memory loss (see Stress).

Nonetheless, good health is not maintained by suppressing anger. Studies show that people who repress their emotions are at a higher risk of developing cancer and having it progress more rapidly. Also, breast cancer patients who express their negative emotions, especially anger, are shown to live longer.[7]

There are psychological consequences that stem from not expressing anger directly. If anger is not expressed, people develop passive-aggressive[*] behaviours that will be detrimental to others around them.[8] Passive-aggressive behaviours are always created from a fear of expressing anger directly. For example, people may be angry with their boss but be afraid of the boss's possible disadvantageous reaction to receiving a direct expression of anger. Maybe, people have been taught that anger is a foolish emotion, which only irrational people use when frustrated by a problem. Perhaps, people have been told that anger is inherently *bad* and used by immoral bullies. The simple thought that emotions are inferior to reason or that anger is a prehistoric expression, although riddled with philosophical holes, is an idea that stops people expressing their anger directly.

The continual challenge of anger is to strike the balance of assertive self-expression from accurate perceptions. There is no *one size fits all*. It is important that expression of anger is appropriate to the situation that created it as then people stop malicious behaviour while keeping themselves from being abusive. At the same time, it prevents people from developing passive-aggressive behaviours that are so destructive to relationships in the long run, and it averts repression that causes metabolic* imbalance and acting-out* behaviour. Hence, appropriate expression of anger stops problems building up externally and internally.

How wrong an observed behaviour is perceived to be is directly proportionate to the degree of anger felt. Anger can be used to understand, implicitly, how unjust an action is believed to be. People can reliably use their feelings, which stem from conscious and unconscious sources, to gauge how angry they truly are. This may sound an obvious statement, but it is possible to ignore or suppress emotions. When people cognitively-avoid* their anger, they are disconnected from how angry they truly are, and they only have generic thoughts of how angry they should be, in such a situation, to guide their judgements. Generic judgements can be used to recognise over- or under-reactions of anger, but purely intellectual decisions are a massively inadequate substitute for the natural process of anger. Understanding different levels of personal anger provides a graph that can be mapped in real-time to the expressions of others. This gives people more accurate perceptions of their anger, but also other people's.

Anger is not a lesser or bad emotion. It can be used abusively, but it's not abusive. A hammer can be used abusively, but it's not abusive. Anger is used to stop many abusive things from happening in the world, yet many people fear it. Even if their fears are unfounded, people will do or say irrational things to stop people doing the things they fear. Fear is a far more unreasonable emotion than anger. This is frustrating as the angry person may be seen as a bully rather than a person who is trying to stop something wrong. The point is missed. The behaviour that made the person angry is overlooked. Offence and a grudge may be taken. A maladjusted fearful reaction is played out.

The fact that abusive people use inappropriate expressions of anger to make others conform to their plans makes the situation all the more complex. Abusive personalities may project false feelings of injustice onto others they want to control. The aim is to create insecure feelings in people. If people think they've done wrong, they instinctively reflect, feel guilt, and fear punishment. They may even backtrack and try to appease the person taking advantage of them. Anger can be used to elicit guilt as part of a guilt-trip. Such abusive use of anger could be delivered in a direct expression or in a more passive-aggressive form – 'God will be angry with you!' Insecure people are easier to dominate. Abusiveness creates and preys on insecurities. No *rubber stamp* of approval is given to such behaviour by anger, but anger can be used to abuse in such a way.

Clarifying where anger comes from is beneficial. What people do with their anger will depend on how reasonable they can be within their context. Having an angry expression without meaning can cause more trouble in the long run because people might misconstrue that it's an abusive attempt to control the situation. Also, it could be misunderstood as a selfish uncontrolled emotional response – mistaken for rage.

Anger motivates people to *stop* something from happening. It is like an alarm bell, saying, 'This is a code red situation.' Anger is an emotion that says 'STOP' or 'DO NOT DO THAT' and it does not usually say 'please?' In its varying forms it's a powerful emotion that is capable of motivating a person in extreme situations (through fury and ferocity) to serious courses of action regarding life and death. This is a reason people are so afraid of anger, but it's also why it's necessary for defence against abuse. Anger will rise to the challenge of any perceived abuse, and it will stay for as long as the perception remains.

The main problem and the defining point is that perceptions are not always correct. People can be too angry or not angry enough. Accurate perception is important. If people are too angry, owing to an inaccurate perception, then they will become mentally, verbally or physically abusive or heavy handed to some degree. This is where people use unnecessary force to prevent something from happening, yet, on the other hand, if people are not sufficiently motivated by anger, because of an inaccurate perception, then they'll be too passive and allow potentially abusive things to happen. The experience of anger is far from simple. Anger is a complex issue. How it's expressed is critical to its effectiveness in stopping an action – without a backlash due to over- or under-reaction.

Interventions, which aim to calm angry people, attempt to get them to reappraise the situation and show any misinterpretations of malicious intent. This is true for abusers who want to pacify their victims and avoid punishment, and it's true for carers who want to calm the hypertensive. The interventions try to change the angry person's view of the world by reducing any perception of ill-intent, so the anger subsides.

If people reflect on their behaviour and find it based on misled thoughts, are they willing to update their perceptions? When people decide they shouldn't be so angry, they may have to experience an awkward situation, admit they were wrong, and perhaps apologise for their excesses. On the other hand, when people decide they should have been angrier, they might have to experience guilt over not having acted sooner, admit they were wrong, and maybe apologise for their passiveness. Are people willing to do this? A balanced view leads to a balanced emotional response, but the cost might be an apology and feeling momentarily awkward through a mixture of embarrassment and guilt. Is it worth it?

Continually ignoring this process will lead people to neglect relevant information and so keep an unreasonable view of the behaviour in question. This ignorance (or cognitive-avoidance) will maintain inaccurate perceptions that create unbalanced emotions, which fuel reactions around the behaviour in question. This is what ultimately leads to abusive and selfish behaviour, not the anger itself.

People are not always right. Their perceptions are often inaccurate to some degree. The fact that people mentally evolve from generation to generation – the micro of the macro – means it's proper to update convictions and opinions about behaviours and situations experienced in life.

To get angry and stop a person who is being abusive is not wrong. To get angry and use *necessary* or *reasonable force* to stop someone using excessive force is not abusive. This is the very definition of justice. Anger and justice are bound together. It is a fundamental right that is written in law for all people in the West. Anger funding reasonable force is a good cause. People should not shy away from acting or speaking in such a way because someone thinks that anger is a bad thing. Do people let someone get away with abuse because another is unsettled by their anger?

There are many people who misunderstand anger. Some think it's a tool for abuse. Others look down their noses, with contempt and disgust, viewing it as an expression that only emotionally illiterate people use. These are understandable thoughts considering that people who were roughly treated with anger are bound to associate the emotion with unreasonable brutes. If they become a parent, they are likely to pass on their fears to their children.

Also, many memes that were passed into Western culture, thousands of years ago, were negative and naive towards anger. Eminent philosophers (such as Zeno Stoic) of ancient times worked from a basis that emotions were inferior to reason, that consequences in life were accepted as fate and that getting angry only made things worse. Such memes were influenced by religious thinking and then in turn influenced religious thinking. It's understandable how thinkers in ancient times began intellectual enquiries with such misconceptions. Throughout civilised history people have tried to make the things they fear taboo. They did not know that emotions were the motivations behind all their lofty enquiries.[9]

Such demolition of emotion was an aim of people in early civilisation. The over-intellectualised revival of memes to purge humanity of emotions by some thinkers in the age of enlightenment can be thought of as a misguided recurrence of a half thought through theory. Nevertheless, the most important of philosophers have never been persuaded. Darwin has probably given the most comprehensive description of emotions to date. A hundred years before Zeno Stoic was on his holier than thou mission to rid the world of emotions like anger (without realising the irony of his moral superiority), the first scientist and most accomplished philosopher, Aristotle, had said:

> For in everything it's no easy task to find the middle...
> anyone can get angry – that is easy – or give or spend
> money, but to do this to the right person, to the right
> extent, at the right time, with the right motive and in the
> right way, that is not for everyone, nor is it easy.

Aristotle concerned himself with establishing methods of using logic. He developed logical thought processes that became the foundation of scientific enquiries. It was impossible for him to understand the evolutionary processes involved in producing the best neurotransmitters to cause nerves to become appropriately affected, or how hormone cocktails infuse bloodstreams. There was no biology to explain the inextricably woven reactions to perception.

Humans look through a cleaner, sharper lens today. Imagine a man who accidently had part of his brain removed (due to a high-velocity shard of metal in a workplace accident) and it was found he had lost his ability to experience complex emotions. No guilt, no worries, no jealousy, no compassion, no admiration, no joy, no sadness, no despair, no anger, yet his intellectual capacity – Intelligence Quotient or IQ – remained within the top three percent of the American population even after extensive tests. That's not such a big deal, right? To some, not having to experience complex emotions might even sound desirous. Unfortunately for the man, who incurred the loss of a substantial part of his secondary emotional processing unit, he found that he could not make a decision and was permanently distracted by facts.

He would stand in a shopping mall for hours in front of an item he knew he needed, but he was unable to choose between the brands on offer. He would compare every minute detail of the products. Their size, fat content, sugars, colour of the packets they were in, their location within the isle, what shop sold them, the sell by dates, the use by dates, what pockets they would most comfortably fit in for transportation, how each would sit in the cupboard at home and so on. It could be said that he was too diligent in his decision making, but that would hide the truth. It was due to a lack of prompts from his right prefrontal lobe that was partly removed in the accident. He had no emotional cues from his higher-brain prompting him to choose one brand over another.

Results from such examples – the above is an amalgamation of two such cases – have taught humanity that emotions play an intricate role in motivation and the cognitive experience of decision making.[10] To separate emotions from cognition is not a desirable experience. It is a tragic loss of part of a system that has taken millions of years to co-evolve subsystems. The brain is so complex it leaves people dumbfounded, with conscious intellectual stupidity, when it's severed from emotion. A conscious mind is like a toddler looking in a mirror for the first time whilst the unconscious parent looks on encouragingly with amusement. Little do toddlers consciously understand how much they need parental guidance.

It is illogical to consider removing emotions. Illogical because it's impossible to do such a thing without rendering people senseless and indecisive due to lacking motivation. Reasoning is intimately bound with the emotions that are its motivations. Zeus did not gift humans intellect. It did not suddenly appear out of nowhere. It developed owing to perceptions that held such activities to be of paramount importance; perceptions of need give rise to anger if someone would maliciously ruin the possibility of attaining or sustaining what's important. Humans could not attain exquisite thoughts without the motivations for them. Given accumulating knowledge, it's increasingly foolish to consider anger as an inferior emotion. All emotions have a place in the evolutionary progress of dealing with reality, and anger has a central role.

Yet there's an important point to remember. If people believe a perception, then they feel the associated emotion whether the perception is true or not. Belief in accurate perceptions is the key to appropriate and just responses. This is no bid to promote rage in society or an excuse to get lost in an impassioned moment of power. Anger is a motivation to stop something wrong from happening. If people believe they have been cheated, they naturally feel angry, but are their perceptions an accurate account of reality? What are they trying to stop? How are they trying to stop it? Is it reasonable?

Anger

Old Norse. *Angr* = trouble, affliction.

1. That which pains or afflicts, or the passive feeling which it produced; troubled, affliction, vexation, sorrow.

2. The active feeling provoked against the agent; passion, rage; wrath, ire, hot displeasure.

Anxiety

Anxiety is fear of perceived future threats.[1] Anything that threatens a structure has the potential to make anyone who cares for it feel anxious. This includes threats to bodily structures, psychological structures, and social structures. The list is endless. The defining point is what people care most about; threats to those things have the potential to induce intense anxiety. People's perceived inability to cope with a predicted challenge is central to anxiety.[2]

It's normal to feel anxiety over one's ability to manage trying events – referred to as being *anxious*. Whereas a person who suffers from anxious experiences continually is referred to as suffering from *anxiety*. People suffering from anxiety for prolonged periods will show signs of stress that have wide reaching neuro-biological, psychological and emotional consequences.

When people perceive an event, they have an emotional reaction to it. Different events elicit different emotional responses. Each emotion is evolutionarily tailored for types of perceived events. Anxiety organises activity in people's cortex to detect potential threats faster than they would do otherwise.[3] For example – excluding brain damage issues, all people detect threatening faces faster than they do friendly or neutral faces, but when people are anxious, they detect threatening faces even faster.[4]

Anxiety is often experienced as pervasive thoughts of negative outcomes to future events. When intense fear or terror is experienced from anticipating potential threatening events, the fearful outlook influences the way people judge other aspects of their lives. This is called affect-infusion*. The negatively affected state of anxiety creates effortful, slow, and vigilant thinking.[5] This is an instinctive effect that makes people think about the perceived threat. It aids a successful resolution for the feared situation. Only, if people cannot find a resolution to the perceived threat – especially if it's an imaginary threat – then this instinctive rumination can trap them in anxiety as they continually refocus attention on a fear they cannot cope wisth.

In prolonged cases of anxiety, people can forget what they originally perceived as threatening, but their outlook has become biassed towards looking for threats. They habitually try to anticipate negative day-to-day issues. The thoughts may not regard direct life-threatening events, but the thoughts are perceived as negative and concern troubled experiences. This process focuses attention again and again on potential threatening events, whether they are imaginary or not, and it reinforces a continuation of anxiety.

The perceptions may be accurate or inaccurate, true or untrue, but anxiety is felt if the perceptions are believed to be true. A pessimistic view of the world can induce permanent anxiety. Pessimistic people not only sound down and stressed when they speak but are experiencing the anxiety that accompanies their perception of the world. People's psychological outlook changes their neurotransmitter and hormone levels according to their perceptions. Hence, they feel the biological effects of stress. Pessimistic people are stressed on a biological level.

The simplified psychology is that when people succeed, positive chemicals are released that make them feel glad or joyous. When people fail, the reverse happens and depressive chemicals are released that make them feel sad, slow, and even lethargic.

Human biology is affected by perceptions of success and loss. For example, the feelings that accompany moments of significant success are contrasted with the feelings that accompany a great loss. If people are told that someone they care for has just died in a tragic car accident, the loss will wrench their minds and emotions. The feelings of shock, denial, anger and despair will all be felt in accordance with the full force of a devastating loss. Yet after several hours of agonising emotional turmoil, they are informed that the information received about the death was erroneous. It was a malicious practical joke. Their lives would have been thrown into chaos for those hours. Because they entered the mourning process, they would feel exhausted by the toll of many depressive emotions associated with loss and anxiety from a suddenly transformed future.

Perceptions alter biological dispositions as long as they are believed to be true. In this way, anxiety can be devastating by reducing people's experience of life through the unseen biological effects of believing bad things will happen.

Serotonin and gamma-aminobutyric acid (GABA) are two of the neurotransmitters involved in regulating stress. Anti-depressants, alcohol and recreational drugs are commonly used socially, for better or for worse, to try to deal with the effects of anxiety. They stimulate or influence the same parts of the brain that are associated with success and loss, but they usually stimulate positive feelings as if success is being experienced.

People use chemicals to dupe themselves, temporarily, in an attempt to counteract the draining chemical effects that their anxiety has created. This can play havoc with people's internal perceptual framework as they subconsciously associate the feelings of massive biological success (stimulated by a substance) with everyday activities. The theory is that this skews decision making on a biological level. The biological memories of massive success are associated with mundane activities, and the natural experiential evidence that the subconscious uses becomes corrupted. This then blurs perceptions of success and loss because of erroneous biological information associated with the memories, or somatic markers[*] – subconscious biasses to cognitive decisions based on previous experience.[6]

States of mind that make people feel helpless or trapped are 'psychological environments' conducive for anxiety. Continuous perceptions of looming harms and past failures drip-feed depressive chemicals into people's bloodstreams and onto their nerves. If prolonged, this stress can accumulate and cause serious health conditions such as cardiovascular disease, later life decline in physical functioning, and memory loss (see Stress).[7] Anxiety is not just an outlook!

Stress Related

Anxiety

Latin. *Anxi-us* = troubled in mind.

1. Troubled or uneasy in mind about an uncertain event; being in troubled or disturbing suspense, concerned, solicitous.

Arrogance

Arrogance is having an inflated opinion of one's self or one's abilities.

It's caused by too much conviction being placed in an inaccurate perception. This misplaced conviction gives people emotions that are too strong for the reality of the situation. Expressions of abilities and beliefs seem out of place and overbearing to onlookers. At the same time, they seem like strong and confident statements to the people expressing them.

The misplaced strength of conviction may fool others into thinking they know what they're talking about. Nonetheless, it's a false security that leads to conflict when around people who know different. This can lead to arrogant people feeling embarrassed or belittled, which results in a bruised ego, and this threatens their perceived social status within a group. It's not uncommon for people holding arrogant opinions to bully a person, who is well informed, from fear of being seen as mistaken and thus undermined by personal error. Arrogance often leads people towards acting in a pushy manner. The scenario created by placing too much conviction in something leaves people on shaky ground. Views are often protected in a defensive manner as errors in judgement are guarded.

Being in a safe, confidential and self-reflective environment, such as a counselling room, is ideal for working through issues of arrogance.[1] Because the embarrassment and loss of status created by others is virtually eliminated, it's much easier to work with the actual inaccurate perception rather than the reactive behaviour. A caring friend can be good to work through such issues with. However the inaccurate perceptions are addressed, they always have to be reflected on and adjusted to better represent reality. This will reduce the misplaced conviction. Then the emotional expressions the conviction funds will be less overbearing and more appropriate.

Arrogance is a weakness. People unknowingly overstep the mark in confident displays that leave a chink in their armour that others can see.

Arrogance also annoys others as it 'steps on toes' and forces untrue issues with strong conviction. It stubbornly refuses to accept truths.

Arrogant views can be passed on from person to person and everyone inherits many. People grow and absorb the convictions of their parents, friends, teachers, groups and cultures without knowing it. It can be very difficult to tell what arrogant beliefs one holds. Personally held arrogant views so often can seem like normal accepted things, so people don't question them. They're overlooked.

In the Visual Cliff experiment, toddlers are placed near a sudden drop in the floor (a visual illusion). Toddlers approach the cliff and glance towards their mothers who are positioned nearby. Mothers are asked to use negative, positive or neutral facial expressions to communicate with their babies (e.g. smiles, nods, frowns, shaking of the head or no expression).[2] The babies' responses systematically and appropriately correspond to their mother's emotional cues. This includes crawling over the edge of the cliff if they are encouraged with a smile. Mothers can encourage or discourage their children with simple positive or negative emotional expressions. This ability to shape a child's convictions around behaviour is disproportionately biassed toward the mother – the primary caregiver – in a hierarchical structure relating to significant others. Just as babies that are several days old have been proven to distinguish their mother's milk and scent, a toddler will not respond to a stranger's emotional expressions in the same way. Babies are genetically programmed to form convictions from their mother's expressions.

Parents instil convictions in their children. This means that until people question their views they are largely directed by the convictions their parents instilled in them. The degree a parent approved or disapproved of a specific behaviour will directly relate to the strength of convictions their child inherits. This natural process evolved so children's behaviour can be appropriately adapted to their environment – to give children a greater probability of succeeding that's based on updates from their parent's experience. This conditioning of conviction happens whether the parent knows it's happening or not. Meme inherited principles are idiosyncratic. They are unique to every individual. This represents the most significant way people can express too much conviction in an ability or opinion without realising it.

On the other hand, people do not only receive thoughts endowed with too much conviction from psychological processes alone. Drug users are very susceptible to developing arrogant views. Their perceptions are sometimes massively altered. They feel the biologically positive feelings that usually accompany experiences of great success. Strong convictions and subconscious biasses are placed in these altered perceptions. The biological sensations, of say elation, that naturally would be created by perceiving massive success are associated with behaviours in no way remarkable.

The theory is that this skews people's biological and neurological memory, for it creates errors in people's instinctive way of relating to the memorised events. The biological portion of the memories – somatic markers[*] – then misrepresent reality and associate massive conviction with thoughts and behaviours that do not deserve such conviction and bias.[3] There are no foundations to those perceptions. No enduring step-by-step process takes drug users to their lofty heights. This represents a mismatch between the subjective[*] value of a memory and reality that subsequently biasses their decisions inappropriately. Long-term drug abuse can leave people expressing weird and wonderful views with a conviction that is hard to justify for the reasonable sober person.

John Lennon once claimed that the Beatles were 'bigger than Jesus'. Margaret Thatcher once said 'there is no such thing as society!' A frequently *high* member of a left-wing pop band that thinks his group is bigger than Jesus. An elected, right-wing, conviction politician in charge of organising British society who does not believe such a thing as society exists. Arrogance is not limited to left-wing or right-wing thoughts. Arrogant views support the psychological architecture of the people that hold them, but people are boldly endowed with too much conviction.

The views *prop up* the inclinations and ideologies of the people that hold them, but the views do not represent an accurate perception of reality.

Although people do not have to be ignorant to be arrogant, a similar situation will also occur for people who use ignorance excessively. Their views will have denied countless reasonable arguments, gestures and suggestions. This again leads to perceptions that are maladjusted and inaccurate to the reality of a situation, so they will hold too much conviction in their perceptions. The arrogance of ignorance is for opposite reasons when compared with the drug user's arrogance. Whereas drug users let wildly *out there* perceptions alter their awareness, ignorant people let nothing in to alter theirs. Nevertheless, both lead to the development of arrogant views.

Arrogance is a troublesome emotion that's related to misplaced and inflated convictions.

Arrogance

Latin. *Arrogantem* = assuming, overbearing, insolent.

1. The taking of too much upon one's self as one's right; the assertion of unwarrantable claims in respect of one's own importance; undue assumption of dignity, authority, or knowledge; aggressive conceit, presumption, or haughtiness, overbearing.

Astonishment

Astonishment is an expression of great surprise. It's created by a sudden and unexpected event. The original word comes from Latin and means 'to be thunderstruck'. Astonishment is an instinctive tactical response which interrupts conscious activity to process unexpected changes in the world.[1] Whilst priming the body for action, it forces the mind to go blank and organises brain processes with an all-consuming receptivity to external events. This emotion, most often measured in milliseconds, is an instinctive preparation for another longer lasting emotion. Astonishment is always bonded to another immediately emerging emotion.

When an intensely sudden and unexpected event happens, much of people's neurological and psychological architecture is shut-off from conscious access. There's a narrowing of focus as attention is redirected to assess the new event.[2] The eyes, mouth and lungs open in synchronisation with each other as a deep breath is drawn and held. The degree to which astonishment assumes control over behaviour is dependent on the intensity of the unexpected event. People's perceived intensity of an event can be gauged through the sound they make as a crowd. The crowd instinctively inhale, and it produces a 'haarrr' sound as the air passes through their mouths and their suddenly opened larynxes on its way into their lungs. More intense events produce a longer and louder 'haaaarrrrrrr'.

Think of a World Cup football match when a player makes a skilful shot in an important game. Flying in a big arc the ball speeds towards the goal. The goalkeeper jumps at full stretch with one hand desperately trying to pluck the ball from the air. On both sides of the stadium the crowd stand up in astonishment. Their eyes, mouths and lungs open in synchronicity causing them to draw a deep collective breath and a 'haaaarrrrrrr' can be heard inside and outside the stadium. They automatically hold their breath. Silence follows the ball's journey. The ball reaches the goalkeeper and passes within a centimetre of his glove before shooting into the goal. The scoring side exhale their pent-up breath in a thunderous roar of celebration as they rejoice. The defending side exhale a collective sigh of desperation, slumping their heads forward, as their lungs deflate.

This describes how astonishment is an initial and neutral emotion that precedes another. The emotion that follows is dependent on whether the event is deemed positive or negative. Upon the goal being scored, one side becomes joyous, amazed and admiring of their players whilst the other becomes fearful and despairs.

This example illustrates the emotion in a way that many people can relate to it. Nonetheless, the football game environment is a simple one. In everyday life the process is much more dynamic. The fear of not knowing what is happening, or will happen, plays a more significant role.

The process is instinctive as a blind person who is told the same story will exhibit the same emotions. In evolutionary terms, astonishment has played the role of making people act appropriately in life-threatening situations. Eyebrows are raised as the eyes open, letting more light onto the pupils. Posture becomes erect as the lungs take a deep breath, raising and firming the torso, as the body is poised to move away from the object of astonishment in the eventuality of danger. Breath is held to enhance the ability to hear whilst reducing the amount of sound made to as little as possible. This may be exhaled with a whistle, big sigh or something similar when the moment has passed without danger.[3]

The arms and hands may be flung out as if to prepare for a fall, protect the head, or push something away. Although the person is securely standing upright, the hands are sometimes thrown down and backwards as if to break a backwards fall or push the body up from a seated position. The expressions are not uniform in their execution and are to some degree individual to the person concerned. The environment, genetic and epigenetic[*] (concerned with gene expressions) disposition all mix to produce a unique expression. One person may hold their breath longer, listening intently, and avoid detection, whilst another might stare wide-eyed. It is like arms, eyes and legs. One arm, eye or leg is just like another, yet all are unique and moved in personalised ways.

When an astonishing event is deemed to be positive, the expression morphs into amazement or admiration. The eyebrows lower, the eyes softly reduce in size, and the open mouth closes as it widens into a smile. When the astonishing event is deemed negative, the expression morphs into fear. Blood drains from the face and hands, leaving them cold, while blood flow increases to the legs as the body prepares to run. The limbs may even start trembling. If the fearful event is deemed to have passed, or be unrealistic, then relief is felt.

Astonishment is instinctive and largely uncontrollable. It's an evolutionary reaction that is neutral and prepares people for an additional emotion that's appropriate to the perceived situation. Amazement, admiration, fear and relief act as extensions to astonishment. In an evolutionary sense, astonishment is an old emotion that's the base of several others that have evolved as direct extensions from it.

Thinking of the environments in which humans evolved allows people to understand what situations emotions have evolved to tackle. For millions of years human needs were acutely more physical than they are today.

One study focused on a distant common ancestor, capuchin monkeys, and decision making. It was found that humans share cognitive thinking biasses with these monkeys.[4] The research concluded that humans have been co-evolving cognitive biasses for at least twenty-three million years (since humans split from capuchin monkeys).

Consciousness emerges – pre-dinosaur – when external events are perceived in relation to the self. This begins the development of unconscious or implicit-memories[*] that will eventually bias behaviour through unconscious emotional responses. The process is finely tuned for millions of years from a slowly increasing vault of subconscious implicit-memories. These are what animals rely on. Instinctive responses develop into repertoires that form emotions such as astonishment, but also others like fear, disgust, jealousy and sadness. As perceptual complexity increases, emotions develop to prepare the body and motivate appropriate responses. The old emotions, such as astonishment, most likely evolved throughout the dinosaur era as cognitive biasses first started to take form in tiny fearful mammals. Over the sixty-five million years or more since then, astonishment developed its extensions.

The prevalence of astonishment throughout the animal kingdom is a testament to its important and incredible success. You only have to startle your cat and dog to view their astonished reaction. In so doing you witness the cross-species possession of the emotion. Just think how wide spread the expression is, and wonder how long each animal has used it. This is a well-developed and fitting emotion that has evolved for sudden and unexpected events – especially life-threatening ones. It has undoubtedly played a role of paramount importance to early life and was a serious factor in evolutionary success.

Astonishment

Latin. *Extonare* = to leave someone thunderstruck.

1. To fill with sudden wonder or amazement; great surprise.

<u>Blushing</u>

Blushing is caused when people think others have learnt embarrassing personal details about them. It refers to mild, tender or moderate feelings involving social circumstances. Blushing *is not* related to life-threatening events or serious offences.

People usually feel exposed when others learn of their personal details. They care about their social prospects and are concerned for what effects such details will have on the judgement of others. The reason it's possible to blush at strangers is because they represent an unknown social impact. People have to care to blush. Feeling exposed and caring what others think is the essence of blushing.

Feelings of wanting to flee the situation are experienced while also having contradicting feelings of wanting to stay. As if to hide, the head, eyes and shoulders have a tendency to move away from onlookers. In this stage the face may become a little pale. Whilst believing that others' opinions have just been reformed, a decision is made to stay and *face the music*. A warm flushing sensation is felt over the face as blood flow is increased to it. Dots appear on the cheeks that then radiate outward into disc-like blotches of reddish pink skin that increase as the blushing continues.

It's notable that if people do not stay and own* the behaviour or thoughts in question, but instead move away and flee, they do not blush. Owning the behaviour in front of others is central to blushing. Most people care how a situation will turn out and if the others' thoughts will turn negatively or positively towards them. They care enough to stay while feeling uneasy and exposed. It's this mentality of standing one's ground, although not aggressively, while feeling vulnerable that causes the blushing or flushing effect on skin.

When people become scared, the blood flow is redirected from different areas, such as the face and internal organs, to other areas, most notably the leg muscles.[1] This instinctive feature evolved to prepare the body to run in the eventuality that escape or evasion from a threat was needed. This is why people can go pale as a sheet in frightening situations.[2] In contrast, when people become angry and stand their ground, blood fills their face and fists, turning them reddish, preparing for fight and the manoeuvre of objects.[3] The autonomic nervous system largely controls this cardiac output, increasing and decreasing blood pressure and flow to and from different parts of the body. Despite the bulk of the functions being unconsciously automated, the autonomic system is not stupid even though its output seems inappropriate at times, for its responses are appropriate adaptations to perception.[4]

Blushing has mild forms of both of the above instinctive reactions. To some degree, people feel like they want to escape a situation but then face the onlookers. The thoughts in mind are not physically dangerous. People don't fear for their lives, but they're concerned enough to consider how others will think of them. The psychological strain is not great, yet significant enough to cause concern on an instinctive level.

People who have been blind from birth still blush. Also, it's possible for people to blush whilst they're alone and thinking about facing someone who has discovered personal details about them. Perception of the incident triggers the reaction.

Interestingly, people only tend to blush on parts of their skin that are exposed to the sight of others. If a woman is wearing a dress that shows cleavage, the blushing that typically starts around the face may graduate down her neck and across her chest, yet restricted to the line of her clothing. It's possible to blush all over the body, but for unknown reasons people tend to only do so on skin that's in plain sight.[5]

People often feel light headed or giddy while blushing. The instinctual processes that move blood away and back to different parts of the body, including the head, must be partially responsible for this. Blushing involves two instincts that, although mild, are at odds with each other. It's not surprising that people feel disorientated when they blush. All the processes are happening while they're trying to consider the thoughts of onlookers and the eventualities that may arise.

If the revealed personal details are desirous in nature, blushing often occurs. The more sensitive people are to the opinions and emotions of others, the more likely they are to blush. Blushing is, thus, considered a refined emotion as it shows that people are not shameless. It confirms that people are sensitive to the perceptions of their peers and use empathy to navigate social situations. Arrogant and ignorant emotions block the blushing reaction.

Blushing

Old English. *Bylscan* = blush, become red, glow.
Old Norse. *Byls* = torch.

1. To become red in the face from modesty or embarrassment.

2. To become red or pink in the face.

Contempt

Contempt is an innate expression of rejection.

It originates from dis-smell (the reflex to avoid a bad smell) and primarily involves the involuntary gestures of the nose as if smelling a rancid odour.[1] Contempt is similar to disgust, which originates from distastefulness and primarily involves involuntary mouth movements. Darwin first described the sensory connection of these two emotions.

Curling under the nose, the upper lip rises. The head tilts away from the offensive thing and leaves the eyes looking down the nose. Muscles at the base of the nose and upper lip moderately contract causing the nostrils to shut in a valve-like fashion. The *looking down the nose* posture is usually accompanied by a nasal snort as if clearing the airways of a toxic odour. These are the hallmarks of contempt.

These remarkable, distinctive features hint at the evolutionary origin as being a reaction to things that smelt offensive. The emotion has now evolved to include behaviours and thoughts that *smell a bit fishy*. When contempt is felt due to the thought of an offensive behaviour, it triggers the original physical reflexes. When these expressions are directed at people, they understandably cause them to become passive and reflect on their behaviour. Does an expression of contempt make people instinctively insecure due to thinking they smell bad?

The nasal nerve is one of only two (the other being optic) that emerges directly from the forebrain. Odours can be smelt at a much greater distance than things can be tasted. Also, people typically smell something before they taste it. Smelling is a close, medium and long range sense. It locates odours nearby while detecting airborne contaminants from miles away. This probably has bearing on the mental characteristics whose evolution is based on this sense. Contempt is an intricately subjective[*] emotion that can be manipulated by the mind in ways that other emotions cannot.

Contempt is a mental attitude that sees another as having contravened a rule or principle. The recipient is moreover viewed as having intentionally broken a rule. It's an emotion that motivates behaviours that enforce social norms and accepted standards. Contempt is an attitude about specific actions, and it marks them as inferior or inappropriate to the situation. Although people may view an individual as contemptible, it's more accurate to say that specific attitudes, beliefs or behaviours are contemptible. The effectiveness of addressing contemptible issues is also more productive when specifically attributed to characteristics rather than persons.

As people can rationalise an infinite amount of subjective rules, contempt can be applied to virtually anything and anyone. Rules can be contravened by others who have no idea of the rules they have crossed. This means that people can potentially be offended by an infinite amount of issues. Such highly malleable reasoning means contempt often reinforces defence-mechanisms[*]. It can be a long term companion of ignorance and pride, where it can be used to reject a great many expressions and behaviours of others. If people perceive an idea, an expression or a behaviour as too costly, inferior or troublesome to consider, they might treat it with contempt as a means of quick rejection even though contempt isn't the most appropriate emotion. In this way, contempt is used excessively by prideful people as part of a defence-mechanism – commonly referred to as snobbery.

Contempt projects an air of offensiveness or pitiful inferiority onto people. If people are insecure, submissive, or have less authority, they may concede to having done wrong when they have not. They may have conceded mentally or in an outward expression of guilt, but in either way they have admitted guilt or shame falsely. In many cases, this is simply due to assuming the other person knows better or it's not worth contending the point with a superior. This compounds problems for people with low self-esteem.

Contempt can be used as a form of control over social situations. One person expresses contempt and the other becomes insecure and passive as this is a natural response to being treated with contempt. In these situations, people expressing contempt – the aggressors – have more freedom to express their views. Yet there may be no grounds at all for expressing contempt. People who are unsure of themselves are especially prone to being dominated in this way.

A group of six holiday makers agreed to divide their luxury chocolate cake evenly amongst themselves. Apart from Lucy and Jack who ate both, on Friday night the holiday makers each ate one of their two portions. They all praised the cake with glorious celebration. Next afternoon Lucy pops back to their rented accommodation for a bag that was left behind. She opens the fridge to have a drink of cold, freshly squeezed, orange juice and sees the chocolate cake sitting at the back of a shelf. She's tempted to eat another person's portion. Lucy's arm stretches into the fridge but then pauses. Almost touching the fantastic-tasting delight, her hand hovers. Having already eaten her portion, she remembers the taste. She thinks, 'No one will know it was me who ate it, and when someone else gets upset, all I'll have to do is keep quiet.'

Pushing the thoughts of upsetting group members out of her mind she takes the chocolate cake slice and eats it, right there, in front of the fridge. Face smeared with yummy chocolate cake she closes the fridge door smiling. Jack enters the kitchen. Lucy almost jumps out of her skin in astonishment before freezing on the spot in fear. They had both eaten their portions the night before. Jack stared at Lucy in contempt because he was thinking of the upset to others she was willingly about to cause. It could ruin everyone's holiday! Jack was a good friend who understood the temptation, so he treated her with compassion, and said, 'To keep the peace, we'll have to buy another cake and leave one of your slices for someone else Lucy.'

The example shows how contempt is felt in the present, and how it can relate to the – cause and effect – complexity of events that will ultimately be detrimental to the future integrity of a group. Contempt senses subtle contaminants with a temporal distance. It's not the cure for what it senses, but it's a marker that says 'WARNING OF CORRUPTION' that aids adaptive responses.

Contempt

Latin. *Contemptus* = scorn.

1. The action of despising; the holding or treating as of little account, or as vile and worthless; the mental attitude in which a thing is so considered. (At first applied to the action, in modern use almost exclusively to the mental attitude or feeling).

Courage

Courage is the ability to stand one's ground or act when fear is present.

The physiological reactions of this emotion are similar to those of fear and anger. Starting from a reaction of fear, people fight against the fear and overcome it. There is always an element of risk involved. Courage implicitly describes the mixture of these two physiologically defensive states. The physiological experience of fear and anger is a cocktail of neurotransmitters and hormones that keep the body and mind on edge. If a courageous state is prolonged, there may be many fluctuations back and forth between the two states. There may be many biological stresses going from one state to the other. Courage is an exhausting emotion.

A common misconception is that courage is a state of existing without fear. This is wrong. The reverse is true. It may be surprising but fear is needed and is the implicit ingredient for people to be courageous. There is apparently a book titled *Feel the Fear and Do It Anyway*. This is the essence of what courage is. The title could have been *Be Courageous*. So it's the amount of fear people feel that determines how courageous they can be, not the lack of it. Just as King Leonidas said to his son in the opening scenes of the film *300,* 'My father taught me that fear is always a constant, but accepting it makes you stronger.'

Theoretically, courage can be used by a person for good or for bad. The intentions are not really the issue. Only the amount of fear overcome is a consideration. This means, at first glance, that bad people can be as courageous as good people. This brings up the other issue that is bound to courage. It's highly associated with good deeds; it has an overall positive perception. This is because of the issue it tackles. Fear is used to intimidate and terrorise people in an attempt to get them to abandon reasonable actions. Abusiveness preys on people who are vulnerable and weak because of their inability to retaliate or inflict injury in their defence.

Terrorising and corrupting those who are perceived as weaker does not take much courage. Abuses usually occur because of a power differential, and a person who lacks an ability to retaliate is used even though it causes him or her distress. This is the essence of abusive behaviour, and it's such deeds that place people in fear.

Courage is seen as a positive characteristic because it's used to overcome the fear that intimidating people inflict on others. This can be on a physical level or a mental level, but there is always a mental element (a perception) involved. Courage is a personal characteristic people use to defeat bullies.

In reality, many sorts of situations occur that require courage and most of them would not be associated with a warrior's reputation. Courage is more frequently found in everyday scenarios when people feel pushed into expressing an opinion they do not believe or saying 'no' to an intimidating person. For example, after having considered the potential of retaliation and intimidation, reporting a burglary and then making a statement to the police. The reporting is a courageous act. However minor or trivial a situation seems intimidation is intimidation, and overcoming implicit fear is a courageous act. Less serious situations are where people hone their senses and where everybody develops a common sense of what *is* and what *is not* acceptable. The strength of people's characters is tested by such experiences.

Cowardice is an extreme inability to stand firm or act in accordance with one's principles when fear is present. Rage is sometimes experienced as the opposite extreme, where recklessness occurs from an inability to act properly due to lack of control when angry or when fury is felt. Courage can be thought of as a tempered experience that is between the two extremes of cowardice and rage. When people feel courage, they acknowledge the fear they are feeling, stand firm, and continue with what they decide is best.

Many people face adversities in their everyday lives and fear the consequences of what could happen if the adversity beats them, such as not being able to pay the bills whilst having children to support or fearing misrepresentation from local malicious gossips. These social scenarios require courage to act when fear is felt. People who overcome such adversities and succeed are admired because others empathise with their ability to stand firm and continue whilst feeling the fear of their circumstances.

Intrepidness whilst acting in the face of serious physical danger is the most commonly understood concept of courage. It is right that people of great courage are recognised for the acts they do. Yet, it should also be recognised that the small increments against injustice, on a personal level, are also a part of a continual change for good. Small acts of courage are happening everywhere, in families, neighbourhoods and societies all over the world. Any fight or single step on a personal level that overcomes fear and intimidation is of value and helps save humanity from being dominated by a climate of fear.

To be fair and just requires the courage of such convictions and no less. If people do not have courage, they will not have a just society. They will live in perpetual victimhood. Courage is needed to support a *standing firm* posture; it's the backbone of justice in any society.

Courage

Latin. *Coraticum* = heart, innermost feeling, as a metaphor for inner strength.

1. The quality of facing danger.

2. Strength of mind when fear is present (backbone).

3. Spirit, liveliness, lustiness, vigour, vital force or energy.

Delight

Delight is a positive emotion that's expressed in moments when people experience joy unexpectedly – just as when an unplanned event happens that turns out to be positive.

An instinctive, uncontrollable smile is a familiar expression of delight. Often people don't realise they're smiling due to being absorbed in thoughts of good news. Delight is a very personal thing that is related to the makeup of an individual's personality. If people find an activity delightful, they would be well advised to revisit that activity. Participating in things that create joy is proven to be good for people on a psychological and biological level.

A possession may aid or even be needed for an experience, but the experience is what satisfies people. This includes the experience of success. It could be gardening, stamp collecting, reading, writing, football, surfing, paragliding, or understanding others. It could be a parent, child, lover, or business partner that causes delight. If people find delight in an activity, it's good for their wellbeing and their immune system. It denotes a high degree of satisfaction whilst resting brain systems that are used for effortful processing; it significantly relieves the tension of accumulated stress (see Stress).

It is possible to find things that delight others, so contribute to their enjoyment of life, and this in turn can delight the delightful person. To focus on and find out what another gains great joy from is not an easy thing. If people have parents that do this for them, they are lucky. To know what delights people is a very useful thing in relationships, but it's important that people do not neglect their emotional health in the process. People often find it's harder to discover or accept their own delights than those of another. Perhaps they feel as if they are being selfish when doing something they delight in. Being preoccupied with one's self is a completely different thing to giving one's self a healthy amount of attention. Humans have to take care of their selves, and doing something that they find delightful could be considered as the equivalent of eating healthy food on a psycho-neuro-biological level. It can be seen as knowing the difference between what people *think* is good for their self and what they *feel* is good for their self.

When people feel positive, their thoughts are automatically biassed towards recalling other thoughts and feelings of a similar nature. This process is called mood-congruence.[1] Positive mood functions as a buffer that enables people to cope with the biological effects of negative experiences with more composure and stability.[2] When people are experiencing positive emotions, they analyse information less whilst using instinctive judgements that rely on their present knowledge base; there's less cognitive processing.[3] This reduces stress on neural analytical pathways, and it allows the unconscious to process past experiential evidence, unimpeded by conscious scrutiny. Positive emotions alleviate excessive neuro-biological stresses – stresses that can accumulate into serious health conditions and memory deterioration later in life.[4] Health problems which accumulate due to the excessive functioning of bodily systems are said to have been created by stress or allostatic-load*.

Negative emotions outnumber positive emotions.[5] Yet, good health is not maintained by maximising positive emotions and minimising negative emotions.[6] Optimal functioning and good health includes both negative and positive emotions as and when they are appropriate to circumstance.

On the other hand, many strategies regarding stress are concerned with managing distress by solving the cause of distress without any consideration of positive emotional states. This is consistent with negative emotions that instinctively focus attention in an analytical way onto negative experience in an attempt to find a solution to the distress. Nonetheless, this instinctive rumination on negative experience is damaging when constant. Positive moods should be considered within any coping strategy.[7] Positive emotions pull people out of conscious analytical rumination and reduce their neuro-biological stress. When a person returns to problem solving, the neural circuits that process that state will be rested and refreshed. Mood management is an important aspect to problem solving too.

This may sound obvious, but lots of people relate to the world in an over-intellectualised fashion, for they do only what they *think* is good for them without any recognition of how it made them *feel*. Some people would place little value in a delightful activity, which left them with a positive mental attitude, if it did not tick their intellectual box of what is good. Yet they have been instinctively satisfied!

Delight

Latin. *Delectare* = to allure, delight, charm, please.

1. The fact or condition of being delighted; pleasure, joy, or satisfaction felt in a high degree.

Despair

Despair is the loss of hope. It is bound to every hope that does not come true. Despair includes such things as assumptions, expectations and anticipations, but only if they include hope (which is an innermost desire that they will come true). Disappointment is the less intense version of despair and relates to assumptions, expectations and anticipations that are less important than hopes.

Hopes are future based, and as their temporal closeness reaches the present they are materialised or lost. When hopes come true, they cease to be future representations, they become real, and joy or elation is experienced. When hopes are lost, they cease to be future representation too, for they become representations of losses. So, as a dream's temporal transition passes from thoughts of the future to past losses, despair is experienced.

The significance of the lost hope relates to the intensity of the despair experienced. When despair is felt, people instinctively become passive, shut down, and often sit motionless with no wish to move. Their heartbeat drops, circulation slows, the skin becomes paler, and facial muscles hang more loosely from the bones.[1] The body becomes limp. Both actions and expressions are affected just like after a big blow or shock to the body.

The eyes become heavy and dull due to reduced blood flow whilst looking vacant with drooped eyelids. Inner eyebrows are often acutely raised which causes the forehead immediately above to wrinkle. In contrast, the outer eyebrows barely move or are even pulled down. The corners of the mouth droop down and outwards which accentuates the centre of the lips lifting into a modest pout. Motionless experience of failure, coupled with the slow blood circulation, makes breathing shallow. The deflated lungs often bring the posture of the body to a slump with the head hanging forward. Deep breaths are taken periodically that lift the torso, head and shoulders before the air is released with a big sigh that drops the head and torso back down. Just existing can feel like a struggle. Big sighs, an unhappy face, lethargy and sedateness are the hallmarks of despair.[2]

> People who promise false hope order despair for those
> who believe them.

Lethargy is an implicit part of despair. The intensity of the lethargy is relevant to the significance of the lost hope, the degree of stress it causes and the ability to cope with the fallout.

Positive emotions biologically and psychologically function as a buffer to cushion the negative effects of despair.[3] Hopes that come true satisfy people on a deep level; they bestow confidence, a sense of self-control, an interest in life, and a positive mental attitude that lasts a long time. So hopes can inoculate people against depressive experiences just like despair. Everyone has hopes and expectations. Mood is deeply affected depending on which hopes are coming true and which ones are being lost. Temperament is possibly influenced too, for despair relates to issues of paramount significance to a person's life. Although the expressions vary with intensity and duration from person to person, extreme fatigue, drowsiness, and apathy are all common to serious cases of despair.

Despair encompasses physiological and biological depressive feelings, heart-ache, and psychological disarray. The cascading psychological fallout goes deep and wide through cortical and sub-cortical neural networks that make people feel psychologically traumatised and perhaps physically ill. Even though despair has a distinctive demeanour, lost hope is often not recognised as the cause. The loss of interest and vacant staring into space are not attributed to the instinctive unconscious efforts that are trying to make sense of the loss.

Sudden feelings of unimaginable loss and a devastating lack of direction in life are experienced in serious episodes of despair. The mind vacates conscious activities and interests. It instinctively redirects into deep unconscious thought. The body is put into a physiologically depressive episode as the mind tries to set a new direction for life that is adjusted to account for the recent devastating news. At face value, people may look absent minded and stressed. This is the outer materialisation of internal chemical reactions created from hormones and neurotransmitters flowing through the bloodstream and affecting nerves with electrochemical transmissions. The process slows people down and makes them feel heavy and biasses their thoughts towards introspection. People are rendered inactive whilst subconscious brain activity is accessing a myriad of possibilities and implementing the best way forward. All of these things often happen without people knowing much about the experience – knowing only that they feel deeply sad and lethargic and have no interest in anything.

For example, chronic mental stress involves many brain systems that include the neo-cortex, limbic system, and hypothalamus. The experience includes producing too much of a certain chemical (calcitonin gene-related peptide or CGRP) that reduces people's biological ability to fight infectious agents, and thus it reduces people's immunity to an array of different illnesses.[4] Depressive emotional conditions pacify people psychologically, neurologically, and biologically. The more intense the condition becomes the more compromised people become, and the more difficult it becomes to function (see Stress).

The unhappy looks or sad body postures are a surface indication of an inner turmoil that is often overlooked and/or verbally unexpressed. This can lead to underestimating the significance of what people in deep despair are experiencing.

It would be very difficult for anyone to suggest, let alone prove, that despair alone is what causes people to commit suicide. It is only responsible to note, however, that serious despair is a critical part of most suicides.

From a theoretical position, people that live entirely in the moment have little chance of falling victim to despair. They have no hopes that can be lost, but they also have no hopes that can come true to satisfy them. People who plan and endeavour to develop aims or achieve an imagined state of existence (such as in a relationship) are the people who are most at risk of falling victim to despair.

Dealing with the future is risky. Any imagined, hoped-for scenario brings potential issues of future despair. How much the imagined scenario means is precisely relevant to the intensity of the despair that could potentially be experienced. If people build their lives around an imagined future, when that future does not come to pass, they feel their efforts are lost and wasted. They may feel that they have fooled themselves and wasted years of their lives. In this respect, short-term hopes and plans are safer and easier to manage as they have less fallout or potential despair associated with them.

The devastation of despair can be harder to take if people have been constructing their lives around an imagined future with a person who then leaves suddenly and they realise the departure has been planned for some time without their knowledge. Not only do people feel fooled, but they have their plans broken into pieces, in moments, without any hope of getting them back. They could not see what was going to happen. They have to start over. The ex-partner is not shocked into despair though. They knew what was coming and had an exit strategy. The jilted are left broken in despair, experiencing the above reactions while they try to move on.

Bereavement almost always includes despair because of people's assumptive view of the world.[5] When people's hopes are based on deep assumptions, they feel despair when those assumptions are proved wrong. Without realising it people naturally make tremendous assumptions regarding the lives of others who are significant to them. For example, people commonly believe and make plans based on family members always being part of their lives until they die in old age. They create an assumptive world to give themselves a working model of reality, so they can make long-term predictions and plans. When a person dies *early*, the hopes related to the deceased are also lost.

The more sudden and violent a death is, the more traumatic the psychological experience is. Because there has been no time to reorder deepest plans, it's more difficult to construct a narrative that makes sense of violently sudden events. When a death is traumatic, more time is needed to recover from the bereavement as the recovery is impeded by deeper, more complicated, despair.

Despair relates to any form of hope for an outcome that is lost, such as working towards a qualification and then for whatever reason failing to gain it or applying for a job, hoping to get it, and then realising that someone else got it instead. These can create episodes of despair in their varying degrees, yet because of the amount of relationships people have, whether they are work-related or social relationships, despair usually relates to people's status with another person or group. After all, it's people that can deceive and take advantage of circumstances, not inanimate objects. This is definitely where most of the despair or heart-ache happens in societies, and it's common for people to react by avoiding future intimacy from fear of feeling despair again. Personal hopes that are entwined with another's hopes can particularly leave people vulnerable to despair. Interpersonal relationships have many unpredictable variables. They are risky things in which to place hope, especially when those hopes are at odds with each other.

Hoping for farfetched dreams will become demoralising if the hopes are unrealistic. It is far more sensible to hope for what is realistic and have those dreams come true. Being able to tell what is a realistic goal, on personal and professional levels, is a very reliable indicator for psychological and emotional stability. This is not to say people should not reach for the stars, only that a realistic personal contribution and time frame should be included. The more unrealistic hopes people hold, the more despair they experience. To underestimate the effects that despair has on people's overall mood is unwise as the results are serious, usually far more serious than people think and plan for. People underestimate despair.

The loss of hope only has to be perceived for the biologically depressive effects to be induced and mood to be negatively affected. People's physical wellbeing is relevant to their perceptions of loss and success. They are affected even if their perceptions are not true to reality. If people believe the loss to be true, they experience it as if they really did lose. Minds are the interface for subconscious recognition of reality. Neurotransmitter and hormone levels rise and fall to perceptions of reality and moods reflect these changes.

Despair is an implicit part of attachment theory* – which has now amassed more than fifty years of empirical evidence.[6] When babies become toddlers, they can move away from their parents, but they have restricted mobility. Part of their instinctive relationship with their parents at this stage is concerned with keeping their parents within a certain proximity. If the parent leaves, the baby will become distressed and begin to cry. Babies have hardly any understanding of time in the early toddler stage. They have no idea that their mother or father will be returning. Babies and toddlers instinctively raise their arms for comfort when they're distressed. Without words they are saying, 'Pick me up and hold me close; I'm scared.' The contact-comfort* of a cuddle for babies and toddlers at this stage should not be underestimated for its significance to dispelling despair. Keeping a toddler's levels of despair low endows them with a secure personality. Cuddles are a primary way humans instinctively reassure their infant's hopes, for cuddling brings babies out of despair.

If the baby's mother (or primary care giver) does not return shortly and comfort them with a cuddle, the baby will experience despair with all of its physiological and biological consequences. If this happens repeatedly, the toddler's memory of their parent will become associated with experiences of despair. If despair is experienced repeatedly in short episodes, the infant will develop an abnormal relationship with their parent and subsequently others in their adult life. In extremely serious cases, when despair is experienced for long periods of time (weeks and months), the infant instinctively detaches from the parent-child relationship as if they had experienced a death and have entered the mourning process. The child's instinctive behaviours, which are built on hopes of parental interaction, are lost. The parent is thus associated with despair instead of comfort.

All the depressive biological effects from hormones and neurotransmitters apply equally, if not more so, to the child's more intense world. This is despair at an instinctual level. It has extremely serious consequences for the child's psychological outlook because it creates anxiety-based cognitive biasses that have effects on attachment behaviour to others as they grow.[7]

Recognising consecutive experiences of despair is important as it can send people into a biologically depressed state. Despair is not just a mental outlook. When innermost plans are lost, deep psychological fallout cascades failures through unconscious neural networks, and this releases depressive chemicals into the bloodstream and onto nerves. Prolonged neuro-biological immune responses cause system-wide stresses that can accumulate to put people at higher risk of serious health complications as they age.[8]

As adults, people must struggle to reorganise and redirect themselves in the midst of the inner turmoil. It can be exhausting. Where hopes are concerned, it's best to adjust them with the most realistic information to hand whilst keeping in mind the risk that will be taken. In this respect, having a few important hopes that are given the attention they deserve can be far more successful than having many. How many hopes can people realistically manage at any one point in time?

When hope is lost, however, all the evidence indicates that people who find meaning in a reconstructed explanation of what happened will adapt more positively than those that cannot or will not explain the situation.[9] After all, this is what the emotion of despair instinctively motivates people to do by forcing them to ruminate on the loss.[10]

Accepting the experience of positive emotion when in a period of despair is difficult because positive emotions pull the mind out of analytical sad ruminations. This can be felt as if it's a betrayal of the memory of who or what has been lost. Positive emotions will help with that rumination if despairing people can bring themselves to experience them. It is highly likely that positive emotion will only be experienced for a short time before rumination begins again. Nevertheless, brief changes in mental disposition and biological chemistry to a positive state will help buffer and alleviate accumulating stresses. The despair will still be sad, but people will feel less lethargic, so the whole process will be healthier than if there's no brief escape from ruminating.

Despair

Latin. *Desperare* = to despair, to lose all hope.

1. The action or condition of despairing or losing hope; a state of mind where there is entire want of hope; hopelessness.

Disappointment

Disappointment is the feeling experienced when an expected event does not come true. The appointment people go to, fully expecting to be seen, only to be told on arrival that it's been cancelled. They lose time and investment and become disorientated at the point they realise things will not go according to their plan. Disappointment and despair are emotional descriptions of this phenomenon. Disappointment is the less serious of the two and not bound to the loss of hope like despair.

Continued disappointment can have serious consequences on people's standard of living. This is true on a physical level and a psychological level. Depression can occur if many disappointments are encountered in succession, especially when no successes or positive emotions cushion the negative feelings. Psychological insecurities occur as anxieties when people think they cannot predict the world accurately. Each disappointment people experience can perceptually be considered a failure. It could be a failure of the world to live up to people's expectations or a failure to make an accurate prediction. Whatever way people view the disappointment, a failure of something to happen is the experience from a subjective[*] point of view.

Disappointment is usually viewed from a psychological perspective, yet its effects manifest physical ailments. The perception of failure produces depressive neurotransmitter and hormone responses. With every little psychological disappointment people also experience a small biological depression. These depressive fluctuations may be minute. Nonetheless, if many minor depressions happen in a row then mood and even immunity to disease can be compromised. The hormone reactions to defeat include prolonged adrenocorticotropic hormone (ACTH) secretion, and this leads to suppression of the immune system as well as other metabolic[*] disturbances.[1] This is more likely if people do not have many positive emotions from successes, over the same period, to buffer the negative experiences.[2]

Researching, planning and working hard are important aspects to succeeding and avoiding disappointment. Active progress towards a goal is essential for success. Nevertheless, overcoming disappointment is not as simple as abiding by such rules alone.

The accurate prediction of future events and the ability to have realistic, achievable expectations is key. In fact, it's a very reliable gauge of psychological and emotional stability. Hence, the issues concerned with managing disappointments are also expectations, anticipations and low-level future predictions. It's healthy to focus on short-term and everyday expectations to see if they're realistic. These expectations may not be as exciting to reflect on as grand dreams coming true, but everyday expectations far outweigh such grand dreams in terms of number and frequency. A success can be considered a failure if expectations are too high. Disappointment can be felt where there should be gladness.

Humans are creatures of habit and changing habits can be difficult. Nonetheless, theoretically, if people are repeatedly disappointed about everyday issues they can try reflecting on their expectations and adjust their perceptions to better reflect reality. Mental assumptions that clutter an outlook can be removed or updated. One misplaced assumption, regarding everyday future thoughts, can repeatedly lead to disappointment. If people reflect on such assumptions over an extended period, it could seriously alter their standard of living. They could release less depressive hormones into their bloodstreams and neurotransmitters onto their nerves. Thus, encountering fewer of those draining penalties that make life less enjoyable.

Disappointment

Middle English. *Desappointer* = undo the appointment, remove from office.

1. The fact of disappointing; the frustration or non-fulfilment of expectation, intention, or desire.

2. The state or condition of being disappointed, with its resulting feeling of dejection.

Disgust

Disgust is an innate expression of rejection.

The expression evolved from vomit-like actions that were used to expel harmful foodstuffs. A perception that a substance is corruptive, toxic or harmful creates disgust. An object or action is thought of as distasteful and treated as potentially corrosive to health.

The lower jaw is pulled down, the lower lip is rolled outwards, and the tongue is moderately pushed out. The head arches back and pulls away from the offending substance. Often the eyes half squint whilst a short burst of air is blown through the lips as if clearing the mouth or throat of something distasteful. Instinctive gestures of pushing something away are common even when there's no physical item to be pushed away. These are typical expressions of mild disgust. Extreme disgust can cause a person's mouth to motion as if vomiting only air with a gaping mouth and tongue pushed fully out (gagging).

Over millions of years disgust has developed from an innate rejection of food to include a psychological appreciation of behaviours. Disgust has evolved to incorporate behaviours that people find distasteful. When these offensive behaviours are perceived, they trigger the original facial expressions for expelling foodstuffs.[1] The higher intellectual processes of assessing behaviours, which are deemed unacceptable and then rejected, are nested upon evolutionary older processes concerned with rejecting food.[2]

Both psychologically and neurologically these processes are part of the same structures. The facial movements of disgust always come into play when people detect anything unusual in the appearance, odour or nature of their food. This is the main indicator of the evolutionary root of the emotion. Darwin first described this over one hundred and fifty years ago.

Infants give the purest expressions of disgust when they taste something extremely sour or bitter. Their whole face is contracted to expel the substance. Eyes sometimes fully shut from muscle contraction as the mouth opens as wide as possible. The tongue is pushed out fully and held there. Whilst holding this impossible pose, they try to blow air out of their gaping mouth to aid the expulsion. As the substance is expelled, their whole body shudders as if from an ice cold breeze which is presumably also to help the distasteful thing on its way.

The expression of disgust in adults is the same only moderated. This is an unconscious action, which primarily turns the bottom lip downwards, accompanied with a modified oral expulsion of air in an expression like 'uurrr'. This is often followed by a minor shudder that looks more for effect than purpose. This is now commonly related to psychological ideas almost as much as foodstuffs.

In our modern world, people who subjectively* find the behaviour of someone in their group unacceptable can often be seen to unconsciously pull their head back whilst moderately pouting their bottom lip and tongue.

Faeces (poo or excrement) is a perfect example for inducing disgust. From an early stage in evolution humans have developed an acute sense of repulsion to anyone else's and sometimes even their own. Through hundreds of thousands of years of avoiding faeces people feel instinctive disgust related to it. Whether it's faeces on their trouser leg or faeces on their face, they instinctively feel uncomfortable with it being there. It's definitely a detestable thing to think of as food. A simple thought of faeces displays disgust's root.

People can use the above idea of faeces as a spring board analogy for any other form of disgust. If people perceive something to be potentially harmful to their health, they reject it. If people think behaviour will somehow affect them negatively, they can view that behaviour as disgusting. If people perform lots of degrading and shameful actions, they may be regarded as disgusting. Yet, on this last point, to say that a person is disgusting is less accurate than to say the thoughts or behaviours an individual expresses are disgusting. Addressing specific behaviours or substances is the effective way to tackle the revulsion of disgusting habits. A person is made up of many things. Unfortunately, people tend to get condemned by loose expressions of disgust – she is disgusting – rather than have a specific behaviour an individual exhibits addressed as disgusting.[3]

It can be difficult for people to separate actions from the people that perform them. When people have not washed for months, have slept on the streets, and carry potentially infectious bacteria wherever they go, it's easy to think of them as disgusting. The only way people can be disgusting is by performing or not performing specific actions though. People in such situations can begin to believe they are innately disgusting – that they cannot modify their disgustingness. These thoughts can rob people of motivation to change. People can actually believe that no matter what they do they will always be disgusting. This is not true.

To clarify how much of an unconscious role perception plays in the disgusting process let us imagine you have an open wound on your leg covered with a plaster. The open wound is covered up and itching. It needs a scratch and that means the plaster needs to be removed. You want to know everything that is going on and look at the plaster closely as you remove it. It has soaked up a little blood, a bit of puss, and is red and yellow. You have only pulled it away a fraction from the skin. You could push it back and let it heal, but you remove the plaster completely and hold it in front of you. After a quick scratch, you decide, from nerves, to quickly put the blood and puss covered plaster back on the open wound to stop you picking it. Only now the thought of putting the plaster back on is disgusting. Perhaps, it's now not clean and could cause infection?

The thought of putting something unclean on an open wound is disgusting. The question is when did the plaster become disgusting? When you partially removed it? When you completely removed it? Perhaps, when air was let in? Or maybe when the plaster was ten centimetres from the wound? Possibly, when it was twenty, thirty or forty centimetres from the wound? At some point in the process of removing the plaster you instinctively felt that it was now a potential risk. You began to think of your own healing bodily fluids as potentially infectious.

So in essence any substance or behaviour that could be seen as toxic or debasing, related to disease, could be seen as disgusting. Just as disease can be passed from one person to another, so can psychological expressions or memes*. Ideas can cause us to act in degrading ways.

Disgust is a highly evolved emotion and extremely subjective in modern use. This is shown perfectly with the example of Darwin's encounter with a native in Tierra del Fuego (located at the southern tip of South America) described in *The Expression of the Emotions in Man and Animals*. The naked native touched, with his unwashed fingers, some cold preserved meat which Darwin was going to eat. The native displayed utter disgust at its softness whilst Darwin felt utter disgust at a naked native touching his food with unwashed hands. The encounter provides a horizon-like scope of the different things people can find disgusting whilst not realising they themselves can seem disgusting too. Disgust is attributed to things in the outside world according to subjective views and social memes, like the texture of meat or a person fingering someone else's food. Did the native not account for preservatives? Was Darwin concerned with bacteria?

This is all well and good when disgust is used in this way. Disgust, however, can be used by people to gain control over a social situation. People can express disgust at others, causing others to pause and consider if their actions are disgusting, and in so doing the others become passive and insecure. This allows the people expressing the disgust to dominate the situation. In this way, disgust is used as a control drama. People can express disgust to faze people into passive insecurity, which is a natural response, and then dominate at the other's expense.

Worse is attempting to persuade people that they're disgusting, so as to compromise their psychological makeup. This is malicious, psychological abuse. It corrupts the internal frame of reference of people who become convinced they are disgusting when they are not. Children are susceptible to such influences. Also, as it will restrict the people's experience of life by making them avoid and neglect aspects of reality unnecessarily, troublesome consequences befall people if they are made to believe that things are disgusting when they are not.

There are consequences to experiencing disgust inappropriately.

When disgust is experienced, it changes the cognitive appraisals of the disgusted to more readily detect contaminants in their environment. Whether it's the texture of food or an intonation of expression, disgust amplifies people's ability to spot potentially sickening features.

When disgust is being felt it biasses cognitive decisions to unrelated things. People are more likely to sell their possessions at knock down prices and pay less than they would do normally for things. A deep sense of expelling something disgusting radiates into general decision making, and people are biassed towards pushing things away and not letting things in.

Accurate perceptions are important. They create an appropriate level of disgust. *How* disgusted people feel is important. Perceptions create emotions if they are accurate or not. If people believe a perception, they feel the associated emotion. Inaccurate perceptions of disgust can extremely restrict a person's behaviour by misadjusting the intensity of the emotion concerned.

For example, some people fear attending public gatherings because other people have sat on the seats before them and potentially left bacteria behind. Strangers may have even put their shoes on the seats. This can be compared to things that people instinctively find disgusting: fluids that emerge from other peoples bodies; a dribble of milkshake that splats on the counter by the till as a women removes a straw from her mouth; standing in someone's vomit. As the potential health risks are different, the perceptions should have different intensities of disgust. Sitting on an ordinary public seat should be the least disgusting, unless it's covered in vomit.

Disgust

Middle French. *Desgoust* = strong dislike,
repugnance; the opposite of 'to taste'.

1. That which pains or afflicts, or the passive feeling
    which it produced; troubled, affliction, vexation,
    sorrow.

2. Strong repugnance, aversion, or repulsion excited
    by that which is loathsome or offensive, as a foul
    smell, disagreeable person or action, disappointed
    ambition, etc.; profound instinctive dislike or
    dissatisfaction.

<u>Elation</u>

Elation is intense joy.

Just as with all the positive emotions, elation is concerned with caring for people and this includes care for oneself (self-respect). More specifically, elation is created from events that will significantly contribute – positively – to particular cared-for people. When hopes come true, people become elated.

Elation is the most positive of feelings, and it's used to describe experiences that can potentially lift spirits to the highest degree. Elation is concerned with extremely high levels of satisfaction, and it's not an emotion experienced every day. It leaves people shining with satisfaction for hours, weeks, and sometimes months after the event. This means it has significant influence on mood. Elation possibly contributes to temperament as it's an emotion of significant fortune.

Sitting on a dune, Rye looks out to sea and marvels at the brilliant blue-gold-red mackerel sunset. Rye was surfing in those waves a few hours ago. He feels a deep sense of contentment and exhilaration that stems from an unknown satisfaction. Rye attempts to explain the experience to Ashley beside him saying, 'I am filled with wonder, but it's more than amazement?'

They turn towards each other and notice the other smiling ear-to-ear. Both belly laugh in acknowledgement and Ashley says, 'We're on a mix of elation and exhilaration.'

There are different levels of elation, and this often is noticeable when people return from a holiday or long adventure. After having an intensely pleasurable time, coming back to a stressful environment creates a contrast between how people felt before they left and how positively charged they are on their return. Many people will recognise the deep biological satisfaction that elating experiences offer. It may be difficult to point to exactly what caused the positivity, but it *feels* unmistakeably nourishing.

Events such as getting married can cause people to feel elated. The glowing woman throughout her pregnancy. The first look at a new born child. Witnessing children getting married or achieving something of great significance in their lives. These things may not cause everyone to be elated as satisfaction and hopes are very personal things that are individual to each and every person. Nevertheless, they do serve as examples of events that can and often do cause people to feel elated.

Positive moods naturally instil a psychological resistance against thinking about negative things that will stress neuro-biological systems. Be that as it may, the perception of a serious threat will interrupt a positive mood as seriously threatening events take precedence over positive ones. This evolutionary adaptation instinctively prepares people for life-threatening scenarios to the exclusion of positive moods.

There are multiple cortical systems and sub-systems that are dedicated to specific emotions, and they're dedicated to processing specific types of information associated with different perceptions.[1] Brain activity shifts to different systems as people perceive different events and experience different emotions. There is accumulating evidence that positive emotional processing is biassed towards the left-hemisphere regions whilst the reverse is true for negative emotions.[2]

Positive emotions work as a buffer, both psychologically and physiologically, to negative emotions.[3] Positive emotions psychologically pull people away from analytical, ruminating thinking. They cause people to act on their present knowledge bases – memory. When in a positive mood, people are instinctively enabled to focus on a broader range of issues, and their thoughts are more inclusive, so they're more creative and flexibly minded.[4] As thoughts are not analytically searching for answers, due to intuitively using current knowledge bases, psychological neural workload is decreased. Activity is reduced in brain areas that process negative searching thoughts. There is a significant psychological relaxing effect of positive emotions.

When this shift in perception takes place, a cascade of biological responses dramatically decreases vigilant and tense states. Amygdalae, situated in each temporal lobe, maintain alertness to fearful and unknown contingencies, and they effectively disengage a load or are put on standby when people experience positive emotions.[5] Neurotransmitters, hormones and sympathetic nervous system functions, which support alert attention to problems, no longer tax neuro-biological systems. As a consequence, the body becomes less tense at a neuro-biological level. Therefore, there is also a significant physiological relaxing effect of positive emotions. They relate to safe environments. Places where people can unwind.

Logically, this suggests that participating in enjoyable activities creates positive emotions that are therapeutic in themselves. Positive emotions relax psychological, neurological and physiological systems related to the right-hemispherical negative emotional processing. Those systems then recuperate to a healthy state ready for when next a problem is encountered. They are not stressed into dysfunction. Switching between left-hemisphere positive and right-hemisphere negative emotional processing describes a process of maintaining balance through change – allostatic*. A healthy balance seems to be achieved through a continuously repeated traverse of brain regions that honours fatigue and rest cycles.

Notwithstanding the difficulties in purposefully achieving such positive emotions, these are significant reasons why positive emotional states should be considered as treatment options to stress, anxiety, and depressive related conditions. As it neuro-biologically pulls people out of negative emotional processing, elation is an emotion that has the power to alleviate, disrupt and even break overly negative cognitive routines.

Nevertheless, a word of caution is needed. As positive emotions lower people's defences, and make people more likely to trust those around them, elation is not an appropriate emotion to be experiencing when in a hostile situation, for it will bias cognitive routines towards being socially relaxed and affable. Because elation is the most positive of emotions, and people react more automatically when feeling intense emotions, people may inappropriately trust those who do not deserve to be trusted. The company in which people become elated matters. It could lead to seriously unfortunate errors in judgment where the most intensely positive feelings are associated to untrustworthy people. Cognitive routines would become biassed towards treating the person with affection, and this would typically be felt as an allure. An unexplainable attraction towards someone who will cause harm.

Elation

Latin. *Elationem*, *Elatus* = elevated, metaphoric sense of lifting spirits.

1. Elevation of mind arising from success or self-approbation, pride of prosperity; pride.

2. Elevation of spirits (in neutral or good sense); buoyancy, joyousness, pleasurable self-satisfaction.

Embarrassment

Embarrassment is an unpleasant feeling that's most commonly experienced when people make a mistake that others see. Embarrassment is highly associated with social interaction and the opinions of others. In many cases, it relates to contravening social rules and normal behaviour.

The initial expression consists of looking down and tilting the head away, typically to the side, to avert the eyes from onlookers. The hands may be brought up to the face as if to hide it from view. Then a controlled awkward smile is displayed as the embarrassed person looks back towards onlookers. The expression usually takes about five seconds to complete.

Perception of these cluster of movements by onlookers shows the embarrassed person's recognition of the inappropriate behaviour, and it promotes compassion and forgiveness from onlookers. The positive appraisal of an expression of embarrassment is not guaranteed though, and it's more likely to be associated with caring, friendly people who value trust, for others seek to exploit such expressions.

Shame will lead to an embarrassed expression – or humiliation with serious contraventions – when it's revealed to others.

A typical scenario of embarrassment is committing a minor social transgression that elicits feelings of awkwardness for people who make the transgression and others who witness it. The fact that others have been made to feel awkward does not create embarrassment. Rather it's the fact that others know that the person embarrassed is now somehow at fault and the opinions of onlookers might be negatively affected. Being scared of social rejection is part of being embarrassed.

Embarrassment is intrinsically related to social pressure. Pain is a physical reaction to cell damage and embarrassment is considered to be related, in an emotional pain-like manner, with the damage being to social reputation. Negative emotions evolved from aspects of pain. The recoiling emotion of embarrassment is to stop adverse damage to future social opportunities.

Embarrassing actions are sometimes followed by mockery and attempts to humiliate. This is often a bid to gain control over the person embarrassed.

People try to make others feel more embarrassed than they should. Because embarrassment is driven by social pressure, it's often used by people to control others who are overly concerned with their reputations, such as people who are excessively prideful in nature. Being aware of social status is a good and healthy thing. Being preoccupied with social status can be a weakness, for instance, it's easier to manipulate a person who is overly sensitive to avoiding embarrassment from malicious gossip.

For people to be able to own* their embarrassing behaviour is important and extremely advantageous. Over time a framework of embarrassing values will develop that enables people to tell the difference between how embarrassed *they should feel* from the mockery and humiliation that *other people would have them feel*. Such discernment is a healthy characteristic to possess, and it indicates a personality that is difficult to manipulate with mockery and humiliation. Banter can be used between friends to build a resistance to overly harsh criticisms.

People are not always fair, and this is never more true than when mockery and humiliation are involved. There are people who would have others believe anything if they thought it would give them control. People can and do gain power through exerting the social pressure of embarrassment – dominating at the expense of others.

Embarrassment has the tendency of making people momentarily passive in nature, so they have less capacity to offer resistance. This is often recognised by domineering personalities as an opportunity to seize control of a situation. This momentarily gives the aggressor an ego-trip from a sense of superiority from gaining control, yet it's abusive for at least two reasons. First, the humiliated person may believe that behaviours are more embarrassing than they actually are. This causes unnecessary avoidance of behaviours and reduces the person's adaptability erroneously. Second, as the mockery or humiliation consumes the concentration of people who are embarrassed, it effectively robs them of an opportunity to reflect clearly on their embarrassing behaviour. This makes it more difficult to learn from personal mistakes. Adding insult to injury muddies the waters. Perceptual load is added. The issue becomes one of trying to perceive accurately between how much embarrassment should truly be felt and how much embarrassment another is attempting to elicit. Accurate perceptions create balanced emotions that are appropriate to the reality of the situation that created them. Inaccurate perceptions create ongoing emotional and social problems as they are inappropriate to the situations where they're expressed.

Experiencing this sort of abuse continually, especially in childhood, may lead to a weak comprehension of embarrassing events. In such cases, embarrassing events are often recognised and memorised only as points of attack, so blurring understanding around personal mistakes and making it more difficult to learn from them. Over time this can create a numbed and under developed understanding of embarrassment. The awkward recoiling feelings of embarrassment become more intense, and they trigger defensive reactions instead of a simple awkward cessation of action. How best to react defensively when embarrassment is felt becomes the issue rather than why the embarrassment is felt.

If people know why they feel embarrassed, it's easier to determine how much embarrassment is appropriate. When people have a reliable internal reference of different embarrassing actions, being pushed around in embarrassing moments by 'oh my god' statements is less likely because they don't believe the hype.

Embarrassment

French. *Embarrasser* = to block, obstruct.

1. To encumber, hamper, impede (movements, actions, persons moving or acting).

2. To perplex, throw into doubt or difficulty.

3. To make (a person) feel awkward by one's speech or actions; to cause (someone) embarrassment.

Empathy

Empathy is the ability to see other people's point of view *as if* through their eyes. People imagine another's experience *as if* they are that person, and they feel the emotions that naturally arise from the perceptions of *walking through* the other's situation. Although empathy is not an emotion as such, when people empathise, they feel an array of emotions from the subjective[*] world they're empathising with. In years to come it may be considered an emotion. Hence, besides being an important concept to grasp, having a description of empathy seems obligatory in a book whose subject is entirely about emotion.

Empathy can be a frustratingly difficult ability to grasp. People get distracted by their outlook and accidentally introduce their emotional material into the process. This perceptual contamination is a common problem with sympathy. Empathy is often confused with sympathy because at face value they are very similar. Nonetheless, empathy is far more useful as a tool for understanding and defining someone else's emotions. It has more potential for comprehensively understanding the subjective reality of another than sympathy – including grasping motives.

Sympathy denotes an experience of people who relate to what another person is feeling due to having felt a similar way, and it's the most natural and prolific means of communication that exists. The experiences do not have to be the same, rather they share a similar consequence. Sympathy works along the lines of identification; if people felt deeply sad after the loss of a loved one, they can feel sympathy for another who has just lost a loved one. Identifying the situation through a similar experience enables people to make allowances for the way another is feeling in the present and will be feeling in the not so distant future. It does not have to be the same loved one for people to extrapolate, so people appreciate the sense of loss and despair the other is experiencing.

Empathy, on the other hand, does not require people to identify a similar experience in their past to imagine someone's situation. People sometimes think that because the empathising process does not rely on common ground that it's less valuable. This is a mistake. Empathy is less personal, in the sense that people are not directly experiencing and recalling evocative emotions from memory. Surprisingly, it is this point that allows more subjective intimacy to develop between people.

Experiences are often too close to the bone or too personal. If someone is talking about something very personal, listeners may not want to associate it with their experience. It could trigger memories that make it extremely difficult to stay focused on what the other is saying. Sympathising can get in the way of developing a relationship with someone because of getting emotionally over-involved, and not being able to detach another's feelings from one's own. Past feelings can get intermingled in the conversation which makes them difficult to separate within the narrative being expressed. These things faze people. Empathy allows people to avoid this sort of fazed state while staying focused on what the other is relating.

In the strictest sense, the emotions that people feel whilst empathising use representations that stem from their brain and their experience. Nevertheless, the emotions are not associated with their past self or their life narrative. The neurological process involves the so-called mirror neuron[*] system. When people perceive an event, their prefrontal brain relays it to the insular region of their somatosensory system, so they associate the perceived event with a sort of role playing unit of their brain that has access to the ways they usually react to those perceptions. These are called their body mapped dispositions (somatic markers[*]). In those maps they have stored real emotional, mental, biological and physiological dispositions they use with relation to the events they are imagining.[1] Thus, they have access to reactions that are true to life associated with the imagined event. The process is done in an *as if* state. A sort of neurological theatre screens a movie of another person's trials and tribulations from a first person perspective. Empathy does not have the same effect as sympathy due to this disassociation with self.

This dynamic creates a professional distance that helps maintain relationships, especially professional ones. It also means that people are not limited to the confines of having similar experiences to another. Empathy lends itself to an appreciation of diversity that is unlikely to develop if people only relate to others in a sympathetic way. People can enjoy the emotional undertones and overtones of another person's related experience even though they share little in common. Sympathy relies on having experiences in common whereas empathy does not. The word empathy is a young word that has been in common use for around fifty years. It is a very new, even innovative, word that describes the perceptual evolution of human interpersonal dynamics.

In the past, some academics and intellectuals have argued over the word. Though these people may have a good understanding of Latin and ancient Greek, they usually have no therapeutic training. It's been argued that empathy is not really a useful word, for it's an American invention to replace the word sympathy which has been used for thousands of years, so no properly educated individual would use it. The intimation is that the word is to be avoided.

Apart from the word being of German origin and coined specifically for its current meaning, the point is that the word is still not accepted by many people as having any distinct meaning other than a synonym for sympathy. This is untrue. Empathy is different and has its own very distinct and unique meaning. No other word describes the experience or the depth that the word implies. Empathy is unique from any other experience for its potential to offer insight into another person's experience of life. It's a process that's invaluable in many situations, such as comprehending a child's view of the world; helping someone with distress and anxiety; ascertaining someone's motives in court.

Empathy also helps people to develop emotional literacy.

Continually focusing on another's perceptions, experiencing the emotions that arise, naturally develops into ways of communicating what is seen and felt. People can learn things from the experiences of others and empathy increases that depth.

There are, however, two considerations to be cautious of when empathising.

First, it's possible for people to empathise too much and lose their sense of identity. People can unwittingly become dominated by another's views even though their intent is to help. When people become too immersed in another person's view of the world, they neglect and forget important aspects of themselves in the process. When overused, empathy creates an identity crisis as people forget the perceptual *as if* boundaries between two subjective worlds.

Second, a biassing experience called 'empathy gaps' exists. Yet this does not strictly apply to empathy as much as it specifically applies to erroneous judgements of future or past behaviour. It refers to different intensities of emotional arousal. When people are in an highly aroused – hot – state (e.g. fury, hunger, sexual), they find it more difficult to empathise with and understand the cognitive processes of those who are in a low – cold – state of arousal. The reverse is true for when people are in a cold state (not furious, not hungry, not sexual) of arousal whilst trying to empathise with someone in a hot state. People in a cold state of arousal are prone to under-appreciate what it will *feel* like to be in a hot future scenario.

These *empathy gaps* in appreciation of feelings also apply to past experiences such as in the morning after experience of trying to make sense of last night's wild behaviour. This is thought to be because people interpret future and past experiences through projecting their current thoughts into an imagined subjective world.[2] But also because their cognitive processing of information is modified depending on what emotion they're currently experiencing.[3]

This *empathy gap* biassing applies more to situations where people are simply imagining a subjective reality. In contrast, *empathy gaps* apply less in situations where people are narrating their experience in a responsive way – the therapeutic environments influencing the aroused state of the therapist. If people are sitting in a room empathising with a person, they naturally begin to experience similar levels of arousal due to perceiving the same narrated content. A therapist's mood would have to be seriously disturbed, by an event that kept him or her in a specific hot or cold state, not to be able to reach and keep empathic harmony because of *empathy gaps*.

Mastering empathy is a highly skilled endeavour, and it's probably the most important tool for defusing conflicted situations on personal and professional levels.

Empathy

Ancient Greek. *Empatheia* = passion, state of emotion.
German. *Einfühlung* = ein 'in' + Fühlung 'feeling'.

1. To see, or perceive, the world through another's eyes.

2. To comprehend the actions and feelings of another by understanding their reasoning.

Envy

Envy is the desire of another's possession. Envy includes a combination of meanings, and it's a complex emotion that often leads to interplay with other negative emotions.

Because the joint meaning can be broken down into three parts, three various expressions of envy exist. One where the envious simply want a possession that someone else has. A second where the envious only want to deprive someone of a possession. A third where the envious want to deprive someone of a possession and take it for themselves. Although envy can fund a whole range of behaviours, it always has these motives.

Originally, envy's meaning was 'to look at with malice'. The word 'possessions' is used here to refer to the entire array of what people can possess: personal characteristics, talents and abilities – not only simple physical items. Envy is experienced as a will to deprive another of pleasure, delight, happiness or somebody. Wanting to deprive another of something is implicit in most envious expressions. Nevertheless, more recently, envy is sometimes used only to describe the desire to be in another's position or to have the same talents as they possess – without a malicious will to deprive. Although, unlike admiration, envy is not filled with positive wonder. It does not have a positive moral overtone. It has the reverse.

Envy, in Christianity, is one of the *seven deadly sins*. This has added a cultural difficulty regarding people owning* their feelings of envy. Defence-mechanisms* are subconsciously motivated denials of experience. They block people from consciously experiencing aspects of reality that would make them feel anxious. If people feel anxious about owning their envy, their subconscious is more likely to push envy out of their awareness. This is one reason why envy can be such a slippery and elusive emotion to grasp.

Another reason is the entwined relationship envy has with jealousy. Envy is often confused with jealously and vice versa. They both have distinct meanings, yet their entwined relationship causes much confusion.

Envy can lead to jealousy, and jealousy can lead to envy (see Jealousy for greater definition of this dynamic). When someone is envious of another's possession, the other becomes jealous (fear of loss due to the rivalry of another) because they would potentially lose a possession.

So, when people are jealous, they feel insecure with the thought that they might lose a possession. At these times, they can become envious of the possessions of the person who is perceived to be depriving them. The jealous can resent loss and seek to enviously take a possession from the person responsible. As it feels like justice, this tit-for-tat vengeance is very seductive. People can think of themselves as righteous when in reality they're simply envious. These emotions can be incredibly powerful. They can be based on fear or lust and associated with idiosyncratic fantastical desires. Hence, both envy and jealousy can have shockingly unpredictable and volatile characteristics.

Although envy can be induced by jealousy, resentment can fuel envy's initial development too. Also, the envious form relationships with others who resent the same people. Envious and resentful people are vulnerable to being used by one another. As the resentful allow the envious to harm those they find offensive, the envious can use the resentment of others. Malicious intentions of envious people are condoned, encouraged, and may even be performed by another's resentment. The envious and the resentful use each other. One has their feelings of vengeance satisfied as the other takes a possession.

When the envious or resentful hurt someone, they can rationalise the malice into an act of justice or even a divine restitution. Rather than own[*] their acceptance of malice, people are willing to believe in a crooked fantasy that conveniently puts their intentions in line with a god. In one swipe of believing in a dishonest perception they absolve themselves of guilt and the fear of punishment, and they may also develop pride.

Partnerships can form due to both parties having a shared goal. Envious resentment of one person, or people, can be created and sustained from such convergent relationships. In reality, this maliciously destructive force is insidious. For example, a parent's actions can be resented by an immature offspring who then forms a relationship with someone who is envious of the parent. These motives are narcissistic. They are not concerned with creating a nourishing environment for children. They are based on obsessive malicious intentions.

Envy has different levels of intensity and pettiness. For example, when people who are perceived as superior do not have a possession their subordinate owns, and cannot get whatever the possession is because they cannot afford it, envy can result. Injustice is perceived and resentment is felt. In this situation, people may become envious of the subordinate's possession. The superior may develop envious intentions of wanting to deprive the subordinate of the possession as it's perceived to threaten their superior social status, yet they perhaps secretly want it for themselves too. This is envy related to resentment, jealousy, pride and vanity. Even mundane experiences of envy often involve multiple emotions that are created from complicated perceptions.

In Western societies envy and jealousy are thought of as bad and somewhat pathetic emotions. This can lead people to avoid addressing their feelings of envy and jealousy. The way for people to dispel envy is for them to accept and recognise what they are envious of and work out why. The emotion is there for a reason. Cutting it out or ignoring envy is not a solution. Ignoring (cognitively avoiding*) envy and jealousy does not make them disappear. It leaves the potentially harmful emotions out of conscious awareness and subconsciously motivating behaviours – referred to as acting-out*.

Envy offers people insights into the makeup of their personality. Should a person justly be deprived of something or are people being malicious due to unreasonable resentment? Why do people want what another person has? Do they feel cheated at heart? Do people believe another's possession would make them happy? Are people in a relationship with a resentful person because it helps to satisfy their envious intentions?

Envy is a complex emotion that is very revealing of people's inner workings and rewarding to work through in therapy.

Envy

Latin. *Invidia* from *invid-us* related to *invidere* = to look at with malice, to envy.

1. Malignant or hostile feeling; ill-will, malice, enmity.

2. To feel displeasure and ill-will at the superiority of (another person) in happiness, success, reputation, or the possession of anything desirable; to regard with discontent another's possession of (some superior advantage which one would like to have for oneself).

3. Also in a less unfavourable sense: to wish oneself on a level with (another) in happiness or in the possession of something desirable; to wish oneself possessed (of something which another has).

Evil

Evil is the most extreme form of malevolence. Evil contains maliciously ill-fitting and unsuitable behaviour towards others. An implicit deeply immoral implication is always implied. Although evil is probably an inexhaustible topic, here are a few key insights.

Just like malevolence, evil is a developed state and not a one-off experience or action. It describes the most serious disregard for people's wellbeing as the psychological and emotional suffering of others is a minor consideration. This disregard can be for several reasons. Sometimes it's due to internal psychological conflicts that are traumatic enough to preoccupy people continually, so leaving them no free attention for considering another's view. In other cases, the neural architecture of a person could be most responsible – a sort of high-functioning autism. A mixture of both of these factors is also theoretically possible. Nonetheless, a severely restricted ability to sympathise and empathise is permanently associated with evil actions.

Likewise, evil actions are highly associated with psychopaths[*]. Psychopaths are people who have an intellectual disconnect from their feelings. They are typically very intelligent, and they can conceive plans and ideas of great intricacy. Also, their intellectual prowess means that they can recognise patterns of behaviour that are deemed acceptable or unacceptable by society, so recognising conforming behaviours enables them to cast a semblance of normality over their behaviour.

A psychopath's decisions are not based on emotions or feelings like normal people. The average psychopath does things because they are accepted, to advantage themselves, rather than because they feel it's the right thing to do. This also means they decide not to do things because others deem the behaviour unacceptable. Psychopaths see the possible disadvantageous consequences to their potential success rather than instinctively feel actions are wrong.

The inability to feel emotions, or being extremely hindered in doing so, means that psychopaths do not empathise or sympathise well. As they cannot imagine what the suffering will *feel* like for their victims, psychopaths can do extremely malicious things that create massive suffering and despair.

In extreme situations, when it's considered more acceptable to 'do whatever it takes' to win, a psychopath's actions are more readily seen as immoral. Their internal frame of reference, built on the advantageous reactions of others regarding what is acceptable or unacceptable in a moderate environment, is no longer relevant. They haven't any reference to make adequate decisions in the new extreme environment. Anything that affects the morale of the people is a moral issue, and psychopaths have a very restricted ability to judge how morale is affected. Many psychopaths go unnoticed in society until they meet an extreme situation and do something shocking. In a wartime scenario, where most people do whatever is needed to stop opposing forces, psychopaths could be responsible for a massive atrocity whilst being unaware of how barbaric and inhumane their actions have been.

In this respect, the subjective[*] attitude of an evil person can be more like supreme intellectual superiority with a strong conviction that others are foolishly motivated by emotions. Feelings and emotions can intellectually get in the way of 'the cause'. This description is like one of a megalomaniac persona (James Bond villains are based on psychopaths) where people are selfish, or narcissistic, because they perceive everyone else as drastically inferior to themselves. This is a very common take on the psychopathic mind.

Nevertheless, it's only responsible to note that a person can become a sadistic psychopath and then learn to feel again. A famous example of such a rare situation is the case of a six-and-a-half-year-old girl called Beth in the documentary *Child of Rage*[*1] (found on YouTube with the title '*Child of Rage – Full Original Documentary*'). Beth and her brother are adopted by a Methodist priest and his wife in 1984. After a couple of months, they learn of the neglect the children suffered, and it makes sense of some of their behaviour. Beth repeatedly hurts her brother by sticking pins in him, without remorse, while explaining explicitly her extremely malicious intentions. She molests and hurts the private parts of her younger brother, yet she does not refrain even when he pleads with her to stop. Beth's behaviour escalates. Because she is found to be sneaking out of her room in the middle of the night and punching her brother in the stomach, her parents realise they have to tie her bedroom door shut while they sleep. Several times she tries to kill her brother and is stopped. Beth openly tells her adoptive parents her intentions to stab them in their sleep with a knife from the kitchen drawer. She wants to do it at night so they can't see her do it, but they can feel her do it, she says.

Beth explains her intended actions to a clinical psychologist in video-taped therapy sessions without any attempt to deceive or conceal. She wants to kill her brother and both adoptive parents. Beth relates her intentions like normal facts and with only a modest amount of shyness. Although vague signs of subconscious resistance appear as traumatic experiences are referred to and remembered, no intense emotions are felt or expressed.

Beth's biological mother died when she was one year old. The psychologist discovers that she has nightmares of a man falling on her with a part of himself, and that it hurts her. Over time it becomes clear that Beth was neglected, like her brother, but she had also been sexually abused. It becomes apparent that she needs specialist help. She was relocated to live with a professional couple, who specialised in working with seriously abused children with attachment issues, at their retreat. Beth receives round the clock attention for every aspect of her life. In time, the professional attention helps Beth and she slowly is able to feel the emotions connected to her actions. Five years later in 1989, Beth has integrated into her community. She is asked, in front of a video camera, about the violent things she used to do to her brother. As she talks of the malicious actions of several years ago, she clearly experiences remorse and then starts to cry before taking comfort in a cuddle.

This is an astonishing example of the psychological transition of a young person into a sadistically psychopathic state, driven by subconscious rage, and the emergence from that state to one where she can feel appropriate emotions. Two thousand years ago, Beth may well have been killed as 'an agent of Satan' or something similar. In the twenty-first century, if there was no intervention for a child like Beth at a young age, it's possible that she would now be an adult people refer to as evil.

A concept similar to 'an agent of Satan' may have been present in Islamic and Christian influenced environments for a few thousand years, although not in Hindu and Buddhist, but the word evil with its current meaning is hundreds of years old rather than thousands of years old. If people would think of an extremely malicious action as a positive thing, and so encourage intense moral corruption, they would be considered evil.

As the word evil conjures up evocative images, it is difficult to use without fazing people. People overly associate the word with religion and depictions of the devil. Many people fear the word evil itself, so they experience minor emotional shock-like tremors when the word is used.

Because of this automatic fearful reaction, people use the word evil to mar, slur or taint the image of others. The word evil can be used to mar person B, by person A. Hence, ironically being an indication of person A's malicious motive. It can be very difficult to use the word evil without it conjuring images of religious philosophy and propaganda. This can instil fear into the conversation inappropriately that's accompanied by all the irrationality and volatility that comes with ideological fear.

These are reasons for using the older words malice and malevolence when describing actions with ill intent. They are both distinctive descriptions for relating the root of an ill-willed corrupting force. What is more, since focus remains on what has been said rather than diverting to fears regarding the devil, they form more accurate perceptions.

Due to its heavily associated religious connections, many people have built up a personal view of what is evil that's based around religious iconography. This makes the evocative powers of the word evil tremendous. Extreme emotions, such as fury, can be elicited against the suggested evil thing as though the subject of the conversation were the very thing pre-concocted as evil. A construct of pure malice, of everything that is unacceptable, of everything that is wrong with the world, and everything that needs to be stamped out at all costs can be associated with the word evil.

Thus the word evil often hinders the flow of communication rather than aids it. The word is used to encourage people to hate someone rather than explain the reality of the situation. The word evil is commonly used by malicious people to manipulate others to hate.

Evil

Proto-Indo-European. *Wap* from Proto-Germanic.
Ubilaz = bad, evil, unskilful, defective, harm, disease.
Old English. *Yfele* = bad, vicious, wicked, the antithesis of good in all its principal senses.
Middle English. *Yfel* = moral badness. Bad in a positive sense. (Bad takes the wider meanings of negative actions, and evil becomes focused on morally corrupt behaviour.)

1. Morally depraved, bad, wicked, vicious applied to a person.

2. The deliberate use of maliciousness or ill-will imposed on others for personal gain, pleasure or thrills (including ego-trips).

Fear

Fear is the emotion people experience when danger is perceived. It's the oldest and most unreasonable of all emotions, yet its aim is always to prevent harm.

The first time people become conscious of a fear, it's reached through astonishment of a negative thing (see Astonishment). When a person is astonished, the instinctual reactions are a preparation for another emotion. Astonishment is the standard instinctive reaction to suddenly perceived events, which usually last milliseconds, that morphs into fear when the sudden event is perceived as negative.[1]

Negative emotions in general narrow attention, but fear redirects and constrains attention to serve fast defensive needs more than any other emotion.[2] Fear has immediate and virtually direct control over many neuro-biological systems. Heart rate and blood flow can significantly speed up or slow down depending on perception alone.[3]

Freezing is an automatic response that takes over psychological processes and redirects attention to scan for a perceived object of fear. Physiological function is instinctively commanded by skeletal muscles to freeze in an appropriate position. A person could crouch or cower while the back moderately hunches into a strangely shaped shrug-like posture. Animals, including humans, often freeze in positions that offer the most camouflage. Immobility is likely to prevent detection from animals whose sight mostly depends on movement. Running increases risk in some situations by releasing a predator's attack response. Different perceptions will bring about different responses instinctively. Freezing is not a mere absence of movement; it's an instinctive, evolutionary, rehearsed act.[4]

If escape is the best option, the heart rapidly palpitates. Pressure increases in the circulation system for pumping oxygenated blood around the body fast. As blood flow is decreased by closing capillaries, areas such as the hands and face become cold while their skin becomes pale, and blood pressure increases in the main vascular system. The legs then become warm from an increased blood flow as they're prepared for running. Typically, the neck and torso muscles move the head away from the perceived threat. Hormones and neurotransmitters prepare the body for action. Hands may shake as the muscles are primed with twitchiness.

These automatic expressions of fear become more uncontrollable, unpredictable and erratic as the emotion increases its intensity and reaches its extreme towards terror. This is partially because humans instinctively prepare for an event according to its perceived intensity more than its probability.[5] Humans instinctively alter their physiological, neurological and psychological processes to best deal with their most intense perceptions. A change in disposition occurs whether the perceptions are an accurate account of reality or not. As long as people believe a perception is true, they instinctively prepare for it. The more intense their perceptions become, the less control people have over these automatic dispositional responses. Emotions progressively assume control of behaviour as they reach towards their limits of intensity.[6]

Fear has been a response to dangerous evolutionary contingencies for hundreds of millions of years.[7] Fear responses were evolving throughout the dinosaur era. It is a primary emotion that is highly associated with the earliest of brain structures, such as the brainstem. At the same time, fear is also entwined in the newest of brain structures, the right prefrontal lobe, which initiates highly evolved social emotions that dominate human interpersonal decisions.[8]

Cognitive decisions will be biassed away from taking risks whilst fear is experienced. Psychological outlook is primed towards recognising ways out, escape routes, of the situation. Risk is the very thing that fear motivates people to avoid.

The newer brain structures are an extension of the older ones. The older structures are necessary for the newer more highly evolved structures to work. Core consciousness depends on the evolutionary older brain structures. Higher faculties and high-definition notions of self rely on the newer structures such as the neo-cortex. If humans lose higher brain structures, and their associated faculties – say through brain injury, core consciousness still remains, and functionality would only be reduced. On the other hand, if humans lose the evolutionary old structure called the brainstem, they have no sense of self and remain in a vegetative state or die.[9]

The brain is formed by many interactive systems that all work together. Systems are seamlessly creating connections between information from conscious and subconscious realms. The brain presents its finding to the imagination on request of a thought in milliseconds. Every memory recall, every word spoken, every solution found is made possible by this process. The entire seamless high-faculty processing, that makes intelligence so distinctive, depends critically on older brain structures. Old and new are ultimately one. They even work as one. Nonetheless, as one is built on the foundation of the other, one of them (social emotions/neo-cortex) cannot work without the other (primary fear/brainstem). Fear is such a foundation to consciousness.

Implicit-memory[*] refers to perceptions that have been stored subconsciously. The amount of unconscious perceptual data is more than humans could imagine, and far beyond anything they could consciously control. As this unconscious data includes automatic lung activation for breathing, heart rate, blood pressure homeostasis[*], and many other biological processes that are necessarily kept out of conscious control, much of this procedural memory is wholly inappropriate for people to control consciously. Even if, by some miracle, they managed to attain the conscious processing power required to do so, a deadly risk would be taken.

Access to these memories is extremely restricted. The ones that are at the top (nearest conscious explicit-memory[*]) of this overwhelming mass of perceptual data are on the tip of one's tongue, or on the edge of awareness. Be that as it may, people can consciously select activities for unconscious automation. Without people realising it, perceptions build into a store of experiential data, until one day they can suddenly perform a complex task without having to think about it. Perceptions of the activities people do frequently amass to be used to re-enact complex activities without conscious attention. Whether it's learning the piano or surfing a wave, people can programme their subconscious by habitually repeating an activity.

As people repeat behaviours over a few hundred thousand years, they develop very precise instinctual reactions to specific events. The reactions are based on a gigantic mass of implicitly stored perceptions. In essence, instinctive reactions are appropriate to the environment in which they developed. Fear has been an instinct for hundreds of millions of years. A mass of data is bundled into distinctive implicit-memories that initiate specific neuro-biological processes when perceptions of a pattern (emotionally competent stimulus*) fit the memory's profile.[10] These are experienced as instincts. A cascade of specific psychological, neurological and biological reactions take place as the emotion of fear manifests in response to a perceived threat. This perceptual representation is pre-semantic*: the profile of a threat can be recognised before people have any conscious awareness of it.[11]

Human integration of fear, throughout evolution, means that it has been hard-wired to the most dramatic biological responses. Fear is a highly evolved emotion associated with thought. To say that fear multi-tasks is a colossal understatement. Fear is felt when intellectually considering possible situations that are extremely complex and sensitive in nature. The range of fear's intensity is tremendous. It's an instinctual response that outranks other instincts whilst being an inherent aspect of many other emotions: anger, jealousy, contempt, disgust, terror and ferocity to mention a few. It has a massive amount of influence over reasoning and habits. It makes people sensitive and protective in nature. Fear, for millions of years, has related directly to mortality and the ability to avoid life-threatening scenarios. When intense fear is felt, similar implicit-memories of the same intensity will be recalled that refer to serious life-threatening situations. The fear is ranked so highly, in people's way of relating to the world, that it will cut through anything else they're engaged in. It has priority status.

This is why fear is so useful when faced with danger, yet it's also the very reason why abusers use it as a form of control. If people think serious danger is associated with a particular path, they will not continue to do that thing unless it's something so valuable that they are willing to face death. The majority of people, adults and children, would much rather avoid seriously dangerous situations for a danger- and stress-free life.

Fear is appropriate when the perceptions that create it are true. Accurate perceptions of threats in the environment create emotions that are appropriate to the reality of the situation. This is a healthy process that enables people to assess and react to real threats. It also enables people to develop an understanding of patterns that occur in life regarding ill-health and mortality, so fear is a healthy and necessary emotion that primarily helps people prosper.

Problems start when people are convinced that something is more, or less, dangerous than it really is. The inaccurate perception causes emotions that are out of proportion to the reality of the situation. This leads to over- or under-reactions. People will overestimate or underestimate the danger in a situation. This means that they will either be too willing to fight, too eager to run, or simply be caught out because they did not appreciate the seriousness of the threat. Phobias and anxiety disorders are examples of how inaccurate perceptions of danger can create too much fear for a given situation.

Fear is an exceptional motivator, and it's incredibly volatile. It can lead to the most unreasonable and irrational actions being taken. This is commonly seen in everyday situations when people panic unnecessarily. Psychological panic can create havoc with thoughts, behaviours and biological processes. If inaccurate perceptions of danger are believed on a prolonged basis, it will create stress on neuro-biological and psychological systems. People's instinctive reactions to fear include heart rate, blood pressure, hormone and neurotransmitter production changes that are meant to accommodate short periods of adaptive activity to shift attention to concentrate on a threat. If a maladaptive response is experienced continually, the organs and systems involved in processing a reaction to that state, and the ones that are neglected due to the preoccupation, will be impaired by accumulated stresses called allostatic-load* (see Stress). Such allostatic-load from continued stress results in serious health conditions, and it's been shown in longitudinal research to predict cardiovascular disease, later life decline in physical functioning and memory loss.[12] Allostatic-load has been linked to high cortisol levels, high risk of cancer and speeding disease progression.[13]

This is the striking truth of fear. It can motivate people in a split second to do incredibly desperate and violent things, yet it can paralyse people and cause disease if chronically experienced. When a threat is perceived to be immediate and real, the thoughts that surround the threat will be the thoughts that press themselves for recognition in mind. Until the threat has gone, fearful responses remain.

The effects of fear from traumatic experiences should not be underestimated. Memories last a lifetime, and this is a serious matter for people who suffer from post-traumatic stress disorder. Especially, when considering that the intensity of a perceived event outweighs the probability of it occurring, instinctive changes automatically manifest as people's dispositions are transformed in preparation for an intense event; just in case it happens.

Natural dangers like mountains, extremely cold weather or wild animals are generally less frequent and less continuous than the numerous relationships most people hold. Most people can go without knowing the serious dangers of walking in the mountains because most people will never be in the situation where they need to know. Only, most people have relationships. To underestimate the dangerous characteristics that another has is to leave one's self vulnerable to those people whenever they are around – vulnerable to potentially terrifying images embedding in memories which last a lifetime.

A healthy sense of fear is a good thing that has the potential to keep people out of harm's way on a physical, emotional and psychological level. Although, as with most instincts, it pertains more to survival in a far more physical and violent evolutionary environment. People can more easily judge threats expressed through body language than gauge the threats of complex social behaviours. The time humans have spent, millions of years, focusing on these physical parameters of survival far outweighs two thousand years of civilised society. Nevertheless, the balance of people's emotional state depends on how accurate their perceptions of the dangers are. Humans are learning to judge what threatening behaviours a new, civilised, highly social and close-knit world has.

As fear is the oldest of emotions, it has the deepest and broadest of influences over biological, physiological and psychological experience. Intense fear is capable of initiating the most primal of deadly feelings – such as ferocity, while mild fear guides people with feelings of concern. Fear is intimately integrated into the highest faculties humans possess. Despite the traumatic side-effects fear can cause, its purpose is always to protect.

Stress Related

Fear

Latin. *Periculum* = trial, risk, danger.

1. A sudden and terrible event; peril.

2. The emotion of pain or uneasiness caused by the sense of impending danger. A state of alarm or dread.

3. Regarding an object or event; the state of fearing (something); apprehension or dread of something that will or may happen in the future.

Ferocity

Ferocity is the most psychologically, emotionally and physically enhanced state for physical self-defence.

The heart palpitates rapidly, and cardiac output delivery is increased selectively to regions such as the arm muscles, trunk muscles, and heart muscles. Blood flow is reduced to other regions such as the kidneys, skin, and gastrointestinal tract as their functions are suppressed.[1] Neuro-biologically, endogenous (natural) painkillers are released to aid actions that potentially incur injuries.

The inner eyebrows pull tightly inwards and down as if to touch each other. As it's stretched down and inwards, the forehead follows the eyebrows causing it to wrinkle towards the centre. Often rising on the edges as emotion escalates, the eyebrows contort. The heart rate increases rapidly to a fast and steady pace. Breathing is fast and heavy to oxygenate the bloodstream and muscles. The mouth is closed. As the jaw is tensed, the nostrils flare to improve airflow to and from the lungs. The mind is concentrated on the offending person or creature. Blood flow to the hands and face is increased, preparing for the fight, which turns them reddish. The shoulder, chest, spine and hip muscles all contract to lift the torso and create a firm posture from which to strike or evade a blow.

There is a conviction present in the mind of the ferocious person that is without rival. Contracting tightly on all features of the face, facial muscles are often at their most tense. The muscles brace and grip the jaw, holding the teeth, as if in a harness. The inner eyebrows are pulled deeply down and inwards by strongly tensed muscles which protect the upper nose with firm corrugated skin. In contrast, the middle and outer eyebrows are pulled up in the opposite direction that creates a V shape to the eyebrows. This allows for the widest angle of vision and lets as much light onto the pupils as possible whilst keeping the face locked in tense protective muscle. The head does not turn far from its central pivot, rather the body will move instead.

There is an admirable, focused concentration fusing and radiating through eyes that are set in a deadly stare. 'One more step,' ferocity says, 'and I will kill you.'

It represents an absolutely resolute furious anger that is coupled with an immovable conviction to fight and do whatever is necessary to stop a perceived threat. Killing instincts are activated. The mind is indomitable. There are no expressions of terror. Actions are motivated by intent to stop whatever is perceived as the threat. This emotional state is witnessed in nature most frequently as a result of parental instinct.

When some animals are faced with a potentially lethal threat to their offspring, from another animal, parental instinct takes over. A resolute mentality to 'do whatever it takes' to protect its offspring often occurs. It may be a bear, a cheetah, a human, or any other animal, but the resolute nature of their decision to protect overcomes any fear projected onto them until their offspring are safe. This leads to a state where an animal is willing to kill while all their fighting instincts are activated.

The ability to think clearly is present to a much greater degree than when consumed by rage. Neither is the ferocious mentally hesitant as in fear or terror. Ferocity is not out of control, but going over-the-top to disable a threat is more likely. The ferocious know what they are doing, and they're willing to do it. They will disable and even kill their enemy without hesitation if it's deemed necessary.

The notable point regarding ferocity is that it's reached through a stance of protection of what's perceived to be most valuable. Values of paramount importance cause ferocity to emerge when they are threatened, so although it's a scary and an unmistakable experience to witness, it materialises to stop something perceived as unimaginably wrong from happening. This is the ultimate expression of physical protection – the pinnacle of anger's ability to say 'STOP' or 'NO'.

People can be seen trying to convince themselves, or others, that a threat they dislike is more of a threat than it really is. This can be seen as an attempt to elicit a ferocious force against the disliked thing. The perception of an unimaginable threat creates ferocity, yet this holds true if people believe in inaccurate perceptions, such as lies. If people believe a perception, they feel the associated emotion.

Ferocity is not a malicious or malevolent mentality that's concerned with wishing ill-health or suffering onto its enemy. The only concern is stopping a clear and present threat to something of paramount importance. Ferocity does not say 'Please?' or abandon protective instinct; it does whatever is necessary to stop the threat. Supported by ferocity for millions of years, parental instinct is probably the most powerful force on the planet.

Ferocity

Latin. *Ferocis* from *Ferox* = wild, bold, courageous, warlike, the ultimate expression of fury or fierceness, in a killing state.

1.   Capable of the most extremely savage, brutal or violent behaviour.

2.   Extremely intense.

Frustration

Frustration is a negative feeling that arises from a perceived failure to fulfil a goal.

This is related to every part of a person's behaviour-orientated life. Everything people put effort into achieving is a potential frustration, such as academic qualifications, continually failing to score a goal, or not being taken seriously when persistently adamant about an issue.

Frustration happens where a perceived goal is sought and attempts to achieve that goal end in failure. The goal could be practical or very academic, such as a ball that continually misses or a high-minded theory that eludes comprehension. Frustration happens to us all. It has very real biological effects.

To a greater or lesser degree, people realise they have goals, and when their goals are not achieved, they feel disappointed or sad. If they feel cheated, they will naturally also feel anger. Because plans can be disrupted, disappointment can accompany frustration. Because things can be lost due to failure, sadness can accompany frustration. Because people can be cheated out of success, anger can accompany frustration.

The hard-wired goal-orientated aspect of frustration gives it much background radiation over people's lives as everyone has goals, whether they realise them or not. Yes, people can become frustrated about not being able to read the daily newspaper as it's continuously thrown in the puddle, by the door, by the paper boy. It is true and irritating. More so for the fact that he has been told not to by his boss three times. The frustration of not being able to read the newspaper is now compounded with the frustration of not being able to stop the paper boy throwing it in the puddle.

People can have their instincts frustrated too, but it's more difficult to notice when this happens. Even though, the consequences are far more serious for self-esteem than not being able to read the daily newspaper.

If continually picking a soggy wet newspaper out of a puddle is having a negative effect on mood, start to imagine the effects of not fulfilling basic instincts over a prolonged period. Mood changes can reach out from the core of one's being. The resulting failures would be felt as very serious things in life not going properly. A serious change in mood accompanies instinctual frustrations.

Nevertheless, it's common for people to attribute no significance to their instincts when they realise they are not feeling good about life. Self-esteem and self-confidence are highly related to these intrinsic goal-orientated motivations. Instincts are goals in themselves, and failure to fulfil them will lead to the same sort of bad and sad feelings people get when they fail at anything else. Only the feeling will be more consequential, more intense. Because instincts have proven to be beneficial for success over hundreds of thousands, if not millions, of years, they can create deeply disturbing feelings.

The problem is that people do not think about instinctual drives in everyday life. Why would people necessarily associate importance with instincts when considering their emotional and psychological health? Rather than being thought of as primary sources of strong feelings to motivate people to keep clean and dry, fit and healthy, provide for children, keep children safe, and stay out of harm's way, instincts are often thought of as fight-or-flight type responses to physical threats. Whether people realise it or not, they all have instincts. If they do not attend to them, there are serious side-effects on mood and self-esteem, for instincts evolved to aid the animal in which they reside.

People can be fulfilling most of their instinctual drives, and so be feeling pretty good with life. They may not be fulfilling quite a few instinctual drives, and so feel distinctly under-par. There are different aspects to every individual; there are many things that people feel they must do. Not doing one of them is not going to be devastating to their lives for the most part, yet if the frustration is stemming from the failure of an important motivation (such as providing for several children), then it's not unreasonable for a person to experience a massive loss in self-esteem, episodes of depression, and despair, in any combination. This means that frustration can lead to lethargy and long periods of stress that could be reinforced by increasing anxiety. In addition to the initial frustrations, these stresses lead to new behaviours aimed at coping with stress.[1] While causing people to have less energy to work with, the neuro-chemical reactions from these negative emotions slow people's bodies down, and even reduce their biological ability to fight infectious diseases.[2]

Whether people admit it or not, they will perceive viscerally* a need to support the children they have. These perceptions stimulate the innate instinctual motivations that are part of being a parent. If people fulfil them successfully, they enjoy the joys of parenthood. If their attempts to fulfil parental goals fail, they will have to live with the frustrations of parenthood, and its associated negative effects on self-esteem. There are of course several aspects to being a good parent. Providing money, shelter and food is only a part of the overall bundle of responsibilities.

There are core frustrations and surface frustrations. The surface frustrations are more easily identified than the deeper sort despite having less of an effect on mood. When core frustrations have been endured over long periods, however, previously minor surface frustrations can cause a person to have intense emotional and physiological pangs, such as sudden outbursts of anger that are seemingly out of proportion to the issue at hand.

Anger and frustration are often intimately linked to one another. When people perceive they have been cheated out of fulfilment, they naturally feel angry.[3] These feelings of anger may be mixed with jealousy when they blame a rival for their loss. When the person blamed is significant to them, feelings of betrayal are mixed with anger, jealousy, and perhaps sadness. People might normally feel only annoyed or moderately angry towards someone they don't know. Nevertheless, in the same situation, when someone they know is perceived to have cheated them, the feelings are intensified with a sense of betrayal that can make people furious. The intermingling of several intense emotions makes it incredibly difficult to decipher what they are actually angry about. People only have to perceive that someone close to them is cheating them, and be tired, for accusations to start flying. The perception may be completely inaccurate, but if they believe the perception, they feel the associated emotions towards the person *as if* it were true.

This can be an awful scenario for people living under pressure with core frustrations. Split-second decisions based on inaccurate perceptions can release spikes of intense anger, spite, resentment, and even hatred towards others. People may be left with a sense of being out of control and unable to manage their feelings, which increases stress.[4] People commonly don't know why they are feeling such strong emotions, and put the whole unpleasant experience down to stress. Stress is a fundamental factor, and it's a fitting description of the feelings being experienced, yet still there's no explanation of why the stress is there.

Let's take a real scenario of a man with four children who, for confidential reasons, is called Mr Nice. Core frustrations once turned Mr Nice, a good-natured Christian father, into an angry man who became verbally abusive towards his children for a year or so. It was disturbingly unpleasant to witness for everyone concerned. The job that he had taken was far from home. It required a lengthy commute which took virtually all of his free time, important time he had previously spent with his family. Mr Nice took the job to improve his family's happiness and prosperity, but over time he came to resent the work for taking away a cherished aspect of his family life. The thought that he was doing it for the family morphed into blame and resentment towards them. Unknowingly, he began to see his children as responsible for his decision.

During the next year, when one of his children would make a typical childish mistake that further frustrated him, Mr Nice would swear and curse abusively at them. Mistakes that would normally only of irritated Mr Nice were transforming him into an uncontrollably verbal brute. It was not until Mr Nice found a job, which paid less and was closer to home, that he had more time to spend with his family. His temper, mood and attitude returned to normal. This return to normal life was also a relief to his wife who had been despairing with how her husband's behaviour had transformed. Working closer to home and having more time with his children proved more valuable and less frustrating than having more money in this case.

Frustration can be a perceptually elusive part of a person's makeup. When seen as a surface psychological experience, its effects on morale and general wellbeing are underestimated. It's hard-wired to core experience. If people are generally fulfilling their core motivations, then surface frustrations will be pretty much the only frustrations they encounter. They will be little more than irritating stumbling blocks or paper boys.

Stress Related

Frustration

Latin. *Frustrationem* = a deception, a disappointment.

1. To be deprived of effect, the feeling of being ineffectual.

2. Psychol: (a) the prevention or hindering of a potentially satisfying activity; (b) the reaction to such prevention that may involve aggression.

Fury

Fury is an emotion of extreme anger.

The inner eyebrows pull tightly inwards and down as if to touch each other. Being stretched down and inwards, the forehead follows the eyebrows and wrinkles towards the centre. Rising on the edges with increasing escalation, the eyebrows contort. The heart rate increases rapidly to a fast and steady pace. Breathing is heavy to oxygenate the bloodstream and muscles. The mouth is closed as the jaw is tensed, and the nostrils flare to improve airflow to and from the lungs. The mind is concentrated on the object of offence. Blood flow to the hands and face is increased, preparing for the fight, which can result in them turning reddish. The shoulder, chest, spine and hip muscles all contract to lift the torso and create a firm posture from which to strike or evade a blow.

There is a tremendous conviction present in the mind of a furious person. Intense and steady, the eyes glare with resoluteness. The movement of the neck is restricted from tightening neck muscles.

Anger is created by a perception of injustice.[1] Fury can be seen as a reaction that stems from a perception of something extremely unjust. Thus, it is a natural reaction to serious injustice and abuse. If people are feeling furious, it's a sign that on some level they have perceived something is seriously wrong.

Nevertheless, feeling furious is no licence to automatically and immediately vent furious feelings at people. Perceptions can be wrong and are often inaccurate to some degree. Making an effort to adjust perceptions to best fit the reality of the situation is often necessary. As there can be serious consequences for those it's unleashed on, fury needs to be appropriate. Being unreasonable will lead people to treat others unfairly by being too furious, or by letting bad things happen from not being furious enough.

A good thing to keep in mind regarding fury is 'doing whatever it takes' to stop abusive behaviour, as this attitude is reasonable. Anything beyond this would be unreasonable and would be considered an offence itself.

Fury is a necessary emotion to combat forms of serious abuse. It can be considered on a sliding scale with anger at the start and ferocity at the end.

Anger – Fury – Ferocity

Fury remains for as long as a perception of serious wrong doing remains. It energises the actions of those who combat injustice over extended periods. People can be motivated to action by fury. They can be motivated to communicate the serious injustice they have experienced. Extended court room battles that last for years can be motivated by fury, and the fury does not subside until justice is done.

The Romans used Furiae (or Furies) as the collective name for female avenging deities sent from Tartarus (the underworld) to punish criminals; this is the origin of the word fury.

When people feel fury, it's important that they check their perceptions to clarify exactly what is seriously wrong. Is it an accurate perception of reality? Is too much being read into the situation? When people get furious with others in their day-to-day lives, it can cause much upset. People may feel betrayed if someone close to them treats them with fury for no good reason. Being too furious potentially leads to abusive behaviour as rough justice emerges.

Sometimes people may feel furious for a reason that evades them. They can use the feelings as solid evidence that at some level they have perceived something seriously offensive. The talent is not to dismiss the feelings as irrelevant, but find what has unconsciously been recognised. The feelings may originate from an outmoded or inherited belief that is partially or wholly not applicable to the situation. The inappropriate perception will then be reasoned out. Although, the feelings may also be an intuitive sign, issued from deep neurological networks, that something has been consciously missed; something that needs to stop.

Fury

Latin. *Furia* = violent passion, rage, madness. The Romans used *Furiae* to translate ancient Greek. *Erinyes*, the collective name for the avenging deities sent from Tartarus to punish criminals.

1. Suggestive of extreme anger in action or appearance.

Gladness

Gladness is a positive emotion that comes from perceived successes.

As with all the positive emotions, gladness is an emotion that arises from caring for people, which includes one's self (self-respect). How people are attached to the things they care about is important. If a person's circumstances are positively affected, the people that care for that person are glad. Gladness always relates to circumstances changing for the better and always describes the positive mood boost that's experienced. Gladness could be considered one step up from pleasure – the most temporary of the positive emotions, yet one step down from joy, for joy describes a reaction to successes of greater significance.

Pleasure – Gladness – Joy – Elation

Positive emotions are primarily concerned with any form of prosperity. Thus, they're also highly associated with the completion of plans and objectives. For example, if a planned day out with a friend went well the people responsible for the outing would feel glad, and they'd experience a minor psychological and neuro-biological lift, yet if the planned event was more significant, involving the achievement of hopes, they would feel overjoyed or elated.

When an attempt to achieve an objective fails, people become frustrated. If people put time and energy into completing a task, it puts a degree of strain on their psychological and neuro-biological systems. All negative emotions, in their varying intensities, narrow attention and cause focus to become more analytical on whatever elicited the troubling perception.[1] People's mental processes are instinctively altered to accommodate problem solving in a more external, slow, and effortful way; this taxes neural pathways and is an instinctive attempt to focus the mind on learning solutions.[2] If the expenditure is met with failure, they will experience more negative emotion, which further stresses their nerves and biological systems, and causes them to become progressively more alert and vigilant. If this continues, it increasingly causes stressful rumination.

When people achieve a perceived task or objective towards a goal, they feel glad. The time and energy they have directed towards completing the task has been effectively used and no more effort is needed. All positive emotions, in their varying intensities, release people from focused analytical thinking.[3] Evidence suggests that there's a left-hemispheric bias to positive emotions and a right-hemispheric bias to negative emotions.[4] Thus, the theory is that to some degree positive emotion instinctively causes people to switch from the brain systems that were being used to focus on the completion of a task, so a neurological shift from searching thoughts based more in the right-hemisphere to more relaxed systems in the left-hemisphere takes place. There is an automatic release of mental, neuro-biological and physiological tension when this happens. Positive emotions are part of the process of perceiving a solution to a problem. They release people from the tension created by a negative emotion that was motivating focus on a problem. Relief is felt simultaneously with a positive emotion.

Negative emotions aid people to achieve goals that then provide them with positive emotion. Emotions are part of the process of maintaining balance through change. Good health is not brought about by maximising positive emotions and minimising negative emotions. It requires optimal functioning of both negative and positive emotional processing.[5]

Gladness is typically accompanied by a moderate release of tension that's associated with the positivity that comes from being able to include a completed task on the way towards achieving a goal. The tasks that can lead to gladness are far more abundant than the joy of achieving the goals they serve. Although the intensity of gladness is moderate, it's the *bread and butter* or *meat and potatoes* that sustains a buoyant mood. Keeping one's self glad maintains a course en route to one's hopes coming true.

Gladness

Old English. *Glaed* = bright, shining, joyous.

1. Having a cheerful or happy disposition.

Good

Good is the feeling that comes from successes and achievements that are perceived to benefit society. Although good is not typically thought of as an emotion per se, the feeling and intellectual notion of good are popular motivations for people. As emotions are highly specified motivations, good may evolve into a bundle of automated actions that are recognised as an emotion. In any case, because of its prolific use and how it influences motivational forces to other emotions, goodness deserves a mention. Although feeling good is probably an inexhaustible topic, here are a few key insights associated with its emotional connotations.

Anything that affects people's morale is a moral issue, so good feelings are associated with fitting and helpful behaviours that contribute positively to people's standards of living. Good is thought of as the opposite of bad. It represents a healthy mentality with a lack of detrimental effects on others. In general, if people think of themselves as good people, they think of themselves as helpful members of society who have principles and aspirations that are beneficial to the environment. In the sense of this paragraph, good represents a degree of improvement and a mentality that avoids guilt.

Feeling good revolves around detecting and avoiding guilt. This can lead to unforeseen problems.

People can feel guilt if their perceptions of a situation are inaccurate and misguided. If people believe a perception, they feel the associated emotion. People who see themselves as good are strongly motivated by guilt, so, inadvertently, they can become the target of people who will play on this consistent personality trait. If good people do or do not behave in a desired manner, they can be the target of persuasion tactics that induce them to feel guilt. As good people will avoid guilt at almost any cost, the manipulation works because they want to avoid any feelings of guilt. Being manipulated in such a way is more difficult to avoid for people who cannot accurately define what guilt is, yet, nonetheless, like to think of themselves as good people.

Thinking of one's self (ego) as a good person can have several unintended consequences. One of the significant side-effects is the desire *not* to own* thoughts and feelings they perceive as bad. Rather than experiencing them with the anxiety they create and wondering why, emotions and thoughts can cause people to *psychologically run away* from their uncomfortable nature. This process is referred to as ignorance, denial or cognitive-avoidance* and is considered a defence-mechanism* when its prompts are from a subconscious source.

The defence-mechanism's role is to stop people feeling conscious anxiety by blocking impulses and thoughts out of conscious view. When people are continually dishonest with themselves in this way, it leads to an underdeveloped personality that cannot relate to the world in regard to the emotions and thoughts that are blocked off from conscious awareness. Only, the people don't care because they believe they are good people.

Over time the denial of experience leads people to develop an ill-fitting personality. This certainly is not good. What's more, the ill-fittingness is not acknowledged as the reasons for the emerging traits are not in conscious view. The perception that people hold of themselves as good is sometimes an ego-trip that concerns the maintenance of their self view in a distorted fashion to prolong the positive feelings they experience from perceiving their self as good.

Behaviour based on reactivity of disownership leaves people susceptible to manipulation. If people have acted in a way that another dislikes, the other can focus on any theoretically possible negative result in an attempt to evoke guilt from misconduct. Similarly, if people have not acted in a way that another wants them to act, the other can focus on any theoretically possible negative result in an attempt to evoke guilt stemming from a perception of neglect. Anger can be used abusively in both of these scenarios to elicit guilt (see Anger).

When the imaginary guilt is perceived in the mind of the reactive *good person*, they may well backtrack on their behaviour. Thus, they are manipulated into changing their behaviour because they simply want to avoid feeling guilt. Even though to backtrack may be the worst decision to make, social pressure from the other effects a change. Only, the change is not adaptive but maladaptive. The adjustment is based on the other's wants rather than an accurate perception of consequences.

If people want to be good rather than good intentioned, the ability to gauge whether actions or inactions will cause undue harm on others – offences that lead to guilt – is a valuable ability. Understanding exactly what guilt is enables people to make secure decisions. As people will have the knowledge they need to decide whether a person's persuasive talk or angry mood is an appropriate expression or not, it will help them to avoid being manipulated by guilt-trips.

One other primary abuse of the good image exists. People represent themselves as good natured to onlookers, so they avert suspicion from their intentions. Because they are free of suspicion, they gain positions of trust. They are then free to act with a degree of impunity in areas where others are vulnerable to their decisions. Passive-aggressive* people are especially prone to this masquerade.

Nevertheless, when individuals are perceived as good for prolonged periods, people find it difficult to accept insidious betrayals. It does not fit with the consistency of their perceptions, so the accusation is questioned repeatedly. Disbelief lingers. This is a normal process that could be considered a type of denial. The problem was believing in a perception of good that was inappropriately associated (see Trust).

Good

Old English. *God* = fitting or suitable.

1. The most general adjective of commendation, implying the existence in a high, or at least satisfactory, degree of characteristic qualities which are either admirable in themselves or useful for some purpose.

Gratitude

Gratitude is a positive feeling experienced towards others who have helped one's self or someone for whom one cares. Theoretically, people can be grateful for any action, sentiment or opinion another expresses that benefits them. Nevertheless, in reality, feelings of gratitude are most often caused by actions or expressions that have *significantly* aided people's states of affairs. When thinking of the person who has helped, a positive warm sensation that radiates around the chest area is experienced.

As it increases positive attachments in relationships, gratitude is a prosocial and moral emotion. When people are grateful, they feel positive themselves because they have been helped, but they also feel the same positivity towards the person who has helped. The positivity is associated with an implicit wish to voluntarily repay kindness. The intention of a grateful person is to repay, and this intention is infused with positive wishes and a joyful heart.

Because it breaks down social bonds and creates tension, resentment is the opposite of gratitude. Resentment slows people's thoughts, making them ruminate on dark and negative issues.[1] Resentment can make people brood over negative thoughts of others – thoughts that can turn hateful. Gratitude makes people feel warm joy that radiates from their chest as they think fondly of another person. Resentment can fuel an envious attitude that seeks malicious revenge whereas gratitude compels people to seek ways in which they can benefit another person's life. Resentment can lead to depression and compromise people's immune systems with an overload of negativity and stress.[2] Gratitude infuses people with positivity, psychologically and biologically, that inoculates them against disappointments and depressive episodes as it acts like a buoyancy aid to mood.[3]

Prosocial is a most appropriate word for gratitude due to the positive respectful interactions it sustains. When people look out onto the world and see selfishness, hardship and meanness in the character of others, the perceptions cause them to be negatively affected, and they become sad and concerned. When people look out onto the world and experience someone aiding them to progress and succeed, their view of the world implicitly becomes more optimistic and cheerful. If people perceive someone significantly helping them reach their goal, they are cheerful in the memories of those deeds and do not find the prospect of returning the favour daunting. They are compelled to contribute with a joyful heart. The initial act of being helped by another is a social action towards them and the appreciation of the act then binds them in voluntary gratitude.

Neuro-biologically, oxytocin is released when people perceive they are grateful, and it's felt in the chest area as warmly radiating joy. These positive feelings get added to an associated network of similar memories. People who have caused gratitude are associated with the positive memories (somatic markers*). Amazingly, social bonds and memories can repeatedly reactivate the neuro-biological release of oxytocin by simple exposure to people or even the thought of them.[4] Oxytocin is a hormone and neurotransmitter highly associated with bonding activities, intimacy and trust. It has potent anti-stress effects that include decreases in blood pressure, heart rate and cortisol levels that can last weeks. Peace and social cohesion of the human race owe much to the release of oxytocin. Released by behaviours which make people feel grateful, oxytocin is a marvellous piece of chemical engineering, or at least it seems so.

Gratitude fuels the creation of other positive emotions (such as admiration, joy, optimism and hope) and compels people to interact socially in a constructive way. Civilisation is partly constructed by the motivational forces that stem from gratitude.

If the repaying of an action feels like a burden, then gratitude is not felt. The warm and joyous feelings experienced with gratitude do not emerge when people feel in debt and obliged to help those who have helped them. Gratitude instinctively compels people to reciprocate behaviour voluntarily. Even if they have no means to repay a favour at the time, they want to at some point. Help is not resented.

Some people will not accept help from others due to having previously felt in debt when others have provided them with something. Unfortunately, as the experience was stressful for them before, this can lead people to reject benevolent acts from others as they do not want to feel indebted again. Some people seek to make others feel indebted to them, so they can feel important and dominant over the people who feel indebted. Although it's possible to mistake the two, especially for young people, this abusive behaviour is significantly different from the benevolence that creates gratitude. Indebtedness is not gratitude.

Also, when children have been neglected, they have not received behaviour from their parents or surroundings that led them to feel gratitude. Neglected people are often surprised when, in their late teens or adulthood, they suddenly feel for the first time a warm positive sensation due to appreciation of another. This is a pleasurable experience, which often leads to a time of mixed bittersweet feelings, when they reflect on how emotionally empty the narratives of their lives have been until that point.

This leads to the defining point of gratitude as *the* prosocial emotion. Gratitude depends on the behaviour of others, but benevolent behaviour has to be perceived for people to feel gratitude. This means that the more prosocial behaviour people are around the more they're likely to perceive benevolence and feel gratitude. Thus, the more likely they are to reciprocate the prosocial behaviour. This in turn creates more gratitude.

Because gratitude depends on the behaviour of others, it's not a simple case of feeling more gratitude about what one has in life. Although, that's not to say people have not overlooked behaviours that would make them feel gratitude if they empathised with individuals who have spent time helping them.

Gratitude is a mental health emotion. In recent empirical studies it's consistently associated with oxytocin and healthy people who have a positive mental outlook. Studies have confirmed that people who feel gratitude are happier than those that do not. Gratitude is one of the best inoculations against negative emotional states becoming unbearable.

Gratitude

Latin. *Gratus* = thanks, pleasing.
Medieval Latin. *Gratitudinem* = 'thankfulness'
from 1560s.

1.   The quality of being thankful; readiness to show appreciation for and to return kindness.

2.   A feeling of thankfulness or appreciation, as for gifts or favours.

Guilt

Guilt is a negative emotion that people experience when they perceive they have caused undue harm to another. The thoughts or perceptions that cause people to feel guilt might be accurate or inaccurate. Perceptions create emotions. If people believe a perception, they feel the associated emotion.

Guilt is an incredibly powerful social emotion of paramount importance to the development of intelligence, yet it's also used to take advantage of people. It can be an intensely abusive tool for controlling others.

The undue damaging effects that people cause others are called offences. Offences correlate to the causation of guilt.

Pain is usually defined as a physical reaction to cell damage. In a similar manner, guilt is emotional pain. When people perceive they have caused undue harm to someone they care for, it hurts them emotionally. The paralysing and recoiling emotional reaction of guilt is very much like a reaction to cell damage, but the cell damage of another. It's to stop undue damage to other people and ultimately the guilty person's future social opportunities – with the thought the cared-for person is an extension of one's self (the extended-self).

There can be far reaching and unpredictable social consequences to unduly harming someone. This means people can fear both the damage they have caused people and the consequences of third-party actions. Fear of damage to reputation, fear of rejection, and fear of punishment may all accompany an experience of guilt.

The experience of guilt causes an array of reactions and outlooks that people further become emotionally affected by – in many ways every day without them realising it. Guilt acts as a guide of 'where not to go' and 'what not to do'. Secondary emotions, such as guilt, are triggered and processed in the right prefrontal lobe, and they're now intrinsic to human social experience.[1] Because of this instinctive use, people often do not realise how frequently they make decisions which partially use guilt to inform those decisions.

Guilt has had far more influence over human development than is commonly acknowledged. One of the reasons for this oversight can be the thought that the Christian Church invented guilt as a method of social mind control. As guilt is an evolutionary, socially intrinsic, emotion that was around long before holy men walked the earth, giving religion the credit for creating guilt is a purely fantastical suggestion. Guilt *is* used as an abusive tool to control people (see Anger). Nevertheless, it's also a natural reaction to the unduly damaging consequences of one's actions.

Guilt is an amazing, complex emotion that can be intellectually fantasised into very obscure meanings with subjective* rules of engagement. Personal interpretations of guilt can strike people to their core and physically, emotionally and mentally paralyse them in a split second. This is true even though the subjective reasoning behind their paralysis may not be understood by those around them. Due to intensely ideological views, feelings of guilt can be far removed from common sense. If people feel guilty, they have a perception that they are doing something unjust or causing unnecessary harm to another. Nonetheless, feeling guilt does not mean that they are guilty because it's their perception of the situation that creates their guilt, and perceptions can be inaccurate or even fictitious imaginings.

Predicting guilt informs interactions with others. People create scenarios in their imaginations to predict the outcomes of their actions. These can be incredibly accurate, yet they can also be completely fantastical. Nevertheless, people instinctively detect and avoid issues of guilt. If people predict a course of action would lead them to feeling guilt, they generally avoid it as that would have damaging effects on their surroundings; it means they won't fit in, and that it's not a good decision. Looking through an evolutionary lens, it's clear to see that if people did something wrong in the distant past, say two hundred thousand years ago, the mistake could have been fatal and resulted in their death or the death of someone close to them. Humans partially learnt to imagine complex and dynamic situations, regarding their personal actions in relationships, to keep their families out of serious trouble.

This prediction of guilt is literally a lifesaver that's evolved into a primary way of keeping people from making mistakes. Guilt always has a moral connotation. Back in bygone eras the effects of mistakes would have had more serious consequences on morale than at present.

Because of the length of time in human evolution where getting things wrong was a deadly affair, it's reasonable to suggest that the reason guilt can create such strong physical, mental and emotional paralysis is due to instinctive suspicions of deadly mistakes. Life was increasingly more violent the further back history goes. Human emotional instincts evolved through those environments, and they reflect specific responses to real challenges faced on earth.

If the prehistoric past is brought into a present day scenario, how would people feel if they sent one of their children to get food alone, because they couldn't be bothered, and their child was attacked or seriously injured? What if people tested a new food on a family member and they died? What if people did not provide enough for their children who then withered and died before their eyes? Just imagine the consequences of being in a pre-historical situation without a mate and having three young children to provide for, or being a child with no parents.

If someone had been responsible for such an occurrence, these are perceptions that could potentially create immense amounts of guilt. It would shock a human to their core. These dramatic examples are to briefly illustrate the serious and deadly consequences of making mistakes for a couple of million years while humans evolved. This would suggest that if people are caused to feel serious guilt about their behaviour, their instincts would relate the feelings to potentially deadly consequences for acting in such a way. Psychologically, an associative network of similarly toned emotions is kept, and when a strong emotion is felt, experiences of a similar emotional tone are brought to mind for comparison, so as age-old instincts would not relay an explicit conscious memory to mind, this would perhaps be felt as deep dread, an omen, or frightful trepidation.

Consequences to mistakes are usually far less severe in modern Western cultures than they ever have been in the entirety of human history on earth. This means that people can unwittingly make others feel as if there are potential deadly consequences to acting in certain ways. Notice that this would typically be an intense fear or sense of responsibility, and not thoughts of death. Expressing intense amounts of anger can induce serious guilt in people. Children are more vulnerable than any others to this type of induced emotional conditioning – which is abusive.

In modern life, people have more opportunities than ever before to re-assess *how offensive* their actions are. If people have done something wrong, it's important to distinguish *how guilty* they should feel, so their reactions are appropriate.

Humans can partly attribute the processing power required to comprehend outcomes of such dynamic situations to the development of their cognitive abilities. The development of human brainpower is related to the computational processes involved in their ability to perceive guilty issues. Human intelligence is bound to the ability to anticipate. Human success is bound to the ability to predict and avoid trouble.

Although guilt is a very effective way to get someone to stop doing something, it's also detrimental to a person's integrity when overused or abused. When the possibility of danger is conveyed to someone as an accurate statement of reality, the amount of guilt people would potentially feel if they were to place someone in that danger would be appropriate to reality. Be that as it may, if the conveyed danger is fictitious, and people believe it, they would think that a danger is present when in reality that is not true. Psychologically, this would create a delusion. The people would experience and express inappropriate emotions surrounding the given situation.

If a child was repeatedly made to feel guilt unduly throughout their upbringing by a significant other, as a means to stop them from doing things, the impressionable child would be made to live in a partially delusive state. They would experience inappropriate emotions with every inaccurate perception of guilt. The child's behaviour would be severely curbed. Their ability to respond would be seriously hindered.

The maladjusted, reactive behaviour would not stop there. Guilt stops people from acting, but it also compels people to act against others where they perceive they should feel guilt. This leads to a situation where people who perceive guilt inaccurately will try to discipline others according to their misguided principles. Believing in a false perception of guilt compels people to create social discords while exhibiting a righteously indignant air of superiority.

Surprisingly, to see if they are just towards others, people need to reflect on their feelings of guilt and the perceptions from which they stem. Feelings of guilt, in this respect, are issues that people can use for personal development that always bear fruit. Imagine people who have been stopped by guilt from behaving in certain ways, yet they discover on closer inspection there's no need to feel guilty (or as guilty). This is a truly liberating experience. One that can have far reaching consequences to self-esteem. This is related to what people believe they deserve on a subconscious level and subsequently to self-defeating behaviours too.

The truth is, on closer inspection, many feelings of guilt have been passed on to people from their parents, significant others and environment when they were young and impressionable. The amount of issues people hold that they have unknowingly inherited from this period, without realising it, is astonishing. Personalities are made up of beliefs that are more concerned with what people inherited than they are comfortable to admit. These inherited guilt issues, which people have become convinced of without realising it, are of great value to personal development. Principles can quickly become out-dated in a fast moving world, yet they do not have to be wholly discarded, for they can be updated.

These principles could have been taught as a form of overbearing and inconsiderate control or as an attempt to guide. The point remains that people inherited them from others who are just as fallible as they are – maybe more so, for those others also inherited guilt issues that they were unaware of. This ultimately leads to the solid conviction that humans are being misguided through inherited principles to some degree. This on a larger scale is an evolutionary process of updating the views, which people have inherited, to be appropriate to current affairs; social evolution in action. Guilt is what determines many of the principles people hold and many of the things they will or will not do. Guilt, or its avoidance, is at the centre of personal and social development.

Nevertheless, guilt is not an easy conviction to overturn. If people feel guilty about something and then realise that they should not feel so guilty, it's usually not as simple as letting go and behaving in a way they previously thought was wrong. Habits of not doing something can be as hard to break as habits of doing something. This difficulty is compounded by doing something they previously thought was wrong or even sinful. Individuals have the final say when it comes to the actual decision of whether they should feel guilty. Perhaps more appropriately the definition should be 'how much guilt' they should feel. Believing in personal judgement enough to overcome the convictions that have been inherited can be a major problem.

A significant reason for this difficulty in challenging previously held principles concerns who originally informed the conviction. Attachment theory* has amassed more than fifty years of evidence.[2] A fitting example of convictions being passed on by a parent is the Visual Cliff experiment where toddlers are placed near the visual illusion of a sudden drop in the floor. When they approach the cliff, they turn to their nearby mothers for guidance. The mothers are instructed to give a positive, negative or neutral expression to communicate with their child (e.g. smiles, nods, frowns, shaking of the head or no expression). A positive response will send their toddler over the cliff. The babies' responses systematically and appropriately correspond to their mother's emotional cues, and no speech is needed.[3]

The conviction with which some childhood memories are encoded is significantly determined by whose expression is part of that memory. If a parent, especially a mother (primary caregiver), or significant other repeatedly expressed themselves in a way that made a child feel guilt, regarding specific situations, it's only reasonable to anticipate greater psychological resistance when challenging those convictions. People have to have the courage of their convictions.

Guilt is useful for issues of self-development as it indicates something people feel they should avoid, and if this is only partly untrue, they have gained an opportunity for self-liberation. On the other hand, if on closer inspection they find greater danger for others than they first thought, they have increased their ability to act responsibly.

There are issues to consider though. The lives of people who think of themselves as good people will revolve around the issue of guilt. They will avoid it with diligence. This makes them an easy and reliable target for persuasion methods that use guilt. People who think of themselves as good become the target of manipulation because it's so obvious that guilt motivates them, so they're often hypersensitive to it.

Nonetheless, manipulation aside, people who feel and accept feelings of guilt are more balanced people than those who do not. The recognition of guilt enables people to act appropriately and fit into their environment. Guilt enables progression while avoiding offensive mistakes that damage social prospects.

People who do not feel guilt are generally dangerous people. They may have chosen to ignore guilt because it would mean they could not pursue a course of action. It may be that they fear thinking of themselves as guilty, and the anxiety created from the thought of the retaliation that would ensue. Ultimately, they are ignoring the very thing that keeps them from doing harm to others. This can lead to people who think of themselves as good and virtuous while ignoring any guilt issues as a defence-mechanism*. They can keep the belief of themselves as good and virtuous people undisturbed as long as the emotion of guilt is pushed out of their conscious awareness. If they treat the guilty in very harsh and unforgivable ways, it would follow that they would have to be harsh and unforgivable to themselves. What they may find even worse is that they would be forced to change their attitudes towards the guilty to continue to think of themselves as just and virtuous people.

It may be surprising that people who do not feel guilt often have rigid personalities and deeply set belief systems. Many people think that those who do not feel guilt are free to do anything they want, but this thought is far from true. They usually do not feel guilt because they do not want to accept the consequences of what they have done, or are doing, due to their belief systems – belief systems they will ignore reality to maintain. People who do not feel guilt can act in desperate ways to maintain their perceived status.

Guilt issues create complex situations to address. In addition to the above scenarios, some people, especially the young, do not realise the full extent of the damaging effects of their behaviour because it has not been pointed out to them.

Also, a difference between personal guilt and criminal guilt exists. Laws change and criminally offensive behaviours in one year are not criminal offences a decade later. If laws represented the degree of undue harm inflicted, there would not be such disparity between criminal guilt and personal guilt, yet laws encompass more than the undue harm that is caused or could have been caused to others. They can include beliefs of how human beings should or should not act. Beliefs that are based on thoughts from thousands of years ago. Some laws include religious ideological inclinations. Such issues can supposedly represent offences to supreme supernatural figures of which only the holiest of men can commune with. Such perceptions are motivating a slow separation of church and state, in the West, that's resulting in judicial laws that represent more closely the undue harmful effects caused by actions.

For example, less than fifty-five years ago in Britain, people who attempted to commit suicide were sentenced to prison as criminals if their attempt failed. Where did their guilt lay? Who did they unduly damage? This inaccurately imposed guilt is also typified by the treatment of gay people. In some countries gays are criminals and in others they are not. Where is their guilt? What undue harm have they caused? In some cultures females are prohibited from educating themselves, and if they attempt to educate themselves, they are shot or executed as examples. Where did their guilt lay? The claims of religious laws cannot be proven, and they're based on beliefs and feelings that mainly pertain to a less evolved era.

Being pushed into convictions of guilt is something people should avoid with great effort, yet when guilt is naturally felt – not imposed – it leads to feelings of remorse. Guilt is a prosocial emotion because its prediction can stop people causing harm to others. When people have done something unjust, guilt-fuelled remorse compels them to repair the damage they have done, and to seek forgiveness.[4]

Guilt is one of the most difficult, significant, revealing and liberating emotions to work with when it comes to self-development.

Guilt

Old English. *Gylt* = crime, sin, fault, fine.
Old English. *Gieldan* = to pay for, debt.

1. A failure of duty, delinquency; offence, crime, sin.

2. Responsible for an action or event; the fault.

3. The fact of having committed, or being guilty of, some specified or implied offence; guiltiness.

Hate

Hate is passionate dislike, and it can be applied to anything or anyone.

The physical expressions of hate are far from uniform. They seem to be an idiosyncratic mixture of contempt and fury. Often the mouth is closed with a moderate pout as the upper lip is braced against the teeth. This stretches the nostrils into an open posture that enables the person to breathe more freely through the nose. Yet almost contradicting this movement, the upper lip moves forward and moderately up causing a partial shutting of the nostrils. The first flared nostril expression is associated with anger, fury and ferocity whilst the second is associated with contempt. This gives an impression that the instinct is to fight what one finds repugnant and wants to avoid. Glaring down one's nose intensely is a common expression of hate which suggests a strong connection with contempt.

The list of things that people can hate is endless: men, women, men and women, washing up, watching action movies, right-wing politics, left-wing politics, those who occupy the middle ground; et cetera.

People's most hated things are often passed on to them from their families or the environments where they spend most of their time. Social pressure is a significant reason for why people hate the things that they do. Ultimately, people's hatred for different things can seriously hinder how well they get on in life.

If resentment is felt towards someone many times, it can develop into hatred. People can inherit views that bias their perception of the world and make them feel mistreated or disrespected. These perceptions may be true or false, but in either case they are troublesome. The troublesome thing about hate is that people do not allow themselves to like the things they hate. That is not to say they would not like them, only that they will not allow for a situation to occur where they begin to like something or someone they hate. In this vein, people deny anything positive to be associated with the things they hate.

Hate does not necessarily describe ill-will towards someone or something, and it's different from malice and malevolence, yet especially when it's created from resentment, hate can include a punitive will motivated by malicious revenge. Ill intent is often meant when hatred is expressed, and this would more accurately be described as malicious hatred, for hate is also often used only to describe an extreme dislike for someone or something. Regardless of the underlying reasons, the word hate is frequently used to express the things people want nothing to do with.

Hate

Ancient Greek. *Kedos* = care, trouble, sorrow.

1. Passionate or intense dislike.

2. To feel extreme hostility towards.

Helplessness

Helplessness is having insufficient ability to influence change. It does not necessarily describe a bad situation although it's usually used in this sense. It describes an experience where people are vulnerable to something or someone and cannot change the situation themselves. Helplessness can completely strip people of self-confidence and mood can be seriously affected.

Serious helplessness and episodes of despair go hand-in-hand. There are many things that can make people depressed. The added complication of being helpless to resolve a situation drains confidence away, and as a result, deepens depressive episodes. This is especially true when the lack of self-confidence leads to a loss of hope. Despair can have the most devastating consequences on morale. Helplessness and despair experienced together can be a suicidal cocktail. Helplessness is seen as a passive inability to act that hinders people's progress. The truth is that it can be a devastating experience which can lead to many other negative emotions.

Even when they have no control, if people perceive they have an element of control over a situation, they remain calmer and panic less. The reverse is also true. When people perceive that they are helpless to effect change, their heart rate and blood pressure increase – especially concerning threatening situations. This leads to anxiety related stresses. If people perceive they are helpless to stop the loss of something, they will first experience anxiety related stresses, and then sad related stresses.[1] If people have a low tolerance of uncertainty, the perception of helplessness alone makes people highly susceptible to anxiety related depression.[2]

When people cannot stop abuse to themselves or a loved one, they feel helpless along with all the other traumatic emotions of the situation. Abuse can be a physical, mental, or an emotional experience.

When people cannot act against the abuse they receive, they may feel shame too.

The reasons for being helpless are many and varied. If people try numerous times to change their circumstances and fail to effect change, in time they will feel helpless as their motivated behaviours are exhausted. This is helplessness due to lacking an ability to overcome a situation. Sometimes, however, it's motivation itself that is robbed. Without motivation people are helpless. Fear strips people of motivation. In these situations people need courage or an intervention from someone else who is willing to help. Interventions of others that aid the helpless can be truly life changing, for they relieve a person of serious stress (see Stress).

Beliefs, theories and principles also have the ability to deprive people of motivation. The power of the human imagination is striking. The influence the mind can exert over behaviour is astonishing. Helplessness that is brought about by false reasoning can be the most difficult to resolve as it's not a simple matter of intervening to stop people taking advantage. The beliefs, theories and principles that deprive people of motivation can have their own defence-mechanisms[*] that protect the thoughts from being changed. Another complication is that beliefs and principles can be inherited, or passed on through memes[*], without the recipient being aware. This can lead people to assume that actions based on false reasoning, which deprive them of motivation and create their helplessness, are just a normal part of their life. Until they are forced to reflect seriously on the issue, no issue is perceived. This creates a scenario where people can be helpless owing to having no motivation, but having no idea why. Perceptions create emotions, and emotions are people's motivations. Inaccurate or misguided perceptions can cause a lack of motivation to help one's self. These kind of self-sabotaging perceptions paralyse people into apathy – a deep lack of interest that could be considered a form of helplessness.

It may sound obvious to state that 'people should avoid getting into a situation where they are helpless around those who would take advantage of them', yet, for whatever reason, people do get themselves into such situations. This can be due to underestimating the potential dangers of being helpless to defend one's self mentally, emotionally, and physically around untrustworthy selfish characters. For people to take a chance that would place them in a situation where they are helpless around such characters is too dangerous; the risk of unpredictable consequences on mood is too great. If trust is broken in those moments, a psychological crisis will be created, and the consequences could last for decades.

Knowing in what situations people are helpless is useful for aiding them to cope, and stopping potential despair. Concern can be focused at those points, aiding people through their potential helpless situations by being ready to support them, and preventing anyone from taking advantage of their position. Standing back allows people to develop ways of coping around their helpless issues while someone is near who is prepared to intervene. Helplessness is always an individual thing that relates to the specific environments and weaknesses where people are powerless to act.

Stress Related

Helplessness

1. Destitute of help; having no assistance from others; needy. (Of persons, their condition, etc.)

2. Having no resources in oneself; unable to help oneself. (The ordinary current sense.)

3. The inability to help oneself.

Hope

Hope is a desire for a most wanted event to come true. It's where the heart has invested in something. Hope relates to internal representations of the future. Typically, the temporal closeness of a hope will be moving towards the person who holds it as he or she fulfils objectives.

Hopes are plans that become subconsciously organised goals for life. The imagination is an interface between the conscious and subconscious appreciation of reality. The five senses, memories, conscious, and unconscious data can all merge within the imagination. In this theatre, plays can be created from any sources of information. Theories, hypotheses, plans, decisions and convictions are formed on what is shown in the sublime skeletal hall.

Subconscious activity uses the data from the imagination for the concerns of making sense of the outer world. When information comes in through the senses and passes through the imagination, additional meaning can be embedded onto the data that the subconscious takes as fact. When ideas in the imagination are imprinted with the deepest desire that they come true, hopes are created.

Hopes are built by what people imagine could be possible. This concerns how a visceral* view of the world is constructed. The organisation of people's highest priorities – hopes – is submitted through the imagination to the unconscious for processing. The processing power of the unconscious is mighty. Raw unconscious processing of hopes creates a psychological architecture from which motivations, inclinations, and disinclinations are issued. Interests and passions are subconscious guides aimed at making hopes come true.

Hope is concerned with priorities and possibilities. The range of possibilities is usually related to what people can imagine – including the most fantastical of all possibilities. Even if an imagined state is completely unrealistic, people can still hope for it to come true. This shows how varied hopes can be. People may see that something is not possible in their lifetime, or for hundreds of years, but they can still hope it will come to pass. They can even pass their hopes on to their children for them to pass on to their children, so each consecutive generation becomes the embodiment of their parent's hopes and dreams. Thus showing how infinite hope can be.

So hopes can be timeless. As long as people do not expect them to come true in their lifetimes, they can imagine that they will come true at some point. As despair is the loss of hope, this enables people to avoid despair for generations upon generations. For as long as people think a remote possibility exists that the desired thing could still come true, hope is alive. In this way, people can hope and work towards things for thousands of years. Besides having the ability to be completely fantastical whilst delivering no despair, these infinite hopes are rare compared to everyday normal hopes.

The hopes that could come true tomorrow, or next year, are the most consequential as their effect is guaranteed to influence mood. These are hopes people cannot avoid seeing, without delusion, whether they come true or not. If a hope does not come true, people experience despair upon the realisation that a dreamed scenario is lost. If the hope is lost, how significant the dream is will determine how much despair is felt. Despair, losses and failures do not nourish people. An opposite effect occurs. Psychological and neuro-biological systems are affected with the equivalent of depressive episodes. This affect induces people to ruminate analytically on the causes of their defeat, so similar sad memories are instinctively recalled to mind for comparison purposes.[1] One lost hope can recall numerous other losses into memory. A hope being lost is felt as the most serious of failures. Losing one hope after another is especially unhealthy. The loss of consecutive hopes can lead to serious episodes of depression.

Unrealistic hopes are a troubling prospect as they have despair encapsulated within them. Nonetheless, everyone has hopes that are unrealistic to some degree. People have to work through the despair as they persevere – adjusting hopes to be more realistic along the way. Hopes have to be tailored to personal circumstances as there is no *one size fits all*. In this sense, realistic represents what is appropriate for the individual in question. How realistic people's hopes and dreams are is a very reliable indicator of how stable they are psychologically and emotionally. Tests have been designed to gauge how realistic people's expectations and hopes are as an assessment before therapy.

Realistic and achievable hopes offer stable psychological health. Each achieved objective on the way towards a hoped-for situation will create gladness. Each achieved hope is felt as a psychological and neuro-biological success that releases positive neurotransmitters and hormones. The results are deeply satisfying feelings, such as joy and elation. These positive emotions disengage the mind from ruminating analytical thinking, and in so doing they release psychological, neural and physical tension.[2] This is accompanied with a boost in optimism which also contributes positively to immune system functioning.[3]

Successes also build an internal sense of control over the world. They develop a sense of self-control, self-belief and security that helps people overcome feelings of helplessness. They make confident individuals who are not afraid to be assertive when they need to be. High self-esteem and self-confidence inoculates people against the negative experiences which everyone inevitably feels from time-to-time. The deep sense of satisfaction that arises from hopes coming true acts to buffer any negative experiences (such as frustration, disappointment and despair).[4]

Because despair is caused when hope is lost, it's sensible to manage the amount of hopes being worked towards. Focusing on a few hopes that all come true is much more healthy and stable than having a dozen hopes of which only a few come true.

Hopes give direction and purpose to life, for they drive people to their desired destinations. They are personalised destinies. Having realistic hopes does not mean the hopes are dull. The achievement of hopes makes people joyous; it also leads to the creation of new hopes that form as an extension of the hopes already achieved. A hope that was once unattainable will become a realistic goal in time. Hopes are built on hopes. People can reach for the stars and be filled with joy along the way.

If hopes are unrealistic, they can be the ruin of people. If hopes are realistic and achieved, they can be the making of people. If people have no hopes, they will spare themselves the possible despair and pain that goes with them, yet they will also deprive themselves of chances to become more healthy, secure, confident, assertive and driven individuals. The defining point is how realistic people can keep their dreams. How many hopes can a person realistically achieve at any one point in time?

Maintaining realistic dreams may not initially be as exciting as keeping high hopes, but achieving hopes is a joyous experience that can lead to higher hopes in time. Achieving hopes is the way people build their ability to predict and control the world. Understanding one's self gives people the psychological, emotional, and physical confidence to enjoy their lives as they succeed.

Hope

Old English. *Hope* = wish, expect, look forward (to something); 'hop' on the notion of 'leaping in expectation'.

1. Expectation of something desired: desire combined with expectation.

2. A person or thing that gives hope or promise for the future, or in which hopes are centred.

Horror

Horror is extreme fear mixed with disgust. In other words, terror and disgust blended together equals horror.

Intense perceptions, generally, cause all emotional expressions to become exaggerated and more erratic in nature. Intense emotions progressively assume control of behaviour as they intensify.[1] Horror is a prime example of such varying extremes of expression. There are initial expressions which always accompany the emotion, for example dramatically raised eyebrows with a corresponding gaping mouth.[2] At the upper limit of horror continuity of expression breaks down and some actions are expressed while others are not.

If a shocking event turns out to be negative, the expression morphs into horror or terror. Horror and terror are both expressions of extreme fear, and they're very similar in their expressions. What separates the two is horror's additional element of revulsion.

The mouth is violently opened, just like terror, and the lower jaw may virtually lock near the chest. In addition, the tongue may be pushed out as if vomiting. Not always, but in some cases, abdominal muscles may contract so violently that vomiting occurs. This is often accompanied by a violent shudder as if shaking something off, which is a common expression of disgust. Perceptions of severe bodily harm mixed with disease or mutilation are what cause classical horrific responses. Horror is a reaction to violently repulsive perceptions.

D-Day, June 6th 1944, one hundred and sixty thousand troops cross the English Channel as they take part in an amphibious landing onto the beaches of Northern France. Veterans describe the rough journey in uncomfortable sea vessels. They say how they aired a willingness to disembark with statements like 'the sooner we get off this damn boat the better'. Next they explain the worst days of their lives. They knew what to expect, yet they walk up the shore in shock. Witnessing the violent scenes shakes them to their cores, and they wonder if they will get out alive. Veterans report feeling sick to the bottom of their stomachs as they walk up the beaches in their units watching the carnage of thousands of allied soldiers. Bodies lay dead, writhing, and twitching from excruciating pain, yet even if it is their best friend that has fallen, everyone has strict orders to keep on marching past the bodies, to give first aid to no one. Under grey skies, sickly zombie-like structures walk with eyes pinned open and gaping mouths as they march through rows of their comrade's mutilated bodies. This was the horror of twentieth-century war.

The *horror* film genre, when analysed, can be seen to create situations that elicit both intense fear and disgust.

A student is walking down a long corridor at a downtrodden college. She notices movement on the floor at the far end of the corridor. Whatever it is, it's moving quickly her way. Lots of running legs and heads come into focus. A troop of big hairy spiders are approaching. Eyes open wide and mouth gaping she stares in disbelief. Shocked, she freezes on the spot. As she turns to run, she feels a sharp stabbing pain in the foot on which she's pivoting. Falling to her hands and knees the sharp pain in her foot gains a hairy sensation. She looks down to see a large spider with its bloody fangs embedded in her foot. The spider is moving around as it tries to gain a more secure location from which to sink a bite. The troop of spiders is getting closer. Horrified, she scrabbles to her feet and runs down the corridor with the spider still attached to her foot.

If people imagine a horrific situation or watch a horror movie, their emotional reactions will be far less dramatic than if they were a soldier walking up the beaches on D-Day. There are different intensities of emotion for being the soldier, imagining being the soldier, and imagining one's self watching the soldier. The more detached a view of the event is, the less intense the emotional reaction will be. Nevertheless, perceptions create emotions. If people believe a perception, they feel the associated emotion whether the perception is true or not.

Horror's expressions are otherwise the same as terror (see Terror).

Stress Related

Horror

Latin. *Horrere* = to bristle with fear, shudder.

1. An intense feeling of fear, shock, or disgust.

2. An intense, painful feeling of repugnance and fear.

Hostility

Hostility is the emotion felt towards a perceived enemy.

It can be a mixture of different negative feelings. Mistrust, contempt, suspicion, jealousy, envy, spite, and malice could be mixed and still be called hostility. Having an overall attitude towards another that categorises them as an enemy, regardless of specific emotions, is what constitutes hostility.

The word 'hostile' is commonly used to describe any unfriendly attitude towards someone. Hostility is characterised by unwillingness to be sociable towards a person or group, yet a reluctance to engage can be caused by many things. Unless a perception of an enemy exists, it's not hostility.

Nevertheless, sometimes, a continuous denial to relate to other people while consistently seeing them as a threat can be taken as a sign of strong underlying convictions that have developmental history. This means that the people who the hostility is being directed at may not be the people who created the negative attitude originally. They are perceived to resemble the makeup of a previous enemy. Such recognition of resemblance can happen subconsciously. People can automatically feel hostility, and act on those feelings without knowing it – known as acting-out*.

The ability to perceive hostility is important. People may underestimate the negativity of another's remarks or actions against them. If they realise that a person is being hostile towards them, they can determine the person views them as an enemy. This usually has a contextualising effect as it prompts people to consider why they are thought of as an enemy. Empathy begins. A key tool in conflict resolution, empathy can give people the information they need to defuse a situation.

If people find that they cannot reason with a hostile person, then at least they have gained insight into why they're receiving negative attention. This enables people to act more appropriately than they could have otherwise, for information is gathered on the reasoning of the hostile person and defences are developed.

Hostility

Latin. *Hostilis* = enemy.

1. Pertaining to the characteristics of an enemy; pertaining to or engaged in actual hostilities.

Humiliation

Humiliation is the negative emotion experienced when being degraded by others in public. It's caused by shame that's made public. Although in exceptional circumstances people can humiliate themselves, predominantly humiliation is due to others exposing someone's shame.

Humiliation is a reduction in rank and self-esteem by bringing to light shameful behaviour – in front of others so people feel demeaned and have less status. Even when an element of truth exists in the situation, the public shame or humiliation is usually overstated and used as a tool to gain control over the social environment. It's most often unfair, and a planned malicious expression to injure and corrupt the view of a specific person in the eyes of others. Yet, sometimes, it's also an unavoidable consequence of justice.

Couples can, and do, humiliate each other and even their children as a way of controlling behaviour. The meaning in what they say is similar to 'you do that and I'll make others think you're disgraceful' or 'I will make you squirm and suffering'. This is as an attempt to condition people's behaviour by giving them a negative experience associated with it (Pavlovian fear conditioning*). Humiliation usually produces intense feelings inside the people who are humiliated. It creates mini shock responses. Feelings of shame, guilt, embarrassment, anger, outrage and even failure can make a person freeze psychologically as the feelings mix with the fear of punishment. The whole experience would be considered humiliating.

This shocking or stressing factor alarms the people on a physical level to avoid such situations, but at the same time deprives them of the chance to explain explicitly and memorise what is going on. This is because people memorise less explicit details when shocked. Humiliation may inhibit a person's actions, but it's not a good educational tool unless the aim is to teach a person how it feels to be increasingly traumatised. It's like a psychological cattle-prod.

Humiliation has little educational merit, and it's predominantly used as a form of cruel social control. The fearful shock-factor makes people alert to threats, yet it severely reduces their ability to think and remember intellectual content. As the memories are then more likely to be implicit-memories* that reside outside the boundaries of conscious reflection, it's incredibly difficult to learn from such events in the present and in hindsight.

Originally, humiliation meant the process of being humbled. The overriding sense to the word now is that of being punished, tortured, mistreated, and generally abused publicly: bring someone to their knees; break someone in public; ruin someone's reputation.

Humiliation is different from feeling humbled. People can feel humbled by the circumstances they find themselves in and it can be an entirely personal affair. No one else has to know for people to feel humbled by events that have taken place.

As humiliation is reducing the social value of a person in the eyes of others, however, those other people are part of the degrading process. Nevertheless, much of the time there would be no sense of *good motive* or *just cause*. It could be to gain control over a social environment with any form of malicious intent.

Because others have to know personal details of the people humiliated, embarrassment is similar to humiliation. An element of social pressure is inherent in both. Embarrassment is the less intense form of humiliation.

As an aim, humiliation is an abusive practice and should have no place in Western, modern judicial systems; it's no longer the intent of the letter of the law to seek humiliating outcomes. Such unjust practices were used in the past by states to horrify the public. The idea was to abuse the individuals publicly as a form of punishment, so others were terrified from repeating the actions of the individuals who were humiliated. Horrific acts could be employed and forced on to the people being humiliated. Humiliation was used, and still is, in many forms of torture. Although it would technically be more of a horrifying act as personal shame may

137

not be present, a prime example of horrific state sponsored humiliation is the outdated practice of tarring and feathering people in public. The inhumane nature of humiliation is what can cause people to break. This is also the reason it's increasingly seen as a more backward and unintelligent way of forcing people to conform.

Humiliation, at its core, is often about getting people to become submissive from the realisation that others view them as wretched, contemptible or disgusting. Causing people so much psychological anguish that they give in and obey. This duress and disgust from others helps those responsible for the humiliation to dominate the submissive and ultimately get what they want. Many humiliating circumstances are created by power-trips based on domination that is ego-centric in nature. This is why humiliation is so heavily associated with abusive personalities. This process of breaking and marring the reputation of people in public can in no way be compared to personal humility or remorse of any kind.

People may not have done anything that is worthy of disgrace, yet lies and inflated truths can be created. This can lead to a group publically abusing someone, but the supposedly humiliated person feels contempt and disgust for his or her punishers. Humiliation is used to make others feel a deep sense of imposed pain, shame, and guilt. The *exposing of shame* or the *imposing of shame* on another while experiencing the feelings of being dominant are the hallmarks of people who purposefully humiliate others.

People seek to corrupt the reputation of others. Not to stop criminal behaviour, but to gain power. Cruel people are willing to cause an effect regardless of morality. They are people who will use power abusively. This can be seen in an ego-trip of being dominant over another human being. 'I am dominant and you will respect my authority' can often be a motive of the humiliating person. 'I will make you feel pain and know what it's like to be publically abused if you do that' is another humiliating motive. Because retaliation is less likely, abuse of all forms is highly associated with positions where a power differential exists. This is true of humiliation.

Nevertheless, humiliation is used on a day-to-day basis in smaller, more unnoticeable doses. It has a far more insidious effect on society than is commonly acknowledged. People who are repeatedly treated in a humiliating fashion can experience serious psychological conditions. Depressive episodes are probably the most common and disturbing effect. A general mistrust of people due to a loss of faith in human nature can be partially responsible for this. Long lasting self-esteem issues can develop as people are forced to acknowledge seriously degrading feelings about themselves. If a false inward acknowledgement is believed, it can create an erroneous sense of shame that can linger for years and even a lifetime.

Gossip is 'unconfirmed as true personal details about others in casual conversation'. Gossip is concerned with the reputation of others, so it's relevant to both embarrassment and humiliation, for both of these emotions relate to social pressure.

Malicious gossip is intended to harm the reputation of others, and it's probably the most frequent situation where humiliation is purposefully *used* in current day social environments. Malicious gossip uses lies and inflated truths to publically humiliate people. This often involves one person within a group singling out someone outside the group to humiliate, and then the group joins in.

Malicious gossip is not to be confused with lively conversations that people have about themselves or their friends and family in an informative and caring fashion. A common charade of a malicious gossip, however, is to present their self as a caring and informative person. As society generally lets people off if their intentions are good, this can be explained as an attempt to avoid being seen as responsible for the trouble caused by misrepresenting people. Malicious gossips want to be seen as good, so they can get away with being bad, for perception of malicious injustice results in anger and aggression towards the malicious agent.[1] A way to reduce someone's anger is to convince them that the damaging behaviour was not intentional. Because many malicious gossips see this, they use it as a tool to pacify the people around them by stopping potential accusations and responsibilities coming their way. When coupled with the passive-aggressive* nature inherent in gossiping, this masquerade makes the effects of malicious gossip difficult to spot. Thus it can go unnoticed.

In history, males have bullied others in their environment mainly by getting them to fear physical injury. Malicious gossip has traditionally been used by female groups to humiliate others into psychological submission by fearing injury by malicious misrepresentation. Therefore, especially through the young adult years where females are typically more socially adept, malicious gossip can be considered as the female form of social bullying.

The malicious gossip uses lies and inflated truths to conjure disgraceful and degrading images of people in the minds of others. This is an attempt to gain control over the social environment and make other people fear them. People do not want others to treat them in a humiliating fashion and spread lies about them in their environment. Malicious gossips make people afraid to challenge their immoral behaviour by fearing rumours of misrepresentation.

Although teenage and young adult women are the most common people to employ humiliation through misrepresentation and manipulation of information, they are definitely not the only offenders. Politics is highly associated with humiliating accusations. Think of the politician who authorises the release of information that will embarrass a colleague or an opponent of whom they are jealous. Humiliation can be used by people to reduce the chances of promotion of a colleague whilst increasing their prospects by eliminating a rival. Humiliation can be used as a passive-aggressive weapon to hurt a victim by corrupting the victim's image in the eyes of others.

As normally females develop greater emotional and social comprehension from a younger age than males, this creates a power differential that can be abused. Humiliation is used to gain attention and social status by reducing the reputation of another. To get the attention of others and gain some social dominance, the malicious gossip attempts to ruin the life of another by singling them out and marring them. This leads to young people all over societies being treated in this cruel malicious fashion by their peers and suffering the psychological effects of being attacked and disgraced. Malicious gossips, just like most bullies, have a tendency to target vulnerable people that cannot hit back.

However people become the target, the malicious gossip seeks to bring them down a notch or two by making them feel small and ashamed in public. This behaviour, in reality, sends lots of young minds into despair.

Social media can be employed to mar people. The effect can be to send them into episodes of depression that can spiral out of control. Sometimes ending in suicide. When a group of girls has influence over a gang of boys, physical intimidation is more likely to be used in conjunction to enforce the malicious gossip. Victims of malicious gossip do not usually speak out, but in these cases victims could also be terrified too, so reducing the likelihood of speaking out further. Just like adolescent boys or men who intimidate and demoralise others to the point of breaking, so do teenage and young adult women who maliciously humiliate others. They can think it makes them cool and superior. It's not uncommon for malicious gossips to walk around like they are most intelligent. 'Look how clever I am, I can humiliate that person.' 'How disgusting is she?' This is the narcissistic ethos to which malicious gossips live.

People are easily fooled, and drawn in to insulting others – missing the true intentions behind the marring and overlooking an immoral attempt to gain control over the social environment by making other people feel insecure about themselves and others. When people feel insecure, they naturally become passive, so this creates an opportunity for others to dominate the social situation.

It can be very hard for younger adults, especially males, to recognise such behaviour. Because they don't want to become the target, it can be so easy for people to duck their heads and let the situation pass. When people do become the target, it can be difficult to control strong emotions that become too resentful, too envious, too jealous, and passive-aggressive in nature. It can be difficult to remember *no shame exists* in talking about the abusive behaviour of malicious gossips to friends, family or teachers. This does not make you like them, and it's not manipulation to air such concerns. Talking genuinely about concerns is completely different from malicious manipulation of conversations.

Just like physical bullying, psychological bullying is detrimental to people's health. These malicious and immoral practices should be seen in the same way that any bullying is viewed.

If in the process of seeking justice someone is unavoidably humiliated from having his or her shameful behaviour revealed, then this would be reasonable as it's raised from a 'need to know' situation. Be that as it may, humiliation *alone* is frequently used to scare and bully people with rumours aimed at corrupting their image in the eyes of others.

Humiliation

Latin. *Humiliare* = to humble.

1. Subdued or brought low in condition or social status.

2. To be made to feel insecure by shame or wounded pride.

3. To be caused to kneel or beg.

<u>Ignorance</u>

Ignorance is disregard of information. The word 'ignorant' is sometimes used only to describe a person who is not aware of something, and without any implication of active rejection. Nonetheless, ignorance as 'the active rejection of information' is described below.

Ignorance is commonly thought of as a bad thing, and in many cases this is true, yet it's also a good and healthy thing to use appropriately – by reducing anxieties and increasing confidence.

As with bad behaviours, guilt is highly associated with ignorance. People consciously and unconsciously try to avoid feeling guilt regarding behaviours that benefit them – behaviours that have an awkward side-effect of being detrimental to others. This conscious process, which pushes out of awareness the uncomfortable emotions or thoughts people do not want to own*, is referred to as ignorance or cognitive-avoidance*.

The perception of one's ability to cope with experiences of life is central to ignorance, and, especially, perception of one's ability to cope with both uncertainty and intensely arousing events.[1] If people fear uncertain outcomes, they are more likely to ignore information and situations that they believe will lead to uncertainty. If people fear loss of behavioural control by becoming too aroused, they are more likely to ignore information and situations they believe will lead them to become highly aroused.

The ability to ignore thoughts and feelings can be a good thing. When thoughts and feelings would lead people to become over aroused, and then to uncontrollable behaviour that leads them to uncertain outcomes (e.g. seduced by images of sex or drugs), the ability to ignore thoughts and feelings can be a good thing. Ignorance gives people a degree of control.

Nevertheless, an issue exists when ignoring material constantly. If people have ignored information around a feared event, they will be less anxious than those who thought about the feared event, yet if a feared event comes true, the ignorant will become more physiologically stressed than those who had thought about it.[2] As long as a situation does not occur where people encounter their ignored fear, ignorance can provide them with less conscious anxiety. If people do encounter an ignored fear, they will be less prepared for the contingencies, and they will be prone to enter a state of crisis, so they will be less able to cope with the consequences.

This helplessness can create serious problems. When people are negatively affected, their attention narrows to focus on the problem whilst reducing their attention to other cues.[3] Furthermore, as emotions reach higher intensities, they progressively assume control of people's behaviour by instinctively orientating their disposition to attend to the intense event.[4] Unfortunately, in this case, that means reinforcing focus onto the feared and ignored content which further stresses their systems. People are then effectively locked into focusing on the very thing that is causing them psychological, neurological and physiological distress. Thus the word 'crisis' is a very apt word to describe the experience when people encounter feared material they have consistently ignored.

These issues are evidence that ignorance is not always good or bad, but it can be either. Ignorance always shows an attempt to cope with reality though.

Ignorance that stems from a subconscious source is classified as a defence-mechanism[*] called denial. A defence-mechanism's aim is to reduce conscious anxiety. The person can then continue with behaviour without consciously spending energy (psychological and neuro-biological) on vigilant behaviours involved in anxiously fearing consequences associated with the behaviour. Guilt can be avoided this way. People who behave in ways that are detrimental to others are frequent employers of ignorance. Continuous use of such ignorance can significantly reduce people's anxiety if they are not faced with the avoided material, but they can be left feeling under-par without knowing why. This is because the *reasons* associated with the *feelings* are not shown in conscious view.

An internal separation between behaviour and feeling is created. A barrier to self-knowledge is constructed. Denial is probably the most frequently used defence-mechanism.

It is important to note that when emotions are pushed out of awareness, either consciously or unconsciously, those emotions continue to motivate behaviours. This is called acting-out*. The problem with acting-out is that people cannot see motivational aspects of their behaviours. They feel compelled to behave in ways they don't understand.

If people are told information that would seriously compromise the makeup of their personality, it can lead to serious mental disarray or breakdown. At these points in time, it's healthy to ignore such information until a time when the information can be managed and integrated with less traumatic consequences. This is especially true when people are told information that is spiteful or malicious in nature. If the material is meant to damage people's mental outlook and cause them a state of mental anguish, then it's best to ignore its validity as its aim is destructive.

Defence-mechanisms are created by the subconscious, and they prompt people to avoid accepting feelings and thoughts that would adversely affect the way people view themselves. Defence-mechanisms can distract people's attention, rationalise information into a less harmful interpretation, or completely deny material. For the most part they are at work without people realising it. They are part of a healthy psychological architecture. If people are self-aware, they may be able to see their defence-mechanisms at work on the edge of their awareness, so the process is not completely out of conscious control.

People can learn to ignore the same harmful things consciously. They can also learn the process of ignoring information that makes them seriously uncomfortable whilst being aware they intend to process the information at a later time. They can create a sort of conscious buffer-zone where they do not fully recognise the credentials of something. Rather they think about it in a 'what if' light until it can fit in with the makeup of their personality without causing as much shock. This is not a cop-out, but a serious appreciation of a psychological consequence.

Again, the conscious filtering process just described is virtually identical to the subconscious one called a defence-mechanism. People's consciousness has been evolving for hundreds of thousands of years and the emergence of an ability to emulate the subconscious processes consciously is an extraordinary evolutionary step. Consciously understanding their motivations provides people with greater adaptability, and broad agreement exists that these are the reasons that humans have developed consciousness of their emotions.[5]

All people have architectural thoughts, with their related neural patterns, in their brains that constitute mental and emotional integrity. People's mental architecture of learned meanings and responses can be modified, but they need to be aware that their mental structures may need time to integrate new information, especially if it conflicts with their existing structure.

Experience has shown that overuse of defence-mechanisms has unfortunate side-effects for personalities. Problems are raised when people ignore more information than is healthy. People progressively have an underdeveloped view on life with very brittle, less adaptive, personalities which exhibit strict defining points. If people continue down such a path, it can leave them in a vulnerable position where their internal frame of reference is overly sheltered from reality. Such a psychological outlook more easily enters a state of crisis if exposed to conventional thoughts and ideals. Ironically, something people use to protect them from conscious anxiety can potentially lead to mental breakdown. The severity of the potential breakdown will be directly relevant to how ignorant they've been.

Ignorance is bliss lived in a fragile glass tower.

The more people ignore the consequences, the greater their crisis will be if and when those consequences come true.

Pride in one's social status is a main employer of ignorance when people wish to maintain an ego-trip. They see their self (ego) in terms of their current social status, so information that is perceived to decrease their social status is ignored or deemed invalid. This is how people subjectively* keep their ego-trip alive. As they could be suggesting that they are prideful, self-delusive, and only interested in the feelings that stem from their unrealistic subjective image of self, people dislike it when someone calls them ignorant. There's an implicit suggestion they're irresponsible people who cannot accept reality. There's an accusation of being selfish to an extent that denies reality.

As it's a main way humans have evolved to filter data – whether they realise it or not – all people subconsciously deny things through defence-mechanisms. This ultimately helps protect them against malicious, or otherwise harmful, information and keeps them from being in a hyper-vigilant state of arousal – distracted all the time. Ignorance is a deep and far reaching issue that concerns complex personalities that are made and structured in considerably different ways. The unconscious can sort through personal issues in a healthy fashion, and gradually filter them into the edge of people's awareness for conscious processing. One of the most important aspects of this process is that the priority given to issues is relevant to the individual's psychological makeup. These issues are ordered according to personal hopes and environmental conditions, and not someone else's agenda.

Thus people should not feel free to ignore everything continually as this will make them prone to psycho-neuro-biological crisis when reality breaches the wall. Ignorance is specifically useful and healthy when dealing with malicious information, yet because they're afraid of being the clichéd IGNORANT person who lives in a crisis-stricken self-delusive world, people can wrongfully feel guilty about ignoring spiteful or malicious comments. The intricate balancing act of allowing, denying, and putting information on hold is not easy. Ignorance is good or bad depending on its application. Even though it may be frustrating for everybody else, ignorance is mostly used subconsciously for health reasons.

Ignorance

Latin. *Ignorare* = not to know, to be ignorant of, mistake, misunderstand, disregard.

1. Not to know, to be ignorant of.

2. Said of a Grand Jury: to return (a bill) with the endorsement of 'not a true bill', 'not found', 'no bill' – to reject as unfounded or having insufficient evidence; to refuse acceptance of.

3. To refuse to take notice of; not to recognise; to disregard intentionally, leave out of account or consideration, 'shut one's eyes to'.

Jealousy

Jealousy is 'fear of loss due to the rivalry of another'.

Although the word jealousy is in common use, many people have no exact understanding of what it means. As many people feel like they have done something deeply wrong if they have been caught in the act of being jealous, simply using the word can faze people quite dramatically.

The dramatic effect is partly due to jealousy's natural intermingling and confusion with envy, one of Christianity's seven deadly sins. A significant reason why many people cannot see jealousy in their self is because it would cause them to feel conscious anxiety. The source of the anxiety is then blocked from conscious view by a subconscious defence-mechanism*. So one of the main reasons why the emotion eludes people is because of an unwillingness to own* it.

Jealousy is a slippery emotion for another reason too.

Envy and jealousy both relate to possessions. Just as much as physical items, the term 'possession' is used here to refer to personal characteristics, talents, abilities, people, and positions. The thought that people are most often jealous, or envious, of material goods is false. The reverse is true. People experience jealousy and envy related to personal connections, characteristics, positions of power, or people far more than simple physical possessions.

Jealousy often leads to envy and envy often leads to jealousy. This entwined relationship is frequently complicated, and it blurs and blends the meanings together.

When people feel jealous, they fear the loss of a possession due to the rivalry of another. As an aspect of envy is 'the will to deprive people of a desirable possession', jealousy may be caused from a possession that someone else envies. When person A is envious of a possession of person B, B becomes jealous.

The intricacy of the interwoven emotions does not stop there. The feared loss has made person B feel deeply insecure, and at those moments the possessions of others often appear more attractive. Person B's jealousy may then morph into envy of a possession of person A. Such tit-for-tat attitudes create a confusing arrangement. Resentment and then justice can mistakenly be instilled into the pursuit of someone else's possession.

Therefore, person A's envy can make person B jealous. This causes B in turn to become envious of person A's possession. A then fears the loss of a possession and becomes jealous, and then wants a possession from B even more. Thus amplification of the initial envy happens, and it starts the process again.

Only, the envy and jealousy are more intense as the rounds get stacked. This potentially endless figure of eight contention is commonly referred to as a vicious cycle. The fact that both jealousy and envy relate to possessions, and that one can cause the other, makes these emotions exceptionally slippery to grasp.

This intricate interweaving of the two emotions is truly astounding. They are not inextricably linked, but their relationship can be entwined to such a degree that it's exasperating to try to tell them apart. Working out which one came first and why they're being felt can be vexing. When people manage to focus on one emotion, it merges into the other. So jealousy and envy often feel elusive emotions to understand. A clear definition that jealousy is concerned *only* with the 'fear of loss due to the rivalry of another' helps tremendously when discerning the complexities of such situations.

Perceptions create emotions.[1] Yet perceptions are not always accurate, so fears, insecurities, and anxieties are not always appropriate to the reality of a situation. Emotions may not be justified, but people feel them all the same. If people believe a perception, they experience the associated emotion.

Jealousy can concern the things that people care about most in the world; this is a significant reason for why it can be a volatile emotion.

Distinguishing jealousy from envy is difficult enough without passionate emotions also clouding the issue at hand – adding yet more complexity to the situation.

Since people's perceptions of a situation are creating their emotions, jealousy can be a frustrating cycle to experience for anybody who is afraid of losing anything valuable. This is especially true when it's another person who is perceived to be depriving people of someone important to them. Jealousy and envy can lead to unbearable and intolerable feelings that are not fully understood. Powerful emotions can bubble beneath the surface of an otherwise calm exterior.

Because people may not be able to own or even recognise jealousy, powerful emotions can uncontrollably motivate their behaviours. They start acting-out[*].

As deciphering the complexities of such a situation can seem impossible at times, all of these elements can make a psychological and emotional subjectivity that's intensely turbulent. Writing down concerns and reading then back a few days later is a valuable aid to comprehending passionate complex behaviour. Emotional literacy is key to understanding behaviour. As they should aim to have a comprehensive understanding of emotion and be explorative, counsellors and psychotherapists can help, for clients can use their professional understanding of emotion.

How valuable a possession is to people, plus the conviction of how real the perceived threat is, will determine how passionate their response will be. What are people willing to do or say to prevent the loss from happening? The value people give to the possession is the initial and overriding factor here. People will first fear losing the possession and then decide how real the threat is. So the conviction in the threat's validity is secondary and generally far more variable than the value placed in what people might lose. Both the perceptions (value and validity) can be changed, with self-reflection or counselling, to a more realistic appraisal of the individual scenario.

The more important the loss, the more powerful the emotions, and the more difficult the reflecting process will generally be. Knowing how important a possession is will help with the reflecting process because it's simpler to identify what possessions are causing what emotions. This is because recognising the connection between an emotion's intensity and its associated possession is more clearly apprehended. It's important for people to be honest with themselves when they judge how much they value a possession.

Emotional literacy determines to a large extent the accuracy of comprehending behaviour. Only the most intelligent creatures can think about their emotions. Conscious reflection on emotion is an evolutionary recent development, and it uses the highest faculties earthly creatures possess. The consciousness of emotion is broadly accepted to have evolved because it offers massive benefits in regard to understanding and adapting to complex behaviour.[2]

Jealously is one of the most common emotions in society, and it does not mean that people are inferior by expressing it. Jealousy is not a bad emotion. It means that people value and care about a possession which they fear losing. If people value something or someone substantially, they can spontaneously react in unpredictable and violent ways. The reaction to perceiving a potential loss can be the bad thing. The emotion of jealousy is an indicator of how valuable a possession is to a person. The actions warranted to keep the status quo are an individual's responsibility. Whether with malicious gossip or murderous rage, here is where people slip up. The course of action people decide upon is what can be the unacceptable, even criminal, aspect in cases of jealousy.

Jealousy is one of the best ways to glimpse how much people truly value something or someone. As one of the most intense and complex emotions, it's revealing, insightful and astounding to work through in personal development.

Jealousy

Ancient Greek. *Zelos* = more often in a good sense
emulation, rivalry, zeal.

1. Troubled by the belief, suspicion, or fear that
    the good that one desires to gain or keep for
    oneself has been or maybe diverted to another;
    resentful towards another on account of known
    or suspected rivalry.

2. In love or affection, especially in sexual love:
    apprehensive in being displaced in the love
    or good-will of someone; distrustful in the
    faithfulness of wife, husband or lover.

3. In respect of success or advantage: apprehensive
    of losing some desired benefit through the rivalry
    of another; feeling ill-will towards another on
    account of some advantage or superiority they
    possess or may possess; grudging, envious.

Joy

Joy is intense gladness created from events of significant success. When hopes come true, joy or elation is felt – whether in play or from hard work. Joy would typically describe the feelings experienced when minor hopes come true. Elation describes the experience of major hopes coming true.

Joy contributes to self-esteem, and it supports healthy moods in several ways. Positive emotions act as a buffer for negative emotions, so besides feeling positive, they help people cope with the challenges they experience in life.[1] Positive emotions orientate people's thought processes to make fast judgements from current knowledge bases – memory – in a creative flexible fashion that uses less cognitive processing than negative emotions.[2] These positive processes generally emerge from success (successes relate to safe situations), so the neuro-biological systems used for alertness turn off, or reduce their load.[3] Negative emotions, in their varying degrees, orientate dispositions and thought processes towards analytical ruminating focus that is effortful, alert and highly directed.[4] This puts stress on the neural pathways and body systems involved in supporting those alert dispositions, especially in fight-or-flight scenarios.[5]

Evidence is starting to emerge regarding right-hemisphere dominance for negative emotional processing and left-hemisphere dominance for positive emotional processing.[6] Theoretically suggesting, positive emotions disengage taxed systems that were processing negative emotions on the right-hemisphere by switching many cognitive processes over to the opposite side. The switch to a positive state reduces psychological (i.e. less effortful problem-solving cognition), neuro-biological (e.g. amygdala alertness, hormone and neurotransmitter production), and physical (e.g. cardiac output, muscle tension) stress in the process. So positive emotions are implicitly associated with relief. While people are enjoying a positive outcome, the more analytical side of their brain is recharging. This is referred to as *allostasis*[*] and means 'maintaining balance through change'.

Feelings of gladness, joy, delight and elation are all created from successful outcomes. Joy is a lasting, not a temporary, emotion and can be regarded as a fruit of hopes achieved. When considering the successful completion of hope and the experience of relief, the emotion contributes significantly to mood and to buoyancy of attitude. Joy presents the world with a rounded face adorned with a smile.

The success that joy originates from could be a personal achievement, yet it could be someone else's achievement too. The important point to note is how it's related to caring. Joy is a gregarious emotion. Joy is relevant to achievements and successes of significance that somehow contribute positively to the lives of the people who are the focus of care. If people see their parents, siblings or children having fun and laughing, they can feel glad or joyous as they witness everybody well and healthy in that moment. When compared to more significant successes, this would produce a positive feeling that would endure for a shorter time and be mild in nature. The event is positive, yet the effects of the event are relatively temporary, for they are relevant to the present more than the future. How long the joy lasts, and the degree of joy felt, is directly relevant to the perception that created it. A perception concerning how much of a positive contribution the event will have for the lives of the people concerned affects the intensity and duration of joy.

For example, if people do something that immensely contributes to the life of someone they care for, over the course of a couple of decades they can feel joy from how that one event helped a person many times. They will carry the joy of that one event in memory, and further joy as its contributions accumulate. That memory will continue to be felt as a success, and the positivity of that memory will illuminate their mood. This is how people can carry joy from one event throughout their lives until the day they die. The more of these events people have contributed to, the more positively the memories will radiate into contentment.

If people do not care for anyone, they cannot feel sad when things go wrong for that person, but they cannot feel glad when that person succeeds either. This is also true of caring for one's self. Experiencing despair or joy depends on failures and successes. When people care deeply about the hopes they hold, the more deeply they feel the outcomes of those hopes. When people hope for another person, they invest some of their well-being in those hopes. If the person fails, then they feel despair. If the person succeeds, then they feel joy. People have to care to feel joy.

The experience of joy is an important part of maintaining a healthy mental outlook, for it relieves stresses that have built up from negative emotions that have been focusing on problems. Joy effectively refreshes neuro-biological systems, and this is reflected in the mood of the person who experiences it. Play and work are important, for peoples hopes are wrapped-up in them, and so too their sanity.

Play is the safe, positive and fun part of the 'maintaining balance through change' that the body instinctively uses to rest parts of the mind and body that are more concerned with focused, negative attention, work. As long as people aren't deprived of their play, the more hopes people have wrapped up in their play, the more potential their play has to release them from their worries (see Hope). Both children and adults, who feel safe in play, work better.

Although it may seem counter-intuitive to care so much about hobbies and pastimes, this rather shallow conscious judgement comes from not appreciating the depth to which such activities instinctively refresh people.

Joy

Latin. *Gaudia* = joy.
Old French. *Joie* = source of pleasure or happiness.

1. A vivid emotion of pleasure arising from a sense of well-being or satisfaction; the feeling or state of being highly pleased or delighted; exultation of spirit; gladness, delight.

Loneliness

Loneliness is the experience of feeling psychologically alone. People can be physically surrounded by people, who they may even know, but feel as if they're alone and amongst strangers. Maybe it's because they do not share any interests. Maybe it's because others seem incapable of understanding a different point of view, and the only way to communicate with the others is by talking about their interests. Perhaps the loneliness could be imposed on them by rejection.

In the modern world, social circles have complicated rules of engagement that some may not be willing to meet. People may completely disagree with the principles of some groups, and they may not have found a social setting in which they're comfortable. They may feel more secure with a lonely life instead. It could be that they've been abused by friends or family in the past, so they find it difficult to trust people in a social setting because they expect to be hurt in some way. A defence-mechanism* whose aim is to keep people safe, but makes them lonely in the process. There are many reasons for loneliness.

The problems with loneliness are multiple too. The inability to care for others and form relationships with them is one of the most significant. Caring for another leads people to feel positive and negative emotions based on the successes and failures of the other. Likewise, the people who care for one's self are also bound to the same positive and negative emotions based on one's successes and failures. At once, people have lost a huge potential for their wellbeing when they feel alone. People look out for their friends and want their friends to do well. When people are completely alone, they have no one in the world to care for or to care for them.

Lack of confidence and inability to relate to others is common for people who have felt lonely for an extended period. Being seen as a loner can invite criticism, and make people an easy target for both physically intimidating and maliciously gossiping bullies. A loner may also be perceived as threatening. This can lead people to withdraw further from society. Being alone reduces opportunities and deprives people of other's perspectives. In this respect, the effects of loneliness on personalities are similar to those of neglect, which may be the lonely person's default experience of life.

Depression is something to be considered regarding loneliness. A pervasive low level negative mood can linger for years and even create a disassociation from society that lasts a lifetime. In epidemiological circles (the science of health and disease in populations) it's common knowledge that socially isolated people are more likely to get sick and die younger than their peers who have the company of a partner, friends or family.

Partially responsible for this must be the accumulation of stresses into allostatic-load* (see Stress) that isn't dissipated from positive emotions. Gratitude is a positive emotion that has potent anti-stress effects, and it's part of how humans maintain a healthy balance through emotional change – allostasis*. Gratitude neuro-biologically relieves the body from stressed states, thus stopping them from accumulating (see Gratitude). When people receive no help from others because they have no one caring for them, they can't benefit from the gratitude. The case is the same for other positive emotions.

Lack of intimacy means that stresses are more difficult to dissipate.

Loneliness

French. *Lone* + *ly* + *ness* = unaccompanied, all by oneself.

1.   Solitary, lone, dejected for want of company.

2.   Sad because one has no friends.

Lust

Lust is most commonly thought of as sexual desire towards another, and it's this definition that is clarified here.

In the past, religious and philosophical thoughts around lust have always been intensely negative. In Christianity, lust is one of the seven deadly sins, and as such, in the West, people traditionally relate such desires to impure devil-like humans who need to be purified with some sort of ritual. This may seem an extreme view for a contemporary Western opinion, yet it's exactly the view that ancestors of the West held, so it is a view that influences present thoughts.

Gradually, over the past few hundred years, there has been an increasing separation of religious and supernatural views from lust. Now it's possible to see lust in a modern and scientific light. Some of the pleasurable feelings associated with lust can now be explained in more practical ways.

The lustful bodily sensations, which people experience from being close to someone they're sexually attracted to, are species wide. Pheromones are chemicals, which the body produces, that instinctively communicate biological information to other members of the species. People communicate with each other about their biological and psychological desire in ways that are stimulating and pleasurable, yet to a large extent out of their control.

People do not consciously produce pheromones to inform someone of a sexual attraction. So they must have subconsciously perceived desirable information about the other to communicate in a subconscious way. When two people, who are sexually attracted to one another, sit side by side, they can enjoy intensely pleasurable feelings without having ever uttered a word. Pheromone secretion is partially responsible for this experience.

People subconsciously recognise aspects of the opposite sex, and this changes their neuro-biological constitution, which in turn changes their disposition towards the person they find attractive. Humans observe shape and silhouettes, odour and complexion, and movement is interpreted as body language. If angry, such cognitive processes become biassed towards using such cues to determine how to stop threats (see Anger). In contrast, lust creates cognitive biasses that use the same information to detect desirability and receptiveness. When people are attracted to someone, their eyes dilate. Although they may not consciously realise these changes in their self, the person they are attracted to will instinctively/ subconsciously recognise such changes in their expressions.

Most people are unlikely to recognise consciously that eyes are dilating, or that similar biological changes are happening. Nonetheless, they will feel positive feelings as their conscious signs of those subconscious comprehensions of the other's biological state. Just as their changing biological state will be subconsciously recognised by the other too.

All of these aspects can be seen as instinctive recognitions of biological compatibility. When recognising on a subconscious level how biologically fitting another is regarding the issue of sex and offspring, the results are relayed through feelings of lust.

Human sexual instincts have evolved over hundreds of thousands of generations, and they indicate successful traits that would be of benefit to offspring. Modern civilised society is a recent development. Two thousand years is a very short time compared to millions of years of evolution. When all the years that humans have evolved through is included in regard to thinking of what their instincts would be relevant to, the conclusion is that the vast majority of people's instincts will relate to a reality that places much greater importance on physical needs of survival. Instinctive appreciations are more relevant to people's physical survival in contrast to their emotional, mental or social needs.

Thus, people can use the bodily sensations of lust as indicators of how well they perceive they're suited to another on a biological level. Nonetheless, this also suggests that it would be foolish to gauge social or mental compatibility using such feelings. These levels of biological compatibility determine to some degree the intensity of people's attraction to one another. If people are around someone who they're instinctively very compatible with, their subconscious senses high levels of pheromones. They may find themselves thinking of the other in a positive light, perhaps even thoughts of a sexual nature. People can find thoughts of a sexual nature coming to the forefront of their minds as they start feeling their instinctive compatibility towards another. Their memories would store this biological compatibility data. This may bias their behaviour towards the attractive person – without them knowing it.

This is not a judgement of either good or bad; it's an explanation that lust is a sign of biological compatibility; it's an instinctive indicator that says, 'Our children will probably be healthy.' Because it's most likely that the lustful side to human nature relates predominantly to physical survival, it can lead to experiencing intense sexual desire for a *socially* incompatible person. The result is that it's perfectly normal to feel a sexual attraction to someone who is disliked or even hated for their ideology. Lust-hate relationships are natural. Nevertheless, a question of caution for lustful relationships is raised: would it be a good emotional, mental and social environment for children?

These aspects of the experience do not encompass the entirety of what lust is. These factors are of great significance to lust though. People cannot come to a reasonable conclusion unless they keep them in mind. If people take this philosophy into consideration, they can deduce, in moments when they feel physical attraction, that they are biologically suited to the person concerned. But this does not mean they will rub along well socially.

The rub along factor can be difficult to accept when people first encounter the intensely pleasurable experience of someone else's physical company. To make a decision on what lustful pleasure indicates can be frustrating to say the least. Younger people and the more romantic at heart tend to lean towards notions of love, fate and destiny. Although lustful experiences may accompany the experience of love, lust by itself is not love. At first people often confuse the two. A deep physical desire can heavily distort people's reasoning and bias their behaviour in ways they cannot recognise.

Lust

Proto-Germanic. *Lustuz* = pleasure, delight.

1. A source of pleasure or delight, an attraction or charm.

2. Desire, appetite, relish or inclination for something.

Malevolence

Malevolence is continuous ill-will towards another, and it's chiefly a developed state of malice. Where a malicious intent is not desired once or twice but continuously, the intent would be called malevolent.

Ill-willed hatred towards a person or group can be a sign of a severely disturbed personality or a psychopathic* nature. When abusive behaviour has been received and given in the past, it has the tendency to desensitise the emotional conduct of those involved. Because of abusive treatment, people can develop a malevolent psychopathic nature, and if properly treated, they can return to normal (see Evil chapter for an excellent example, or search YouTube with the title '*Child of Rage – Full Original Documentary*').

In the West, judgements of lawful guilt are based on malicious intent. If a person is proven to have been malevolent towards a victim before the incident in question, it's far harder to prove potential innocence or lack of ill intent. This is due to the malevolent person having been proven to be desirous of inflicting harm onto the other for some time, so making it difficult to prove the victim was not harmed intentionally.

Whether a perception is true or not, perception creates emotion.[1] If people believe a perception, they feel the associated emotion. Negative emotions, in their varying degrees, change psychological processing of information towards a perceived problem, and they induce effortful analytical thinking. This has the tendency to make people ruminate on problems that they cannot solve. This is especially true if the perceptions are of an intense nature, for people's dispositions orientate to the anticipated intensity of an event more so than the probability of the event happening.[2] The more intense harm malevolent people wish onto someone, the more their dispositions will be prepared for an intensely negative outcome, and the more their thoughts will ruminate on those issues.

This focus on a negative stream of thought is then reinforced further by negativity bias – a natural bias to focus on a perceived negative event rather than a positive event of equal intensity.[3] An animal giving priority of attention to deadly negative events, before positive events, is more likely to survive with offspring. This negativity bias makes sense in an evolutionary perspective. Nevertheless, believing an imagined negative perception can trigger such biasses. This maladaptive responding to perceived events is common to mental illness.[4]

Malevolence is a mentality addicted to thoughts of wishing harm onto another, so much so that it can change the malevolent person's disposition to one of extreme negativity. Resentment, envy, jealousy, hatred, contempt and hostility could all be part of a malevolent disposition. Malevolence implicitly stresses psycho-neuro-biological systems which support negatively affected states (see Stress). This chronic stress can seriously compromise people's ability to function, and this includes their immune system's ability to fight infection.[5] Because it describes a prolonged state of extreme negativity, malevolence is an unhealthy experience that can have long-term health implications.[6]

Ill thoughts directed towards others, most often, cause anxiety and guilt – from thoughts of the consequences – which may reach extreme levels. Any form of malevolence can quite reasonably be considered a sign of underlying internal personality conflicts. It's reasonable to suspect some intensely opposing internal feelings that appear as conscious or unconscious anxieties. Malevolent people can consciously and unconsciously perceive their self as going over-the-top, which can create defence-mechanisms* with self-sabotaging behaviours.

Sometimes, where malevolent people are too frightened to own* their violent impulses, they could suffer from projection*. They may erroneously attribute the feelings from those impulses as originating from someone else.

Nevertheless, in many cases, the essence of malevolence is the surfacing of unresolved serious psychological conflicts from the past. A person in the present may resemble an aspect of those past conflicts. The person illuminates the memories, and this triggers the overwhelming negativity. When the person in the present resembles a person in the past who's deeply resented, unknowingly the feelings of resentment can be reattributed to the unrelated person in the present; a process called transference[*].

Both of these disturbing conflicted states can work off one another. They can blend into a virtually indecipherable connection that perpetuates negativity.

For example, when Zoe first meets Charles, he reminds her of a domineering person from her past, and she begins to believe Charles is a domineering personality as she's seen his type before (transference). Zoe then experiences malevolence towards Charles that she cannot own, and she then misinterprets it as originating from him (projection). Zoe believes that Charles is a dominating personality who wants to hurt her. Believing it to contain malicious intent, she reacts aggressively to a question he asks, and Charles in return gets angry with her for attacking him. Zoe determines Charles's anger to be a validation of his domineeringly malevolent personality.

Unresolved serious mental conflicts breach into present day scenarios is such ways. The issues can be worked through, usually in therapy, by gradually remembering the original perceptions to progressively build a mature narrative for them. Nevertheless, this relies on the malevolent person wanting to resolve the feelings of overwhelming malicious hatred, being literate enough to articulate experience, and being willing to work through traumatic memories. People do not always want to work through such issues. Especially when considering that resentment could be fused into the ill-will, the malevolence may be deemed just, so it could feel like a betrayal of one's self to abandon it.

The difference between being willing to use physical force to hurt someone if it's necessary to stop them doing something abusive and simply willing an experience of harm and suffering onto another is important. The

165

critical distinction is that one intention is to *STOP* someone from doing something wrong whereas the other intention is to cause *SUFFERING*. Although a person may experience suffering as people use whatever force is necessary to stop the individual doing something malicious, the aim is *not* to cause a person to suffer, but to stop the malice.

Malevolence desires harm, illness and suffering.

Malevolence

Latin. *Malevolentia* = the wishing or the disposition to wish evil or ill-will onto others, ill-will.

1. Of persons their feelings and actions. Desirous of evil to others; entertaining, actuated by, or indicative of ill-will; disposed or addicted to ill-will.

Malice

Malice is intent to harm. Maliciousness deals undue harm onto people. It has a morally corrupt reputation and is highly associated with cruel unnecessary action. It does not specifically describe a satisfaction derived from inflicting harm onto another, for the appropriate word would be sadistic. People can strongly desire to harm another seriously because they think it's what the other deserves, and this would be classed as malicious intent.

Malice is one of the principal concepts that underpin the laws in many countries worldwide, and all Western states, so the perception of malice governs global behaviour. The concept of malice shapes the liberties people experience. In comprehending what is wrong and discouraging it the progress of humanity is formed. Through imposing penalties and restraining people from being able to abuse, humans achieve a continually progressive state of existence. This is why malice is used as a point of judgement in law courts.

Nonetheless, it's more than just a judicial concept. Malice is a central part of human evolution. To be able to decide where and when someone crosses the line between necessary force and abusive ill-will allows people to decide where intervention is needed. Most laws grew from everyday perceptions of actions that were deemed to be just or unjust. Understanding malice allows people to comprehend more fully the workings of humanity, and the cogs of society. It allows people to be more just in their personal lives, and it enables them to see injustice as and when it happens.

Most people would agree that there's something wrong with gaining satisfaction from inflicting pain on people. Not as many people will agree that there's something wrong when only pain is inflicted on another though. This is because of the technical point that justifies the use of fighting and self-defence. When stopping people from doing serious wrong to someone, it may be necessary to cause them pain in the process. The technical point is that the intention is to *stop* them from doing harm, and it's not an intention to cause them pain or gain satisfaction from causing pain.

This is the pivotal point between good and bad, lawful and unlawful, moral and immoral. Malice is a far reaching principle that all lives revolve around. Defining where guilt resides often depends on determining if malice is present. The central role bestowed to malice in courts of law was not a lucky occurrence that stuck. Judgements that determine if the accused is innocent rely on the discernment of malice. Did the defendant inflict pain to hurt the plaintiff or was it to stop the plaintiff from doing something wrong?

On a personal level, if people are gaining pleasure from inflicting pain on another, they are not being malicious but sadistic. If people were planning on inflicting pain on another because of what the other had done, so the person suffers, the pain would be maliciously inflicted.

A revenge-like quality is highly associated with malicious actions. Constant malicious thoughts can be seen as the path to unbridled malicious hatred or malevolence. In reality, it's not uncommon for victims of a crime to want the criminal responsible to suffer.

Philosophically, revenge is differentiated from justice. Pure revenge has no specific limits to its punishment, and it can be full of malicious intent. Justice seeks to stop abusive actions, cause restitution of losses, redistribute ill-gotten gains, and to keep members of the public safe from malicious actions.

Most people will think about doing harm to another at points in their lives. This is not to say they are all malicious or sadistic people. Perceptions are not always accurate. To be just, people have to reflect and decide whether it's truly necessary to inflict harm onto another to stop them from doing something wrong. To harm someone who doesn't need to be harmed is malicious.

Malice

Latin. *Malitia* from *Mal-Us* = bad to us.

1. Bad quality, badness; chiefly in moral sense, wickedness.

2. Power to harm, harmfulness; harmful action.

Optimism

Optimism is a positive mental outlook towards future circumstances. Optimists are people who implicitly believe that positive outcomes will materialise for them. The inherent expectation is a general improvement in circumstances.

Rather than the outcome of specific goals, an optimist's positivity depends on the perception of general goals being achieved. People can express their optimism about a specific deal or how well they predict a specific outcome will turn out, but this would more accurately be described as an expression of confidence in a specific outcome. Unless the meaning of such a statement was saying, 'I believe this outcome will be positive, but if it's not, I'm sure things are going to be all right anyway.'

This focus on general improvement is true to the original meaning of the word. Originally optimism referred to a philosophical concept regarding the belief that 'the greatest good will prevail somehow'. This concept caused the creation of a classical satirical work called *Candide*[1], by Voltaire, which is considered part of the Western canon, and it brought the word 'optimism' into popular language more than two hundred years ago.

Candide was Voltaire's way of shooting holes in his day's philosophical concept of optimism. It portrays a young man, called Candide, who has been indoctrinated with the philosophical notion that 'the greatest good will prevail somehow'. The novel then follows his journey as his comfortable lifestyle abruptly changes for the worst. He is thrown into a world of hardship for himself and the people he cares most about. Candide is continually disillusioned and loses his appreciation of universal optimism by recognising that the notion 'the greatest good will prevail somehow' significantly depends on personal circumstances.

The source of an optimist's resilient expectation of positive outcomes is a line of scientific enquiry. It has been proven that optimists have healthier, more adaptive, immune system functioning, and their positive mental outlook infuses adaptive ideas, attitudes and judgements towards a positive outcome.[2]

This positive offset is often associated with the perception of control people believe they have over an outcome. A perception of control has been proven to reduce stress hormones within individuals that believe they have an element of control over an outcome – even when they have no control whatsoever.[3] These two aspects (expectation of positive emotion and lack of stress) of an optimist's disposition make their likelihood of becoming ill lower, and their likelihood of recovering from an illness better than non-optimists. This direct link between perception and immune system functioning is starting to be evidenced. It's understandably significant to mental, emotional and physical health.

People's perception of their ability to cope with a situation is also highly associated with both reducing stress and adapting behaviour towards success. The perception of one's ability to cope *effectively* with *affective* – emotional – consequences is important to the stability of one's personality.[4]

As portrayed in *Candide*, the experience of optimism is not entirely positive. Theoretically, two principal factors can significantly contribute to an optimist's perception of the world.

First, a dispositional optimist's outlook – a person who intrinsically expects positive outcomes – can derive from their attachment style. Amassing more than fifty years of empirical research, attachment theory[*] shows how children learn to interpret the world through their association with their primary care giver, evolutionarily the mothers.[5] If toddlers are met with an appropriate and secure response when expressing their fears and needs, they implicitly inherit a disposition that's positive in nature. The majority of all stressful events experienced have ended positively, and their needs have been satisfied. On the other hand, if toddlers express their fears or needs and they are met with no response (or an inappropriate response) repeatedly, then the perception of the world they inherit becomes fractured with anxiety and maybe even despair. This anxiety laden outlook is part of the child's implicit-memory* that accumulates over time and is used to predict future outcomes. The predictions bias their perceptions towards interpreting negative future events.

This, extremely concise description of attachment theory, gives an idea of how repeated positive and negative outcomes accumulate in a child's memory, and how they're used subsequently to bias interpretation of future events. As illustrated in *Candide*, people can be dispositional optimists because they have always been around positive outcomes.

Second, ignorance or cognitive-avoidance* can be employed to block or suppress losses from being consciously recognised, so sadness is not experienced. The same mechanisms can also be used to block fears of future outcomes that would otherwise make a person feel anxious. It has been proven that people who cognitively avoid thinking about their feared outcome experience less stress hormones than people who do. Only, the low trait-anxiety of high cognitive-avoidance is offset by elevated physiological arousal (stress) if the cognitively avoided event is encountered.[6] The dynamics of avoiding recognition of negative possibilities can therefore underpin optimism by eliminating stressors that would contradict a perceived positive outcome, but at the risk of the person becoming overwhelmed into a state of crisis if an avoided feared stressor is encountered (see Ignorance).

When unknown combinations of the two main considerations above are factored in, the analysis of optimism is complex. The satirical appraisals of optimism are concerned with both. The first consideration above regards the conditioning effect of positive circumstances and warns of the naiveté of wholeheartedly thinking 'the greatest good will prevail' without concerted effort. The second consideration regards the ignoring of feared possibilities and the experience of crisis when the ignored possibility happens.

Therefore, the health benefits that are evidenced as associated with optimism seem to apply more, but not exclusively, to the first consideration regarding attachment theory. It must be stated that success experienced repeatedly, with or without a secure attachment figure, would theoretically create the conditions for implicit-memory that are associated with dispositional optimism. Even if the occurrence of such a situation is difficult to imagine.

Additionally, attachment to a significant individual, who positively contributes to a person's life consistently, should not be underestimated for its ability to instil optimism and cultivate gratitude. When children mature and reflect on the memories of someone who purposefully contributed to their life in positive ways, the affect is often gratitude (see Gratitude). Not only does such a lucky child remember general positive outcomes, but they are effectively inoculated with a mass of memories that make them feel gratitude towards those who are significant to them. Gratitude is *the* prosocial emotion. It's an elixir of life. The health benefits of such a vault of memories is immense.

When considering optimism, it's important to keep in mind that both negative and positive emotions are needed in appropriate proportions for optimal healthy functioning.[7] Healthy mental, emotional and physiological states are not maintained by maximising positive emotions and minimising negative emotions. Combinations of both positive and negative emotions are necessary for a person to adapt to changing and unpredictable circumstances.[8]

Optimism refers to one's perception of coping with both known and unknown challenges. A general improvement in quality of life materialises due to positive outcomes. Negative emotions such as frustration, anger and disgust are often needed to cope with challenges and achieve positive outcomes.

The association of optimism with repeated successful outcomes suggests that a person's level of optimism is generally malleable. That it's adjusted to their recent – months to years – history of success. If people continually overcome everyday stresses, no matter how small they are, it will contribute to their accumulation of implicit memories. Especially when it's coupled to gratitude, this accumulation of subconscious feeling from positive outcomes seems to be at the heart of healthy optimism.

Optimism

Latin. *Optimum* = the greatest good or best.
French. *Optimisme* (1737) = 'belief that good ultimately will prevail in the world' brought from philosophy into popular usage by a satire on the idea called *Candide* by Voltaire, considered part of the Western canon.

1. Confidence regarding future success.

2. A general expectation of positive events.

Pity

Pity is the feeling of tender concern for people in distress.

Especially in unfortunate situations, where people are perceived to be experiencing distress undeservedly, pity was originally understood as relating to sadness or despair. Pity can be a sincere experience that allows people who are feeling distress to realise others understand their predicament. If people know that someone understands their experience, it can be a relief. A clarifying voice that reflects on the unfortunate circumstances is a reassuring comfort that helps people gain perspective on their situation. When the unfortunate situation has implications for another, it's reassuring to know the other is not angry, for it removes the fear of punishment that can add further load to an already stressful event.

A problem encountered with pity is when people's pity is based on beliefs that the misfortune is due to a mistake caused by inferiority. As the inferiority can be deemed a contaminating behaviour, this can lead to pity being associated with people who *look down their nose* in contempt at the unfortunately distressed. A patronising air is created from the mixture of kindness and contempt. The distress of others is treated with a caring facade that masks the hidden feelings of contempt. As feelings of being judged and potential social fallout are added to the already stressful experience, this hinders more than it helps.

So, nowadays, pity has two definitions. First, people are genuinely reflecting on another's distress (e.g. sadness or despair). Second, that people are being patronising by *looking down their nose* at another for getting into such a predicament and faking kindness.

Pity

Latin. *Pietatem* = piety, affection, duty.

1. Sympathetic or kindly sorrow evoked by the misfortune, suffering or distress of another.

2. To disregard feeling angry at someone who has caused us offence as their mistakes were due to them being inferior, and the distress that they are in is their fault. To look 'down one's nose' at the mistakes or distress of another.

Pleasure

Pleasure is the most temporary of the positive emotions: a here-and-now emotion.

As it's associated closely with bodily states and the earliest of evolutionary developments, it's possibly at the root of all positive emotions. It can be intellectually difficult to separate the physical sensation of pleasure from the emotion of pleasure. This is because they are so closely related, and there's a physical component to emotional pleasure.

As its opposite, pleasure is usually contrasted with pain. While the experience of pleasure elicits a smile, pain elicits the expression of a frown. Pain is something people want to keep away from and not repeat. Pleasure is something people seek and repeat. Pain relates to the detection of, feeling of, and protection of cell damage. Pleasure relates to perceptions of things that will contribute positively to cell structures.

Sadness and despair are forms of emotional pain. Rather than direct physical damage, they relate to negative social circumstances. Gladness and elation are forms of emotional pleasure. Rather than direct physical stimulation, they relate to positive social circumstances.

Pleasure is highly associated with the functions of the body. It serves the necessities of biological regulation in instinctual ways. The amount of pleasure people gain from different foods and beverages will depend on how much they have consumed of those items. If people have been doing an intensely physical activity for several hours, the taste of food and drink will be more pleasurable than if they had done no physical activity. People will gain more pleasure, in these cases, from items that have a greater calorific or hydrating value. This is because bodies need more calories and water when they have been active. People need more food, and the taste of the food is more pleasurable, so this urges them to consume more and receive more calories. The water people drink after exerting themselves tastes intensely more pleasurable than the water they drink when they are fully hydrated. The heightened taste compels them to consume more.

This is evidence of an evolutionary homeostatic* – maintaining balance through change – nature to the sensation of pleasure. Pleasure is not only concerned with the perception of positive sensations, but also the perception of how much of a specific substance is good at a specific time. Pleasures are sensitive to needs. Mineral content, vitamin content and basic calorific values are simple examples of the body's continuous regulation of its environment using pleasure. Thousands of bodily processes are detected and regulated in a similar automated/instinctual manner. These processes have broad variation. The body states they encompass range from muscle tension to wavelength detection.

A twenty minute daily exposure to sunlight has been shown to reduce blood pressure by about ten percent. To phrase it another way, being without sunlight exposure increases blood pressure by about ten percent. The sensation of pleasure from sunlight on skin is also a simple example of pleasure's relationship with a need for a vitamin. Humans create vitamin D when their skin is exposed to ultraviolet B (UVB) radiation. It enables the body to absorb calcium. Without enough vitamin D bones grow misshapen or become thin and brittle. Vitamin D protects older people from osteoporosis. These biological needs are related to how strongly people are attracted to sunlight.

When people are sitting in a coffee shop waiting for their friend, they suddenly feel pleased to see their friend walking through the door. People feel relief as their fears reduce. The friend has contributed to their feelings of safety, but also to their social prospects. The thought that they have not been stood-up causes anxieties to reduce. They are pleased that the planned meeting is taking place. This regulates mood by lowering anxieties and bringing their sense of security closer to a comfortable level, which reduces tense vigilant dispositions and frees attention and energy. People experience the most basic emotion of pleasure without knowing there's a biological reason for it.

People feel the physical pleasure of the tasty food and refreshing water sliding down their throat, but they also feel emotionally pleased with themselves, for as the food and drink goes down, it nourishes their bodies. Just as people feel emotionally pleased sitting in the sun on a warm day when their body temperature is just right. Just as sitting in the coffee shop feeling pleased a friend is there too. There are physical and emotional aspects to pleasure. Whether people are oblivious to it or not, there's an underlying aim of maintaining balance through change that's the basis of pleasurable activities.

Pleasure is used to describe positive feelings that stem from vastly different sensations, yet it's always as an expression of a small amount of positive feeling. The more an event will contribute to people's social lives, the greater the amount of positive feeling experienced, the less likely pleasure will be used to describe the experience. Gladness, joy and elation are expressions of greater positive feelings. They relate less to the physical here-and-now and more to social outcomes. They relate less to the body's internal state.

Pleasure can be here one moment then gone the next, for it's a fleeting sensation that can last seconds, yet it may continue for hours with constant stimulation of a short-lived sensation. When it ends, pleasure isn't felt as a great loss, for it's less consequential than joy and elation. Pleasure is a commonly available feeling that can be experienced with much greater frequency than any other positive emotion. As a body's homeostatic need for items changes hourly, opportunities to fulfil potentially pleasurable needs are virtually constant. Hence, although it may be a temporary and mildly positive emotion, it's possible to experience it abundantly. A lot of small things experienced frequently can have a very positive, bubbly effect on general mood.

As people can participate in pleasurable activities without fearing great loss of positive feeling when the activity ends, pleasure's temporality can have an attractive quality. Delicious food served in small and varied amounts with complementary drinks is well known to create a pleasant setting. Groups of people can experience the same things as pleasurable. They can have mildly positive feelings, over the course of an evening, without risking much of an emotional slump afterwards. When subconscious anxieties of maintaining food and drink intake are eliminated, conscious attention stays focused on the discussion at hand. Thus a host can provide a positive yet stable social setting for people to mingle.

Although being in pleasurable company may lead to opportunities and encounters that can be greatly fulfilling, the pleasure itself does not lead to this satisfaction. If people think that continually doing pleasurable things will create a great sense of satisfaction or happiness, it's a mistaken assumption. This is something to be considered for people who distract themselves from feeling the despair of a situation with pleasurable activities. Pleasure will not fill a hole created by despair. Just as it's not a solution to regret, remorse, guilt or shame. Though it can introduce a well needed interruption to stress, pleasure does not address the anxieties of social emotions.

For a theoretical example, alcohol dramatically affects the body's gamma-aminobutyric acid (GABA) neurotransmitter process. GABA is associated with relaxation and the reduction of stress. People may find consuming large amounts of alcohol pleasurable because it acts as a homeostatic agent that biologically symbolises the achievement of solutions to psychological and biological stresses. It facilitates the same biological processes that would be experienced if they had found solutions to their stresses. When the alcohol wears off, the GABA process reorganises itself once again to the psychological stresses that have not been addressed. Alcohol allows people to dupe themselves, and to biologically forget their stresses. As it does not maintain balance through change, it's a false homeostasis. Because it compromises body systems and reduces people's ability to function, it reduces their ability to solve the stresses that caused them to drink; it's added load. This is the reason people cannot drown their sorrows. Rather than a solution, excessive alcohol is a distraction from social stresses. Such excessively distracting guilty pleasures often have the unfortunate side-effect of adding stress in the long run.

Pleasurable sensations are the bubbliest of feelings. Pleasure goes on and off the boil, and it's there one moment and gone the next without causing shock when it's absent. The things that people like create pleasurable feelings, and those feelings often unknowingly have an underlying objective related to a balanced bodily state.

Pleasure

Latin. *Placere* = to be acceptable, be liked, be approved.
Ancient Greek. *Plaxos* = level surface, flat, 'to become flat'.

1. The condition of consciousness or sensation induced by the enjoyment or anticipation of what is felt or viewed as good or desirable; enjoyment, delight, gratification. The opposite of pain.

2. In a strictly physical sense: the indulgence of the appetites; sensual gratification.

3. Psychology: denoting the theory that the drives to achieve pleasure and to avoid pain are basic

motivating forces, or instincts, in human and animal life.

4. Man (or woman) of pleasure: one who is devoted to the pursuit of sensual pleasure; a licentious person.

Pride

Pride is a word of two halves. One side is the description of a positive mental respect for personal characteristics, talents, abilities and decisions well made. The other is used to describe a way of viewing one's self in a distorted fashion, so to prolong a superior image of one's self that ultimately leads to unfair biassing personality traits.

Evolutionarily, pride is innately nested onto neural architecture that rewards important achievements. The chin and nose are held aloft as the head tilts back. The neck is openly displayed. A smile adorns the face, and the chest is pushed out. In significant victories, arms are often raised to head height and above and sometimes air pumped with clenched fists – a sort of vertical orgasm. Blind people instinctively exhibit the same features, and other animals display pride too, so it's not only innate, but it's a cross species social emotion. Pride instinctively conveys a perception of success, yet it can manifest in two sharply contrasting ways.

The two descriptions seem to be polar opposites, yet the single word is in common use. Pride frequently describes something that is extremely positive whilst at the same time being used by many others to describe something that is extremely negative. Often people initially think that there's only one meaning. People tend to learn one meaning for the word, usually the one their family uses, and they stick to the initial meaning while learning to acknowledge the other meaning too. This has the tendency of creating a time where people realise and address the issue. Until this point is reached, there can be many misunderstandings when people use the word 'pride' in conversations.

It may seem a very simple thing to resolve and hardly worth mentioning as people can take on the additional meaning when they first learn of it. In reality, it's usually not that simple. The concept has important and complex overtones. It encompasses several emotions in one descriptive state. It takes time to develop personal meaning around each description. Pride is a sharply negative emotion to some people whilst being an admirable quality of success for others. This creates ongoing misunderstandings and sticking points in conversations unless people define the two accurately.

The easier description to define is associated with satisfaction from decisions well made. This concept is heavily associated with personal achievement and success. Pride can be placed in personal characteristics or talents that lead to success. Specifically, pride is often used to describe success over adversity. In this sense, people can be extremely proud of others, and parents will undoubtedly recognise this as positive.

Appreciation and confidence in one's abilities is one of the most significant aspects of self-esteem. Self-esteem inoculates people against a wide range of depressive scenarios and allows them to succeed in the face of adversity.

When people doubt someone and that individual has the courage in his or her convictions, makes sound decisions, and succeeds regardless, it's these points in time that typify the essence of pride in the positive sense.

Appreciation of courage, talents and decisions – all wrapped up in a bundle of positive regard. Whereas admiration is filled with overwhelming wonder, pride is filled with overwhelming positive-regard created from appreciation. Pride says 'I am really impressed with that decision!' and 'I am really impressed with the way you handled that!'

The negative form of pride is unflattering.

A strutting puffed-up peacock is the negative emblem of pride.

In ancient texts, pride was the first of the seven deadly sins, but it was also said that all other sins stem from pride. However exaggerated this view of the negative form of pride is, it's an historical account of how wary ancestors of the West were in respect to pride.

The negative description of pride is heavily associated with an excessive appreciation of one's own achievements. This leads to an inflated sense of status that becomes the basis of one's self-esteem. In this respect, pride can resemble arrogance. A preoccupation with a perceived social status creates a sort of vanity-orientated pride. Fear of losing a perceived status can lead to different behaviours aimed at stopping the loss. When the potential loss of status is caused by another, jealousy can lead to an array of other negative emotions through envy (see Jealousy and Envy). When people fear the loss of an important status, overly reactive behaviours based on snap decisions can become preoccupied with stopping the perceived loss of status at any cost. These unjust and purely selfish reactions typify the negative description of pride.

Snap decisions that are based on pride can be acted-out* in milliseconds and to a large extent go unnoticed by either party in a conversation. People commonly notice, in hind-sight, that they're being prideful when they reflect on their motives, yet because the problem with the situation has been created by their reaction, they have difficulty accepting they acted in a pathetic way as this would threaten their sense of status. People like to think they're always in control or at least would like others to think so, and that's a reason why people push the thought of their pathetic impulsive behaviour out of conscious awareness (see Ignorance). Pride can enter into a self-delusive cycle with a motive of maintaining status by ignoring information that would jeopardise the current feelings of self-esteem. Feelings that are based on an inflated sense of status. Pride has got its definition of unreasonably maintaining self-interest due to such biassing. Even though others can clearly see that people are being selfish and unreasonable, they cannot admit it to themselves.

The elements of this description of pride are overvaluing of status, air of superiority, and contempt for others. This can be seen in terms of an ego-trip where people think of their self (ego) as being of great importance, and more valuable than others around them. Although, because of the overvaluing of their self-concept, if the truth were to be known, their status and ego-trip would be threatened, so the self-delusive aspect to this form of pride is employed. This denial of new information (ignorance or cognitive-avoidance*) can be seen as an attempt to prolong the ego-trip. In so doing, the side-effects of excessive confidence and self-esteem are created. The self-concept is prevented from updating.

Contempt can mentally be used to intimidate people, and it has a long-standing relationship with pride. Proud people exhibit their superiority over others by walking around in a puffed-up fashion. Radiating self-confidence, they hold their nose aloft as if not to smell nearby inferior persons. In doing so they express contempt. This spectacle can make recipients of the contempt feel insecure; it can induce passiveness. The prideful people are then at liberty to dominate the situation. Pride and contempt coupled together can be used to probe the confidence of others. A survey of reactions that may be taken advantage of is noted. A passive or submissive response suggests a person is open to domination or befriending.

Pride

Old English. *Pryto* = congratulate (oneself).

1. A high or inflated sense of one's own qualities, attainments, or estate, which gives rise to a feeling or attitude of superiority over and contempt for others; inordinate self-esteem.

2. A feeling of elation, pleasure, or high satisfaction derived from some action or possession, 'to take pride in'.

Rage

Rage is an intense, short lived, period of anger that's out of control.

Rage is used to describe a state where people are susceptible to making bad decisions due to a loss of control, caused by intense anger, which reduces their ability to think reasonably. The uncontrollable nature defines rage from other emotional states fuelled by anger. People can fly into a rage and make a situation worse from being unreasonable, and this often creates regrettable circumstances. So rage is seen as a crude, unthinking emotion.

As people experience intense emotions, their attention narrows to focus on the subject which is arousing them, so the amount of cues they can pay attention to is reduced.[1] The psychological and neuro-biological processes shift to cortical regions that are most appropriate to process the perceived situation.[2] People are less conscious of their behaviour, and they rely more heavily on automatic ways of relating to events. When emotions are reaching their limits of intensity, they progressively assume control over behaviour.[3] At times like these people act more on instincts and learned dispositions (habits).

As oxygenated blood flow is instinctively increased to areas such as the muscles, heart, face and the hands, rage is physiologically characterised by increased heart rate and blood pressure. At the same time, blood flow to the intestinal tract, kidneys and skin is reduced and their functions suppressed. Natural (endogenous) painkillers are released from the brainstem to make bodily damage more bearable.[4]

The entire body responds in this way, so people are appropriately composed to engage with the perceived event. Although it does so automatically, rage does stress people's systems to rapidly adapt. A healthy person can adapt to such situations with a moderate biological tax as long as these adaptive behaviours are not constantly engaged. If they are constantly turned on (due to a misperception or not), it will place serious stress on the neuro-biological components and even reduce people's ability to fight infection.[5] Such continuous stresses have accumulative effects over decades that are related to metabolic syndrome*, primary hypertension* and cardiovascular disease.[6]

Rage is highly associated with periods of intense frustration and perceived malicious injustice.[7] Rage is commonly seen when people believe a person has cheated them. Especially when the person perceived to have cheated them is known intimately, feelings of betrayal mix with anger, and a sense of loss; this can cause jealousy which can then cause an array of negative emotions through envy and resentment. All these powerful emotions will create a cocktail of hormones and neurotransmitters that will tax thinking, making it turbulent and laboured. So the out-of-control nature of rage is highly associated with feelings of betrayal that erupt when a significant other is perceived to have acted maliciously.

Although rage will give people a brief state of heightened instinct to act upon in a physical situation, people will not be as tactical or reasonable in that state. They are blinded by rage. This is why it's considered a liability when compared to furious anger or ferociousness as it's possible to be astonishingly angry yet still in control of one's faculties.

When in a state of rage, it's difficult to defuse heated situations. The restriction on higher faculty thoughts whilst being swamped with intense emotions severely reduces thought capacity. If people saw a friend who became enraged in a heated social situation, it would be a good idea to keep an eye on any defusing points that arose as the enraged are more likely to miss them.

Rage can be considered a choice of fight rather than flight and on a par of intensity with fury but uncontrollable.

Rage

Latin. *Rabies* = madness, rage, fury, be mad, rave.

1. Violent uncontrollable anger.

2. A fit of violent anger.

<u>Regret</u>

Regret is a sad emotion people feel when an opportunity has been missed or if they have caused an unfortunate situation for themselves. Sad emotions cause thinking to become slow and revolve around the origin of the negative experience. This happens instinctively to force people's focus onto the issues involved, so they're more likely to identify what caused the emotional pain and avoid it in the future.[1]

Sadness is created by a perception of loss.[2] It also relates to things that have happened. Sadness is past orientated and if people fear for a loss that has not yet happened, the appropriate word for the emotion is anxiety.[3] Similarly, regret relates to perceived failures that have led to loss, but, specifically, when the loss could have been prevented. If actions or decisions people have taken lead to an outcome where they lose a possession of value, they would naturally feel regret.

The word 'possession' is used here to describe talents, positive feelings, jobs, and people – not just simple physical items. The perception of any personal mistake that prevented any positive situation from happening can cause regret. As mistakes could lead to hopes being frustrated or destroyed, regret may be accompanied by frustration and despair. In this way, besides experiencing an unfortunate situation, people also become negatively affected, and these emotions are intensified by the perception that the whole scenario could have been prevented.

Although regret can be created in an instant, it can linger for years. If people feel that they have missed an opportunity with someone who is significant to them, they may always regret missing that opportunity. People may not be able to describe why they feel so disappointed and find it difficult to come to terms with a deep sense of longing that they cannot fully understand. Regret can reach deep into the heart and make people feel incredibly desperate with the recognition of lost hopes. Since regret includes things that didn't happen because of action or inaction, loss of potential relationships are encompassed within its scope.

Sometimes regret can be a scary emotion because people do not know why they feel such strong sadness (which could be subconscious despair). People might feel as if they have done something deeply wrong, but usually without any sense of guilt. For when guilt is present with a mistake that's been made, the more appropriate emotion is remorse.

Effects of regret can range from sad mild disappointment to gut-wrenching despair depending on how significant the mistake was. The perception of value attached to the loss may be accurate or inaccurate.

Frequently, as if they have perceived something subconsciously, people cannot fully explain why they feel so deeply about an issue. They have a notion that something means a lot to them in some unknown way, yet the only sign they have is the strong feelings that stem from deep within. Regret can signal how significant a possession is through subconsciously created feelings. People can become unsettled by this, for they feel they should reconsider their actions, but the only evidence they have to support such reasoning is deep feelings.

As a result, people often question their emotions when feeling regret: 'Do I trust my subconscious perceptions to value such things for me?'; 'Is that reasonable?'; 'Do I trust my feelings or not?' The whole process can seem disturbingly unscientific.

Sometimes there will be no possible future opportunity or reunion. People will have to make the same decision about how much a possession really meant to them, based on their feelings of loss, but knowing they will never have an opportunity to correct it. This is why regret is highly associated with unresolved sadness and despair.

As they will be used to inform future similar situations, valuations are important. Reflective judgements will create conscious and unconscious biassing guides for future decisions. Once a valuation is believed, it will create psychological (and subsequently behavioural) dispositions that influence both thought and instinctual propensities. The depth to which people feel regret can be considered as the depth of subconscious recognition they're experiencing. If people do not feel regret for their mistakes, they have not learnt from experience, so they are doomed to repeat them.

In some cases, regret can be accompanied by a hope that another chance will come along, so the damage once created can be somewhat repaired. But often no realistic hope may still exist, and people may fear accepting the despair. The character of regret is sorrowful mourning that brings about sadness and despair. The effects are very sobering and have a tendency to cause people to reflect on the amount of time they have in life.

Regret

Old French. *Regreter* = long after, lament someone's death, to remember with distress or longing.

1. To feel sad or disappointed that something has not happened.

2. To feel sad or guilty that something bad has happened.

3. To feel sad that an opportunity has been missed.

Relief

Relief is the emotion people feel when a negative strain is lessened or stops.

When a potentially negative event is being considered but then perceived as no longer a threat, relief follows the preparatory emotions of surprise, astonishment and shock. Whilst considering negative events, these preparatory emotions introduce varying degrees of stress into the individual. Momentarily people may become scared, fearful, horrified or terrified and then tension is released as relief as the threat is recognised as false.

The release of negative emotions typically induces a notable 'sigh of relief', from exhaling the air that has just been instinctively inhaled and held by one of the preparatory emotions (see Astonishment). This is also true for the corresponding slump in posture and relaxation of the instinctively tense neck and torso regions. Together these reactions of the head dipping, shoulders slumping and sigh of relief are the actions that are most associated with an expression of relief.

Nevertheless, stress can relate to events whose perceived position is further into the future. If a taxing endeavour is perceived to be in the future, people will subconsciously orientate their disposition to be ready for when the event is anticipated to happen, especially feared events.[1] Intense emotions cause attention to narrow and focus, with a sense of urgency, onto the eliciting event.[2] Emotions also progressively assume control over behaviour at higher levels of intensity.[3] These aspects are brought into action as emotions intensify in relation to how close the event is (both temporal and spatial proximity affect the orientating response), and negative events outrank positive events for priority of dispositions.[4]

Future events that people are only partially conscious of, but anticipate, can cause an increasing state of alertness. Changes in psychological information processing styles, neuro-biological releases of hormones, and physiological tenseness orientate people's dispositions to the anticipated event. Conscious and subconscious perceptions of how close the event is to materialising determine the time when people's dispositions begin to change in preparation for it. Neuro-biological systems, such as the amygdala and its numerous associative systems, are activated and maintained relevant to people's anxieties.[5] By reorienting people's dispositions in preparation for an anticipated event, these systems and subsystems can tax current unrelated behaviours. In this process, physiological responses are activated by and then biassed towards the perceived event – intensity of an anticipated event outweighs the probability of it occurring.[6] If people hear news that an anticipated negative event will not be happening and they feel an instinctive relief, it's partially because of a release of subconsciously organised systems that have been preparing for the event.

Relief can relate to any form of stress, anxiety, failure, jealousy, envy, injury, or any negative tension people are experiencing or expecting to experience. If people have an excessive work load that is causing them stress and anxiety, they will experience relief if their work load is suddenly lightened. Relief describes the mental, emotional and physical experience of relaxation after feeling tense.

Relief is the sudden withdrawal of negative experience, and as such it's not pleasure. Whereas relief indicates a negative thing that has lessened, pleasure indicates things that are nourishing, especially regarding the body's state. Nevertheless, the release of tension and effort that were being spent on maintaining a taxing vigilant disposition can be used for positive purposes once they are released, so pleasure is highly associated with relief. Pleasure can even be associated with obtaining an agent that creates relief.

Positive emotions are always associated with a release of tension. Negative emotions cause thinking to become more analytically effortful (searching) and focused on a specific problem. Positive emotions cause thinking to rely more on current knowledge bases (instincts and learnt information) with an inclusive thinking style which uses more categories, so flexibility and creativity are increased whilst using less effort.[7]

Accumulating evidence is showing that negative emotions are biassed towards right-hemisphere functioning and positive emotions are biassed towards the left-hemisphere.[8] A theoretical base that sits well with the allostatic[*] suggestion that negative emotions aid the accomplishment of a goal, and when that goal is achieved, a positive emotion is experienced. Therefore, as the switch from negative to positive emotion happens – a shift from right-hemisphere effortful thinking to left-hemisphere relaxed thinking, the right side's load is reduced, so it can recharge. Thus relief is implicitly coupled to positive emotions as well as a reduction in negative tension.

Relief

Old French. *Relief* = alleviation of distress, ease, assistance.

1. Ease or alleviation given to or received by a person through the removal or lessening of some cause of distress or anxiety; deliverance from what is burdensome or exhausting to the mind; mental relaxation; hence also, entertainment, sport.

2. Ease from, or lessening of, physical pain or discomfort.

3. An agreeable change of object to the mind or one of the senses, esp. that of sight.

Remorse

Remorse is a mixture of regret and guilt that stems from the recognition of an offence.

Regret is similar to remorse in the sense of having done something regrettable and having deep sorrowful feelings associated with being responsible for the unfortunate consequences, yet whereas regret can be caused by a preventable unfortunate situation, where no offence has been committed, remorse specifically refers to the undue harm caused to another. The major overtone of remorse is regret, but it's specifically regret about an offence that leads to guilt.

Remorse is a sign that people are taking responsibility for the undue negative effects they have caused another. Remorse requires empathising or sympathising with the victim of offence. People who are genuinely remorseful do not want to commit the act again. They are genuinely sorry for what they have done.

For these reasons, remorse plays a central role in Western courts of law. Judges and juries will endeavour to see if people, who have admitted guilt, feel remorse for what they have done. If they are remorseful, they are unlikely to commit the crime again. There will usually be clearly defined circumstances that led up to the crime being committed, and the remorseful person will usually provide a clear narrative of what happened. When people are sentenced for a crime, the remorseful will receive a sentence that is less severe than those who are unrepentant and feel no remorse.

Unremorseful people will continue to be a threat to civilised society. They have not consciously acknowledged the undue negative effects of their behaviour. Unremorseful people are still motivated by the same psychological architecture that leads to undue harm being imposed on others.

Remorse can be thought of as the point at which forgiveness starts. Nonetheless, this does not mean that remorseful people will not be punished. Although punishment and forgiveness are two separate things, in reality one often follows the other. Even when people are understood not to have intended any injury and are remorseful for what they have done, if the crime is serious, there's something of an unwritten rule that people must also take their punishment before being completely forgiven. Just as if undergoing punishment willingly is a necessary deterrent to stop re-offending and a sign of true remorse.

This leads to the two significant theoretical arguments for what stops crime.

First, remorse is the most significant way in which people could refrain from repeating their crimes. Although remorse may be the best deterrent for stopping future offences, an offence has already been committed, so it's not a perfect solution. People also need to possess the ability to feel (sympathise or empathise) for the victims of the crime to feel remorse.

Second, 'fear of punishment' as an intended deterrent would theoretically suit those who – for whatever reason – cannot empathise with their victims, so they cannot be remorseful. Fear can prevent people committing an offence in the first place. Yet it's not as reliable at stopping reoffending as there's not necessarily any respect for the would-be victim. Fear of punishment can also cause people to become rebellious and commit offences due to feeling dominated.

Two further important factors also complicate the 'fear of punishment' issue. According to the findings of research, *certainty of punishment* is much more important than the *severity of punishment* in deterring criminal behaviour. The likelihood people will get caught and be punished is a greater discouragement, to would-be criminals, than a severe punishment alone.[1] The fewer people in a population that agree a specific behaviour is offensive, or the fewer people that are willing to report offences, the more unreliable fear becomes as a deterrent. Thus fear is unreliable when not enforced in a uniform fashion, is unnecessary for people who feel remorse, and causes rebellious offences if misused.

Until the beginnings of civilisation, selfishness, outside of the family unit, was the most dominant mentality in evolution. When the person who is unduly harmed is a family member or someone known intimately, people feel remorse to a much greater intensity.

Throughout early evolution people concerned themselves with caring as far as the nuclear family. Then in time the care included the extended family. Then eventually people began to care for communities several thousand years ago when societies first developed because of farming.

Due to survival being the motivating factor, stealing in early evolution would have been considered nothing more than competition. Stealing clearly became redundant when people began living side by side in ever increasing numbers. Farming caused humans to become close knit gregarious people who had food in greater supply. The likelihood of getting caught stealing in a developing small community would have been very high, and the consequences of being thrown out of the community would have been severely threatening.

Also, because a farming community can produce food, stealing food would have been less of a survival issue. So, stealing of food would have gone from being a desirable activity to an undesirable one. The likelihood is that it would have caused more upset than it was worth.

Instincts which developed over millions of years have, however, a tendency to dominate more recent faculties that allow people to empathise. When instincts are no longer needed because of a change in behaviour, redundant impulses continue as propensities that urge similar ways of behaving, and the perception of negative consequences becomes people's motivation to refrain. Perceiving negative consequences for one's self and empathising with the undue negative effects on community members are two different things. The former has been about since the dawn of consciousness. The latter is but a matter of civilisation.

Whether it's accurately judging someone else's remorse or accurately judging someone else's distress, people are suspicious of new abilities like empathy. This relates to how selfish people's attitudes are, and thus how selfish people assume others to be. If people cannot accept the undue negative effects their selfishness has caused others, how can they understand or trust the legitimacy of the remorse another expresses? People's inability to accept someone else's remorse can say more about themselves than anyone else. Remorse is not a selfish emotion. The infinitely unfortunate thing is that it's always preceded by an offence.

Nevertheless, punishment is dealt judicially to the remorseful as well as the unremorseful. This is partially because empathising is one of the newest human evolutionary abilities. People are not proficient in knowing whether another is truly remorseful or acting for a more lenient sentence. This does not negate the credibility of remorse – only a human's ability to gauge it properly. This is a significant reason why remorse is rendered as an insufficient, unreliable and untrustworthy characteristic when it comes to complete forgiveness.

Regret can simply describe sadness over a missed opportunity without any implied guilt. Remorse is a deeply sad and guilty experience created by owning* the offences one has committed.

Remorse

Latin. *Remordere* = to vex, disturb or to bite back.

1. Moral anguish arising from past misdeeds.

2. Distress caused by the guilt of past offences.

Resentment

Resentment is a bitter emotion that people feel towards someone who's perceived to have committed an offence and got away with it.

The damage that resentment can create to people's lives is usually underestimated. When used to drive a wedge between relationships, resentment can be a divisive tool that third parties play on to manipulate those who feel resentful. Resentment is also highly associated with envy, stress and depressive thoughts. People entrap themselves with resentment without knowing the seriously damaging affects that occur.

Perceptions create emotions. If the perceptions are accurate or inaccurate representations of reality is beside the point. If people believe a perception, they feel the associated emotion.[1]

Perceptions of deliberate and malicious injustice are proven to cause anger.[2] Resentment is anger regarding a past offence where the resented person is perceived to have got away with the offence. A method for reducing both anger and resentment is to reconsider whether people deliberately caused offence.[3] If after reconsidering their position a decision is made that there was no deliberate will to offend, a situation that could have led to great negativity could be defused as the anger subsides.

Unlike anger that can be a pre-emptive strike to prevent a possible offence from happening, resentment is always a reaction to a perceived offence that has already occurred. This includes injury to pride. If people are taken advantage of or not credited for the things that they've done, they will be in prime resentment territory. This perception of injustice can make the resentment difficult to let go of, for it leaves people stuck in a negative experience because it somehow feels 'just and right' to continue, and a betrayal of themselves to quit.

This can lead to a cascade of complex negative emotions being experienced, yet they can be unexpressed as they simmer below an apparently calm exterior. The situation gets more complicated when the perceived mistreatment originates from people who are intimately trusted. The feelings of resentment are intensified and mingled with a sense of treachery. The already difficult situation is amplified with deeply unjust feelings that are far more difficult to shake. People commonly feel intensely resentful towards someone who is significant to them, perceiving a friend as a traitor where others would receive only moderate resentment.

Negative emotions cause thinking to become slow and ruminate on the subject of displeasure.[4] This is an evolutionary strategy to aid problem solving automatically, yet it's not best suited to resentment. When people think around a specific emotion, they have a tendency to bring to mind memories with similar emotional content for comparison purposes (a process termed mood-congruence[*]).[5] If people have trouble dispelling similar, yet unrelated, thoughts from their mind, it can seriously increase their negativity. In turn this makes them ruminate on those thoughts more. Ever deepening spirals of ruminating are possible. The resentfulness causes a powerful bias towards negative thought cycles that people can feel helpless to control.[6]

The more intensely people feel resentment the more helpless they will be to break out of the negative thought cycles. This happens for one major reason. Emotions progressively assume control over behaviour the higher their intensity becomes.[7] Interacting with psychological processing, this automatic control of behaviour is on a neuro-biological level, and if continuous, it results in serious stresses being placed on an array of bodily systems.[8]

The biological effects associated with loss, failure, anger, betrayal, fear, contempt, disgust, jealousy, envy, and more, are often entwined with resentment. Many other emotions can be indirectly fuelled by resentment. Emotions can intermingle into one experience which has resentment at its core. The cocktail of neurotransmitters and hormones associated with each emotion, along with the physiological states they induce, can be disguised by the resentment that binds them together. Stress can accumulate, and it's not simply a psychological outlook, but a biologically depressive experience that reduces people's ability to function across the emotional, psychological and biological spectrum, encompassing the immune system too.[9]

Perceptions from the frontal lobes are relayed to the amygdala, limbic system, hypothalamus and brainstem. These brain regions have control of many of the autonomic nervous system's functions. As the metabolism* (chemical processes that support life) begins to adjust breathing, blood pressure and hormones to best suit the perceived situation, changes begin to alter inner organ functioning.[10] If a defensive disposition (anger or fear related) is called for, people's inner constitutions change accordingly: increased heart rate; increased lung capacity; suppressed digestion; suppressed kidney functioning; muscle firming; natural (endogenous) painkiller release. A different variation of these changes is used for defeat, and yet another for anxiety. If these changes are prolonged, they seriously disturb metabolic efforts to support life and suppression of the immune system begins.[11]

The perceptions that cause these autonomic changes do not have to be accurate or appropriate to a situation. Perceptions only have to be believed for their associated emotions to be felt. The more intensely perceptions are believed, the more rapidly neuro-biological responses begin. Urgent perceptions assume control of bodily resources. When these responses are short and appropriate to a situation, the body responds for the necessitated duration then it returns to normal healthy low-stressed functioning. This 'maintaining balance through change' is referred to as *allostasis**, and it's completely normal.

Nevertheless, if these system stresses are prolonged, the systems involved are put under a heightened risk of complication. Other systems whose duties have been neglected are also put at risk. As such loads accumulate over decades, people are especially prone to serious health complications due to accumulated system stresses (see Stress).[12] This is referred to as *allostatic-load**.

Physical exercise can aid metabolic activity (e.g. heart rate, blood pressure, lowering glucose levels), and in effect refreshes many body systems, so physical health is seen as a serious factor in preventing *allostatic-load* from accumulating.[13]

Resentment is created when people perceive they are treated unfairly and the mistreatment has gone unpunished. Often because they do not express their anger or feel they cannot express their anger. The perception of unpunished, unfair treatment creates a slow burning anger that often becomes expressed in an indirect, passive-aggressive[*] manner. Feeling resentment towards someone continuously, especially when unexpressed, may lead to suppressed feelings of hatred manifesting over time.

Resentment is highly associated with envy. When these two emotions are coupled together, and acted upon, the situations that result can create many other detrimental emotions. Malicious actions are often motivated by resentment. People use the resentment as justification for actions they would not normally condone. Detrimental emotions motivate detrimental behaviours which create detrimental scenarios for the resented person, but also the resentful person and everyone else caught in between. The resentful can attack someone, use humiliation, or try to mar reputations by inciting outside parties to resent the individual too. This sort of malicious envy is often motivated by resentment.

The resentful and the envious are vulnerable to being used by, or using, one another. Envy's temptation flirts with a resentful attitude. The resentful have abnormally low defences to oppose envy, for if the envious seek to deprive the same person of a possession, a dark attraction implicitly dances before them.

Resentful people can find themselves condoning, encouraging, and even performing actions that aid another's envious intentions. Both have a vested interest. One's vengeance is satisfied while the other gains a possession. They are both unopposed to malice being inflicted on the same individual or people. Relationships form between resentful and envious people because they share a destructive goal (see Envy).

The resentment can be false though. When people have a resentful nature, they often vent their angry feelings onto others to relieve their underlying negative mood. Studies show that people release accumulated anger onto easy targets that are perceived to deserve resentment in some way.[14] For example, if people perceived that unidentified person A evaded punishment for an offence, the next time they perceive unrelated person B committing an offence they are more likely to sanction elevated levels of punishment. Just as if person B were responsible for person A's past crime. People have a tendency of backdating punishment for earlier evasions of justice. This rough justice is largely done unconsciously, and it's more of a venting procedure than an act of integrity. People have a tendency to carryover resentment and release it onto the next person they have a chance of punishing – a sort of transference*.

For example, unemployed people who receive benefit are easy targets who are vulnerable to being attacked in this way. They can receive the resentment that people are too afraid to direct at their boss. Many people with resentful attitudes do not express their anger toward their superiors, so instead they wait to find someone who they believe cannot retaliate, and someone who is perceived as lower in hierarchy is perfect for their venting of resentment. This abusive redirection of negativity is aimed at someone who is perceived to be offensive (typically in some minor way). This makes it harder for onlookers to see the negativity as abusive manipulation. Besides, the onlookers may do the same, or even join forces to create a venting mob of resentment, all looking sheepishly back at their boss, but not knowing why. People can even believe they are acting with righteous indignation. The truth is that even when the victim is offensive, the amount of resentment imposed on them is vastly out of proportion; it's a carryover of resentment.

The mass of negativity can seriously affect people's mood and lead to denial of detrimental emotions, behaviours and situations that have ultimately been created by the resentment. People don't want to take responsibility for the destructive situations that have been created by their misdirected resentment. People do not want to feel like the guilty one. It feels unfair to view one's self as guilty when feeling resentment. Also, people fear becoming the target of the sort of resentment they are treating others with. This means that the resentful feelings may be protected by the defence-mechanism[*] of denial (see Ignorance).

Nevertheless, denial is certainly not the only side-effect when resentful thoughts are being harboured. Irritable and touchy feelings regularly arise when a resented person is in the vicinity. This is a hallmark reaction of resentment. Anger arises when the person, who is the focus of resentment, is recognised positively by other people or even animals. Yet the anger and envy, fuelled by resentment, motivate actions unknowingly because people have ignored the negative emotions that stem from their resentment. This is referred to as acting-out[*].

If people disown or deny the emotions they feel, the emotions are still being created. The denial only pushes the emotions out of conscious awareness. Unexpressed anger of any sort will cause people to act in destructive passive-aggressive ways. When people cannot consciously accept the emotions they feel, it complicates everything. Not only do they act-out the feelings unknowingly, but if they realise that their behaviour is part of the problem and wish to address their passive-aggressive offences, they cannot recognise the emotions that are motivating the offending behaviours.

Frustratingly for everyone else, others cannot discuss the feelings directly either. When another mentions that their actions seem to be passive-aggressive, contain anger, envy or resentment, they do not know what the other is talking about. They may even take further offence at the seemingly unprovoked accusation and slur on their character, creating more resentment they cannot recognise.

If people are emotionally illiterate, a similar situation is created. Just as when people are in denial, they cannot recognise the emotions being referred to. Much worse is when people are both afraid to feel emotions and emotionally illiterate. This creates defence-mechanisms that are frustratingly difficult to address, even for professionals.

One of the most serious effects of resentment on health regards the underlying feelings that can accumulate. Very significant changes in mood can occur. A pervasive negative outlook can stimulate depressive neurotransmitters and hormones. The result is serious episodes of depression that can go unnoticed and denied for long periods of time. The troubling aspect is that resentment is more common in people who hide their feelings. Not expressing feelings can be extremely self-defeating in these scenarios. In serious cases it can lead to pathological passive-aggressiveness.[15]

For example, when people do not express their concerns it creates a situation where they could be feeling unhappy and angry towards someone, yet faking happiness or disinterested contentment. This situation itself could be a path to depression and passive-aggression while others have no idea. If inexpression is also coupled with denial of personal feelings (not just hiding them), it sets in place attitudes that are extremely conducive to orientating people towards a state of depression and passive-aggression. The astonishingly detrimental thing is that nobody knows it's happening, not even the people it's happening to. If the anger was expressed overtly, it would aid others who care to recognise that there's something wrong – before mood has become too affected.

Another aspect to a developed resentful personality is the sudden outburst of negative emotions. Betraying the apparently calm and collected mood that has been presented to date. Small outbursts of anger may appear from nowhere. These sudden lashes of outward aggression are incredibly important insights into people's present makeup, and a sign that issues of resentment are a possibility (although frustration would have to be ruled out).

Because people can subconsciously recognise that their consciously ignored behaviour is unfair, a whole array of self-defeating attitudes can be created from continually feeling resentful. This to a large extent can be a consequence of inaccurate perceptions of everyday issues that lead people to feel wronged when indeed they are not. Misunderstanding can be a key factor in feeling resentment and to what degree the intensity of those feelings are felt. As resentment is easily confused with justice, rejection can ensue if the resentful feelings are challenged with a heavy handed approach. A hammer is not the tool for this job. In such cases, resentful people are likely to push away the people who intimately care about them. This scenario often induces depressive episodes whilst leaving the resentful isolated and unwilling to accept help from those that care most.

The resentful are particularly vulnerable to being manipulated in such isolated positions. If abusively envious personalities recognise resentment in another is directed towards someone they are envious of, they could encourage the resentment by modestly agreeing with it. While seemingly endearing themselves in sympathetic expressions, abusers can subtly split people apart by gradually eliciting feelings of hate. While the resentful are being used, they start to care for the person abusing them. Unthinkable situations can materialise when people resent an offspring, parent, partner, friend or colleague.

Whenever challenging resentful feelings, just like passive-aggressive behaviours, they are best addressed with one tentative challenge at a time. Whatever the reply, a remark that refers to a resentful attitude being seemingly over-the-top needs to be followed by a retreat. The typical defensive reaction of people defending their attitude should be accepted – regardless of its content. To overcome defence-mechanisms it's important that the resentful person does not feel under attack. Then, although a tentatively challenging comment may not seem to have caused any change in attitude, it will be thought about as a reasonable point. In time, single tentative remarks accumulate into unthreatening objective reasoning.

Stress Related

Resentment

Latin. *Sentire* = to feel.
French. *Ressentir* = feel pain, regret.

1. Indignation or ill-will felt as the result of a real or
    imagined grievance.

2. To hold bitter feelings towards somebody for a
    perceived transgression.

Sadism

Sadism is gaining satisfaction from inflicting pain on another. Dominating behaviour is frequently associated with sadism, but specifically when it causes distress. As sadism is one person asserting his or her excessive will over another whilst finding the distress that's caused pleasurable, the definition has vast scope because it's not limited to physical pain. Sexual dominance, parental control, teacher discipline and pupil revenge could theoretically all be classified within this definition if pleasure is felt at observing another's distress.

Nonetheless, it's possible to inflict incredible pain onto a person whilst on the battlefield, protecting one's self or loved ones without being considered sadistic. To inflict injury, distress or suffering, no matter how severe, is not enough for the act to be sadistic. When the aim is to stop someone from committing an action perceived as abusive, it's a just cause. Forceful behaviour would be classed as sane and lawful if the force used was reasonable – even if the person died.

The definition of sadism always includes satisfaction that's gained from another's distress. To wish someone else to be in pain or cause someone to be in pain is not enough for those acts to be sadistic. A child wanting to find out what happens when they drop another child on its head, although disturbing, is not sadistic. These acts may not be seen as completely sane, but they would not be classed as sadistic acts. They may be malevolent, malicious, callous, unfeeling, cruel, evil or many other things, yet they are not sadistic as long as there's no satisfaction derived from the suffering inflicted.

Unless there's some form of subconscious satisfaction involved, consciously creating a scenario where people are satisfying their self by inflicting suffering on another is almost unimaginable. A subconscious satisfaction would point to a deep perception being present that has created a strong impulse – compulsively motivated – them to commit the act. People may suggest that a wrong or deeply misplaced perception may exist in the mind of a sadist, yet the reasons for sadism have proven beyond explicit understanding at present.

Perhaps it's owing to a set of neural networks, normally separate, linking because of a physical abnormality or an accident. Possibly an ancestor receiving significant and regular rewards for torturing people then associated the pain of others with personal satisfaction, and it's passed on through epigenetic* lineage. Conceivably it could be a manifestation of prolonged successful malevolence. The behaviour could be simply learnt from parents. A mixture of all of these or something distinctly different. No one can say for sure. However the satisfaction came to be there, it's reasonable to say there's a subconscious satisfaction associated with the perception of others' distress.

People make the mistake of thinking that sadism relates just to distress from physical pain. In reality, the mental and emotional pain of others is far more common. Females and males can be sadistic. Exerting excessive control that causes distress and is enjoyed is probably the most common form of sadism. Intimidation and humiliation are used to cause distress that's enjoyed, for these provide an implicit power-trip. Sadistic thoughts are often associated with domination fantasies.

The original word comes from the Count de Sade of France as stated below.

Sadism

French. *Sadism* = the name of the Count (usually
called 'Marquis') de Sade (1740–1814) who was
infamous for his crimes and the character of
his writings.

1. A form of sexual perversion marked by a love of
    cruelty. Now understood as cruelty that evidences
    a subconscious craving and is apparently satisfied,
    sexually or otherwise, by the infliction of pain
    on another by means of aggressive or destructive
    behaviour or the assertion of power over that
    person; also, loosely, deliberate or excessive
    cruelty morbidly enjoyed.

Sadness

Sadness is the negative and depressive emotion that accompanies a perceived loss.[1] Sadness relates to events that have happened; it always refers to the past. If a person fears a loss that has not happened, the emotion is anxiety.[2] On a perceptual level, the effects of a loss are virtually indistinguishable from that of a failure.

Sadness makes thoughts slow while refocusing the mind on the cause of the loss.[3] It forces the mind to pay attention to the issues involved. Specifically, resulting in elaboration around the loss to help identify what caused the emotional pain, so that similar future situations can be better managed.[4] Sadness is a motivtion for change.

Sad thoughts are linked together in associative networks within the brain. Other memories that share the same emotional tone have a tendency to be recalled for an elaborative comparison. This is termed mood-congruence*, and it's often unnerving.[5] People may find themselves remembering many sad experiences that bubble up and influence how they look upon present issues. A sad or depressive turn of events affects other everyday experiences. Instinctively, people prepare for a narrative building process by putting other aspects of their life on hold. Other interests seem viscerally* dull and uninteresting.

The subconscious trawls through an experiential archive of similar sad memories. Then it presents potentially relevant content in the imagination for conscious veto or accreditation. A narrative explanation for the incurred loss takes priority over mundane activities. If the memories that bubble up do not add clarity – to the current sad loss, they can be dismissed. A haunting memory around the time of such losses does not mean the content is relevant, but that it's similar in tone. Especially when people have busy lives, setting time aside for such a sad process of affirming and disregarding associative memories can be annoying.

Also, to rest and recuperate after a physical blow is accepted as normal, yet recognition for such a restorative period after a non-physical loss is rather scant. People are largely ignorant of the narrative building period. Accurate narrative explanations of loss lead to a faster and more stable recovery that better supports longevity. Similar mistakes are less likely to be repeated. People will significantly improve their future health with the ability to better manage similar stressful situations.

Pain is a negative physical reaction to cell damage. Sadness is an emotional form of pain where the damage is done to social prosperity owing to loss. The depressive and unpleasant emotion of sadness is to stop damage to future prosperity by adjusting the current psychological architecture. A reflective state is induced to ensure an explanation of how the loss materialised.

Sadness acts as an emotional marker for hindsight. The experiential evidence can be used by the subconscious at a pre-semantic* level. To own* the loss, experience the emotion, and recognise what caused its creation is important. When a similar situation is perceived in the future, the emotional marker will be a part of memory – personal learned dispositions – and will prompt adaptive behaviours.[6]

Nevertheless, there are important cognative biasses of which people are best made aware. Sadness is the 'out with the old and in with the new' emotion. The evolutionary core features of sadness create deep feelings as motivation to churn up the past and renew the attitudes towards the cause of the problem. A side-effect regarding money exists. Decision making on unrelated topics can be affected by this earthmoving disposition. People who are experiencing sadness are more willing to sell their possessions at a lower price than they would do normally, and buy possessions at a higher price than they would do normally. People become far more susceptible to the 'here why don't you try this to cheer you up' approach to marketing. They are more likely to become indebted when depressed.

Sadness has its own distinctive facial features. The mouth and cheeks show a frown. The eyebrows are scrunched together low in the middle of the forehead, a sign that a state of action is not engaged and inward reflection is on-going. The head often hangs off the shoulders looking towards the ground. Thoughts and actions become progressively slower, and the elimination of tears often accompanies the depressive feelings as their intensity increases. As serious damage to social prosperity is perceived, people cry. Perception of significant change to social consequences, not the recoiling pain, seems to be the cause of tears, for people cry when they're elated too.

Facial displays of sadness instinctively evoke sympathy from onlookers (see Sympathy).[7] As shown in sympathy-related physiological responses and expressions, the perception of someone else's distress causes overt attempts to help from children (as early as eight months old) and adults.[8] Humans predominantly use the eyebrows and cheeks to detect sadness.[9] Expressions such as a hung head and shrugged posture act as further indicators of the emotion's intensity.

Amazingly and admirably, sadness appears to be millions of years old in origin. Although the experience of sadness will vary with the degree of consciousness a creature possesses, vast amounts of creatures potentially suffer it. This is inferred from its neurological execution site within the brain. The midbrain is located at the top of the brainstem. Many of the reactions of sadness are initiated from an execution site in this region called the mesencephalon.[10]

An experimental medical treatment for people suffering from Parkinson's concerned the midbrain. The team provided laboratory evidence of what happened. Treatment involved inserting electrodes into the midbrain's motor nuclei. The placements of the eight electrode points were two millimetres from each other, and there were four on the left side and four on the right. To gauge which point gave the optimal result for the patient, a low-intensity, high-frequency electrical current was passed through one electrode at a time.

Perspective of the two millimetre gap is enhanced when it's understood that neurons are measured in thousandths of a millimetre, and over eighty billion neuron cells reside in the human brain. A number of electrodes positioned two millimetres apart cover a vast expanse in terms of neuron populations, like different cities in a country.

The doctors were testing the implanted electrodes in a patient when something extraordinarily unexpected happened. As a current was passed through one of the electrodes, the team behind the screen waited to see if improved motor function would result. But the patient diverted the focus of everybody's attention with an abrupt change in mood. Slumping forward, she suddenly stopped talking and cast her eyes down. A few seconds later she began to cry. A few more seconds and the tears were flowing. The emotional episode caused the doctors to be distracted from looking at her motor functions. This was a Parkinson's sufferer in distress, and they were naturally sympathising with her; what had happened to make her experience such distress?

A few more seconds and the patient started talking about how deeply sad she was. Then how she had no energy, how she'd had enough of life, and how it was pointless. She displayed increasing intensities of sadness that rapidly reached despair. She said she was worthless, and that she was scared of this world and wanted to hide in the corner.

This is when the physician controlling the treatment had an idea. 'The change in the patient's disposition could be a result of the electric current being passed through her brain?' he thought and promptly stopped the process.

A minute or so later, the patient had another abrupt change in disposition. She began talking in a light-hearted manner as she had been before the shocking experiment. 'What was that all about?' she said in astonishment. 'Where did that come from?' She couldn't explain where the sadness had originated from, or why it escalated to despair.

Just as if neurotransmitters and hormones had been released from a deeply sad thought, the current had activated motor nuclei of sadness. She had uncontrollably experienced the motor functions and associative mentality of the emotion. The astonishing abruptness was due to the direct electrical current. In usual circumstances the motions of sadness would graduate slowly. Normally, the initial impulses stem from a sad perception in the prefrontal cortex before being relayed to the execution site in the midbrain. The electrode had bypassed any need for the natural triggering of the motions.

The motions of sadness are most often triggered by thoughts in the cerebral cortex, and they relate to a perceived event – an emotionally competent stimulus*.

The newest parts of the human brain are integrated with the earliest parts, and all work as one. Although it may seem like it, the brain is not one unit. Brains are comprised of many systems that have evolved at different times and at different rates. The gradual evolution of different systems took hundreds of millions of years. Nevertheless, all the systems are inseparably integrated with one another. All the systems are inter-dependent. They work seamlessly. The systems that are hundreds of millions of years old, like the brainstem, have frequent instructions from the newest systems such as the neo-cortex. The fluent communication between the old and the new is constant. It is indispensable. The older parts of the human brain are essential for consciousness.[11] They will never be redundant.

Loss has psychological, emotional and biological effects. Depressive neurotransmitters and hormones are released into the body's systems when loss is perceived. A slump in biological, psychological and emotional states is experienced which corresponds to sad electro-chemical reactions. Sections of the midbrain region are inextricable to sadness. This is an intimate and influential part of the nervous system, for it has many neural programmes that directly alter metabolic* – chemical balances that maintain life – processes.[12]

Failure does not have to be experienced directly. People become sad too when a person they care for fails. The more direct the loss is, the greater the affect is. The more intimately the person is known, the stronger the feelings will be. This failure has the widest possible context and includes anything that's perceived to deprive cared for persons of rewards. Time, somebody, something, or even ideas; it really doesn't matter. A perception of loss is all that's required.

If more failures are perceived than successes, depressive territory is looming. Mood will become slumped. The neuro-biological and psychological effects of repeated failures, without success, take their toll. Successes release neurotransmitters and hormones that stimulate positivity in the brain. Tense neuro-biological systems are relaxed. Thoughts flow more freely. If people do not have enough successes, they will become depressed to some degree.

Perception controls this process. An imagined failure still has the same biological effects as a real failure. If a perception is believed, the corresponding emotion is experienced. Prolonged inappropriate emotions stress and disrupt people's metabolism, and this includes suppressing immune system functioning which leaves them more vulnerable to infection (see Stress).[13]

A small amount of sadness on a regular basis is not a detrimental thing as long as successes are at hand to buffer the effects. The intensity of people's sadness will be greater if a failure is perceived to be highly significant to their prospects. Just as serious successes produce elation, significant failures cause despair. Nonetheless, lots of little losses are not to be underestimated. They can build up sadness, so mood becomes significantly affected. This is above all true when losses are incurred continuously.

People can be sad when doing well, but someone they care for experiences serious failures. When consequences are significantly negative, sometimes people stop caring for others who are habitually self-destructive or have a very serious illness. If people have only a few successes in their lives, the negativity of someone else's sadness can be overwhelming. This is a largely unconscious activity. Even though they may look uncaring to onlookers, people may detach from a person they know who's unwell because they subconsciously fear becoming too sad. This is a defence-mechanism* called 'withdrawal' that stops people becoming too depressed. A statement to condone or sanction this is not. A statement validating the psychological withdrawal that many people have experienced with the people they care for most, it is. Everyone has to care for a person before they can withdraw. As anxiety and guilt creep in from perceptions of potential neglect, and questions of loyalty are raised, people often find it difficult to come to terms with their exit.

In general, if successes outweigh failures, then depression is offset. The immune system's operation is healthy. To find and do anything that leads to success on a regular basis has positive effects on health. Successes contribute to self-confidence by creating a sense of control in the world that will reduce anxieties and contribute to a positive mental outlook (see Optimism). Success and failure can be imagined as a bank balance. Too much failure or loss will put people in the red, and their mood becomes negatively affected.

Sadness

Middle English. *Sad* = serious, grave, unhappy.

1. Overly serious, gravity of mind or demeanour.

2. Of persons, their feelings or dispositions: sorrowful, mournful.

3. Of times, places, actions, etc.: characterised by sorrow, sorrowful.

4. The feeling of things sorrowful; distressing, calamitous, lamentable.

Satisfaction

Satisfaction is the emotion that arises from being positively affected by the fulfilment of a goal. It literally means 'enough'.

Negative emotions cause thinking to become slow, effortful (in a searching manner), and narrowed onto the object of concern. This aids people to overcome problems. Positive emotions, such as satisfaction, are associated with quicker lighter thinking, which recalls current knowledge bases. Positive emotions cause more creative and flexible thought processes which spend less time focusing on specific things.[1]

Accumulating evidence is revealing a bias of negative emotional processing towards the right-hemisphere, and a left-hemisphere bias for positive emotional processing.[2] Although, considerable hemispherical overlap occurs. More than forty billion neurons reside in each hemisphere. The many systems that comprise those eighty billion neurons are not split down the middle into neat distinct zones.

Negative emotions aid people to focus their minds onto a problem and spend effort thinking about a solution, but this taxes the systems involved in processing a negative state, and they may become stressed. Positive emotions emerge on successful completion of a problem. They are associated with a release of the taxing effort of negative emotions. Satisfaction pulls people out of slow effortful thinking, as they're freed from analysis, and makes their conscious thoughts faster. This coincides with a shift from right-hemisphere to left-hemisphere processing. This is felt as neurological relief that allows the taxed systems to recharge.

Satisfaction has two significant aspects associated with success. One is the physical, neuro-biological and psychological release of tension that's felt as relaxation. Another is the amount of benefit received from whatever has been gained – e.g. the quantity and variety of nutrients in a piece of food. It includes the fulfilment of emotions that stem from an instinctual level as well as a conscious process of reasoning. A mixture of *how much* effort was spent and *how much* positive infusion takes place determines *how much* satisfaction is experienced.

On a philosophical note, there must be some form of satisfaction used on a neuro-biological level for homeostasis* and allostasis* to function. Bodily processes for different systems are engaged and disengaged according to the priority of their task's completion. A symphony of bodily resources is conducted with precise timing to maintain health. Immediate concerns take precedence, and there must be some way of determining when a process has done enough, so another process can engage.

Therefore, the following theoretical possibility exists. Homeostatic neuro-biological release of a process is the evolutionary origin of conscious satisfaction; social satisfaction is nested with neuro-biologically satisfying processes. People have many plans and hopes that maintain their social prosperity; does it not make sense that the reason they feel satisfied with one activity is so they can move on to another in a form of social allostasis?

A large part of perception is processed by the subconscious. Just as with biological allostasis, the unconscious measures the success of an aim that's in place. Conscious objectives may be aligned with motives that are not consciously acknowledged. Satisfaction is an emotion which stems from deep unconscious layers, but it reaches conscious appreciation. When people complete a goal and feel it's a much more significant success than they thought it would be, it suggests a motivation linked with a deep motive, a motive that goes beyond conscious understanding. The feelings of contentment and relaxation that stem from a success are valuable indications of just how much the goal truly means to people. Feelings of satisfaction are the pointer on a gauge of personal prosperity.

People can have an intellectual aim they work towards and complete, yet feel dissatisfied with the outcome. Not because of failure, but because it does not feel satisfying. It's possible for this to happen whether one day or one year was spent working on the fulfilment of the goal. This might be taken as a sign that the goal was not aligned with a deeper motive, not associated with instinct or hope. If the rewards of success were not fulfilling, a washed-out feeling would typically be experienced. Satisfying deeds contribute positively to people's state. The more positively things contribute, the more satisfying they are. People's state relates to deep and wide-ranging aspects of their life. Satisfaction is an idiosyncratic affair. Apart from being associated with instinctive needs, it also entails the relevant nutrients (physical and social) people need to recuperate from activities that are en route to fulfilling hopes.

Satisfaction originally described performing an act set by a priest which would atone for sin. To satisfy a creditor, on a bank balance sheet, is another view of satisfaction that's unrelated to religion but has the same overtone. This tone is also contained in the present day description of satisfaction that's used in the broader sense to explain any form of fulfilment. It is not only related to fulfilling a perceived holy agreement or a financial contract.

If a lot of energies are spent in pursuit of a goal, which doesn't have enough positive effect upon achievement, the result is dissatisfaction. Completing goals that are not linked to instinct or hope is dissatisfying. Stress is increased by dissatisfaction. Emotions keep balance through change, for they are allostatic motivations serving biological and social needs.[3] Satisfaction is an *enough* part of the allostatic process.

People perceive reality with the entirety of *their* senses and choose a course of action based on those conscious and unconscious perceptions. When those personal objectives and goals are achieved, satisfaction is experienced.

Satisfaction

Latin. *Satis* = enough.

1. The action of gratifying (an appetite or desire) to the full, or of contenting (a person) by the

complete fulfilment of a desire or supply of a
want; the fact of having been gratified to the full
or of having one's desire fulfilled.

2. The feeling of having enough; to supply fully
the needs of; of putting an end to (an appetite, a
want) by fully supplying it.

3. The feeling of being furnished with sufficient
proof or information; of being assured or set free
from doubt or uncertainty; to be convinced.

Scare

Scare is an expression of alarm at finding a modest danger worrying. Being scared is an expression that shows an experience of mild fear. The motions associated with being scared are moderate and represent the mild intensity caused from a perception of danger.

Being scared is reached through surprise at a negative thing. When a person is surprised, the instinctual reactions are a preparation for another emotion. In one fluid motion the mouth, lungs and eyes open in coordination with each other. The opening of the eyes also lifts the eyebrows. The heart rate increases a few beats a minute. A little gasp of air is drawn and held to aid hearing.

When a surprising event turns out negative, the expression morphs into scare. The eyes open more as they fix on perceived danger, so the eyebrows are pulled further up which wrinkles the forehead. Another quick breath may be taken that moderately erects the posture from an inflated chest area. The muscles around the mouth become quite loose.

The body may freeze as if to evade notice. Blood is drained from specific areas of the body, such as the hands and head, making them cold. The skin of such areas becomes paler from decreased blood flow. As they are preparing to run, blood is pumped to the legs. The head is typically lowered, as if crouching, and the back may be moderately hunched into a strangely shaped shrug-like posture. A brief expression of surprise can be seen milliseconds before the face becomes more serious and worry stricken.

The word 'scare' comes from frightening the timid or shy.

Scare

Old Norse. *Skjarr* = to frighten, timid, shy.

1. A sudden fright or alarm, especially with little or no reason.

2. A general state of alarm; a panic.

Shame

Shame is distress caused by personal feelings of disgrace. It stems from a perception of one's self having thought or acted in a self-demeaning manner. When people feel sick with their behaviour, it's called shame. Withdrawing from social interaction, when one has debased one's self, is a central motivational force of shame. It regards ceasing action that is damaging to one's self; behaviour that may be ongoing and difficult to change. Blind people exhibit it, and this suggests it's innate.

Shame is related to any action perceived as degrading, either directly or indirectly, to one's self. If people do something that would ultimately corrupt their personality, that deed would be deemed shameful – especially actions that give short-term pleasure with a result of long-term disadvantage.

Expressions of shame have been shown to evoke sympathy from onlookers.[1] Overt displays of distress are met with overt attempts to help from both children (as young as eight months) and adults – shown in sympathy-related expressions and physiological responses.[2]

This shows that innate social expressions elicit innate responses.

Nevertheless, people express shame in front of those who care for them for wise reasons. People can aggravate distress. If shame is shown to someone, embarrassment will typically be felt too. Shame, more so than other forms of distress, is difficult to deal with socially. People commonly withdraw from the situation to escape an overwhelming sense of dread. There are good reasons for such caution. Some people seek to cruelly punish shameful acts, so the withdrawal is not pointless.

Cruel persons seek personal details that relate to others' shame as a means of corrupt social control. This is done by disseminating the shameful knowledge, to specific people at specific times, to cause social misfortune by humiliation. Uncomfortable truths can be used to blackmail people by threatening them with social calamity if they do not meet specific demands. Malicious talk about others' shameful private details is used as a weapon to cause a traumatic injury to rivals (see Humiliation).

If their professional services are contracted, counsellors, psychotherapists, psychologists and psychiatrists are bound by confidentiality. They have to act in their patient's best interest. They have a duty of care. Above all, it's sensible to express shame to others trustworthy in matters of mental health, so at least additional distress is avoided.

Pain is a physical reaction to cell damage which appeared very early in the evolution of species. It's hundreds of millions of years old. Shame is emotional pain. Things that impact social circumstances can damage people's ability to succeed. Shame is, however, arguably, only thousands of years young. Shame is associated with the right-ventromedial prefrontal cortex; as this region is associated with high-functioning, human social decisions, it's considered a sophisticated behavioural reaction.[3]

When a shameful deed is made public, a person will feel embarrassed or humiliated too. If this damages social reputation, the social prospects of the humiliated person are damaged. Fear of social rejection is highly associated with shame. The internal recoiling is to stop damage to social opportunities in the future.

Other negative emotions are highly associated with shame. Sadness, anxiety, regret and despair can be indirectly experienced through shame. Feelings of failure or loss are implicit, so shame inherently makes people sad (see Sadness). Also, people experiencing shame are contemplating the undue harm they have caused themselves (guilt for damaging one's self) and damage to their future opportunities (see Anxiety). Shame could be described as guilt from self-harm that leads to anxieties. Shame feels like remorse for one's lost hopes.

Dreams and opportunities are not automatic things. Hopes are made true from effort. If people destroy opportunities that would lead to their prosperity the result is sadness or despair. The contemplation of how such consequences will negatively affect the well-being of significant others will result in guilt being felt too. Shame is a complex emotion because of all the other emotions associated with it.

To commit a social faux pas – minor social stumble – would lead to embarrassment rather than shame as it's not a serious degrading of nature. There are hardly any social consequences to such minor mistakes, so they are easily disregarded. Whereas embarrassment always relates to others knowing of someone's error, shame can be an entirely personal affair that requires no recognition from others. If someone else tries to impose shame, it's an attempt to humiliate.

When a perception of shame stems from an accurate appraisal of events, it's far better to accept the feelings rather than avoid them. Yet this can be difficult as the feelings of shame are uncomfortable to own*. Often people want to push the emotion out of awareness.

Perceptions create emotions, whether the perceptions are correct descriptions of reality or not. If a perception is believed, the associated emotion is experienced. If people believe a perception about their acting in a degrading way, they feel shame. Pretending that such emotions are not there causes troubling behaviour. Suppressing shame only pushes it out of sight. Behaviour will continue to be unconsciously motivated by the shame without any conscious oversight – a process referred to as acting-out* that would be felt as a strong feeling of wanting to withdraw, but without the specific reason that shame reveals. This will also elevate unconscious anxieties associated with cortisol-related stress levels (see Stress).

Both shame and stress are highly associated to addicts.

The experience of such an emotionally charged state makes for a seriously worrying cocktail of neurotransmitters and hormones. As shame instinctively causes people to withdraw, it often places addicts in a position where they are vulnerable to perpetuate, or relapse, on that which they are addicted. Next day, they feel additional shame for what they could not help from happening, and the process begins again (see Helplessness). Their health deteriorates and their psychological and biological systems are increasingly stressed. As the addictive substance usually relieves them of negative experience momentarily, temptation dances in their mind. Withdrawn and feeling overwhelming negative emotions is not a conducive environment to escape an addiction that offers instant relief. However temporary that release may be, due to the overwhelming intensity of negative experience, it's grasped as a reflex to alleviate the excruciating emotional pain.

Notably, a non-stressful, helpful environment to share one's shame can make all the difference. When people don't have to be completely alone with their shame, stress is reduced, and excruciating emotions are less likely to be experienced, so temptation's promise of relief holds less value.

Theoretically, suggesting that shame evolved in an environment where withdrawal was made from the wider community back into a nucleus of trusted, helpful and compassionate people.

Accurate perceptions of shame are indications that behaving in a specific way will lead to the ruin of hopes. They are important markers of damaging behaviour. There are several reasons it's difficult to own shame. One is that it will include despair created from any related lost hope. This means it's uncomfortable for people to accept shameful feelings but of paramount importance that people do. If people ignore their shameful actions, they will be unaware of parts of their personalities that are self-defeating, so anxieties are created that cannot be resolved. Future success depends on being able to accept shame, which stems from accurate perceptions, as this creates motivations to avoid repeating the behaviour.

The opposite is true for any inaccurate or false perception of shame. People must reject reasoning based on such foundations. Believing that thoughts or behaviours are shameful when they are not will lead people to attribute self-destructive properties to thoughts and behaviours that do not deserve such convictions. This imposes inappropriate boundaries on people and limits their ability to adapt. If this happens many times (e.g. in childhood), it would create a metaphorical straitjacket for their personality. Feeling shame wrongfully can seriously hinder peoples' progress in life, for it can leave them bystanders who inappropriately watch opportunities pass by.

People's lives will be adversely affected if they act shamefully, ignore they are acting shamefully, or accept imposed shame. Every aspect of shame relates to the creation of unfortunate circumstances. If people feel personally degraded, and it's not because of their behaviour, they should not feel shame.

Intensity of shame should be equal to the adverse consequences the behaviour in question has caused or will cause. The most appropriate intensity of shame will be created by accurate perceptions of just *how* detrimental the behaviour has been.

When shame makes the body recoil from a specific action, it leaves an uncomfortable and powerful memory. Such memory informs future decisions. An internal frame of reference is constructed of the world which informs responses. Shame is encoded into memory with a social footnote saying 'Withdraw!', 'Do not repeat!' or 'Avoid!' Feeling shame is a painful experience and part of a natural process of avoiding highly specific behaviours.

Shame

Proto-Germanic. *Skamo* = Feelings of guilt or disgrace, to cover oneself.

1. The painful emotion arising from the consciousness of something dishonouring or indecorous in one's own conduct or circumstances (or in those of others whose honour or disgrace one regards as one's own), or of being in a situation that offends our sense of modesty or decency.

Shock

Shock is a state of disorientation that arises from serious, sudden change.

Two major definitions of shock exist, and they are both different intensities of the same experience. The first describes the initial response to an intense and sudden event whilst the second explains the ongoing reactions to that event. So the term shock describes primary and secondary experiences to intensely sudden events. Both definitions are described below for greater distinction. If the shock is mild, only the initial reactions emerge. The more intense and sudden an event is, the more likely primary shock will lead to secondary shock.

When trying to understand shock, it helps to know that intense emotions assume more control over bodily processes than milder emotions. Instinctual responses to perceptions automatically express themselves as emotions become more intense. Responses are unconsciously processed from perceptions, and the content of perception is partially formed from imagination. The more intense the perception, the faster this unconscious processing happens. Vivid imaginations create stronger emotions.[1] This remains true if the perceptions that have informed the mind are inaccurate or even complete fantasy. If a perception is believed, the associated emotion is experienced. Emotions are idiosyncratically expressed, so individual differences in expression become more erratic with intense emotions. Nevertheless, recognisable themes form the basis of shock.

First, there's the mostly psychological experience of being shocked. Emotional reactions to sudden and unexpected events take an order of intensity that starts with 'surprise', next is 'astonishment', and finally 'shock' is the most intense. These emotions are usually measured in milliseconds or sometimes seconds, and shock can be exempt from this rule of thumb as it's a reaction to the most intense perceptions. All of these emotions to sudden and unexpected events prepare people for another longer lasting adaptive emotion that follows. In this respect, shock is always intimately bonded to the beginning of another emotion, yet whatever emotion shock morphs into, it will be filled with wonder.

The eyes, mouth and lungs open in synchronisation with each other. A fluid motion that raises the eyebrows and opens the mouth wide whilst a sharp audible breath is drawn and held.

Shock is instinctual. Blind and deaf people show the same emotional expressions, and it's also seen in many animals. Eyebrows are raised, as the eyes open wide, removing them from obstructing vision and letting more light onto the pupils. The posture becomes very erect as the lungs take a sharp deep breath. Muscles around the inflated torso, the neck, back and hips are tensed. The body is firmly poised to run away from danger or evade a blow, yet as if to attempt not to be noticed by a dangerous creature, the body may be rendered motionless. The breath is held to reduce noise that could be noticed and to improve hearing. Senses are primed to detect any sign of a threat.

Owing to the intensity of the event, the breath may be held so tightly that people turn faint or choke, for the heart rate increases rapidly. Dizziness can occur through lack of oxygen which compounds the overall feeling of being dazed.

People often push hands out in front, as if to prepare for a fall, although they're stationary. Although people are already standing, hands are sometimes thrown down and backwards as if to break a backwards fall, or perhaps to push the body up quickly from a seated position. Arms may lift up over the head as if to protect it from a falling or flying object, yet there's no such threat. Often people motion as if to push something or someone away although nothing or nobody is there. These expressions are not expressed in a uniform manner between people, for they're individual to the person concerned, stemming from instinct, learnt environmental dispositions, and from epigenetic* code.

These are commonly experienced instinctive reactions to sudden and intense events. In these initial moments there has been no decision made as to whether the sudden event is positive or negative. Shock prepares the body's posture to adapt to either outcome, and part of that process is readying the body for activity just in case it's needed. All the preparatory motions, such as keeping quiet by holding the breath and freezing to prevent attracting attention, are enacted in case they're needed. As early humans evolved, their shorter lives were occupied with continuous physical labour. Life-threatening events would have been common. These instinctive preparations would have given precious life-saving seconds in a life-threatening emergency.

When such a shocking event turns out to be positive, the expression morphs into joy or elation. The eyes reduce in size, lowering the eyebrows, while the open mouth widens into a smile. The exhale, of pent up breath, may sound like screams, or cries of pain, as the muscles are so tightly contracted around the rib cage that laughter is rarely heard even when the event is elating. Instead deep breaths and erratic cries of joy with strained, fluctuating facial features are often the result.

When the shocking event is negative, the expression morphs into terror (or horror if there's an element of disgust). The blood drains from the face and hands, leaving them cold, as it's redirected to the legs that are prepared to run. The limbs may even twitch as they ready for movement. If the perceived danger passes, then immediate relief is felt, often resulting in a massive sigh from forced exhalation of pent-up breath that lunges the body forward.

These are instinctive initial reactions of shock that are dependent on the intensity and suddenness of a perceived event. Shock is an evolutionary reaction that's neutral. It prepares the body and mind for an additional emotion that's appropriately adaptive to perceived events. Elation, terror, horror and relief are emotional reactions that act as extensions to shock.

Second, shock is an intense reaction that shuts body systems down, so that resources can be focused on something else that has suddenly become a priority.

This is commonly experienced when people fall or land on a hard surface in an awkward position. Consciousness can literally shut down as people faint or drop off to sleep. This is an instinctive attempt to stop activities that are not vital. It prevents movement in case of a serious physical injury. Shock can occur if an injury has happened or not. A serious jolt can send people into shock. When believed, a fantastical perception of a serious injury is enough.

The shutdown is to assess injuries. It is an instinctive safe guard that could be compared to a spinal-board that ambulance crews strap to people. When people have been in an accident, they're strapped down to keep them from moving. It's a precaution against an unseen injury inadvertently paralysing injured people when paramedics move them.

Whereas superficial pain has the tendency to create a fight-or-flight[*] response, visceral[*] pain acutely reduces activity and often leaves people dormant.[2]

In a similar way conscious processes reduce. The shutdown leaves people existing in a shock-like daze where they're unable to think as they would do normally. Shock can happen without people being physically hurt. It can also be a response to positive and negative news. Hearing about seriously consequential happenings is enough to send people into shock.

How significant an event is perceived to be determines how shocked a person becomes. The ability to use normal mental processes is lost as the mind is focused on something else. The mind is trying to factor in the new information. Consciousness is affected. The ability to attend to detail becomes diminished. In varying degrees of time, higher consciousness vacates its residency. The lights are on but nobody is home.

Shock experiences have a range of intensities that often have considerable overlap with fight-or-flight instincts. A true example of moderate shock with fight-or-flight overlap is the case of Martin. He was riding with his friends on a hire bicycle one night in London. They were on a lad's night out, and all had one pint before hiring bicycles to travel to a different location across the centre of London. As they stopped and pulled their bicycles up onto the path, they looked at the spectacle of theatres, hotels and shops along the Strand before setting off once again. They hurried onto the road in front of a red double-decker bus. Martin was the last to leave the path and was at the back of the group. He didn't expect the other bikes in front of him slowing down as they descended the large curb, so he had to brake for a second.

The double-decker bus came to a stop, but it was too late. It consumed the rear wheel of Martin's hire bike. He was standing on the bike peddles and looking back to see the huge red structure towering over him as it happened. The bike was ripped backwards under the bus as Martin's body continued forward with his legs getting stuck on the handle bars. In a corner of his mind, a perception of his body being pulled under the bus, entangled in the hire bike, took hold.

London double-decker buses have amazingly good brakes. The bus had stopped on a penny. Martin was now standing on the road with his feet in between the front half of a bike and the red monstrosity lurching inches from his back.

Trying to cheer Martin up, his mates pulled the bike out from the bus and joked of the accident. The bus driver, six foot five inches tall and attempting to control his anger, found his patience being tested owing to a group of lads trying to make the experience funny whilst offering no apology. A passer-by, Jake, had to mediate, and he asked Martin for the hire bike number to diffuse the situation. The bus driver could take the unique code from the back of the bike for insurance. Martin handed Jake the bike whilst gesturing he didn't want to approach the bus driver himself.

Martin didn't notice he'd passed his valuables, in a bag on the front, with the bike to Jake. Martin had no physical injury but he had entered into a fight-or-flight process. It had limited unnecessary thinking and primed his instinctive implicit-memory* to heighten the speed of his physical reactions. He had natural analgesia – painkillers – flowing in his blood stream and was instinctively focusing on body movements. Yet that was not all. A large proportion of Martin's attention was being redirected from conscious to unconscious control as it tried to assess what the consequences of the event were. These processes were limiting his higher faculties. Martin couldn't speak more than a few seconds at a time and kept forgetting what he'd said.

After Jake had aided the bus driver, he went back to Martin with the bike and said everything was sorted. Martin nodded and then went to walk away down the Strand leaving Jake with the hire bike and all his valuables. Neither Martin nor his friends recognised he was in shock. They had no recognition of the neuro-biological process that Martin's body had engaged.

Fortunately Jake, the passer-by, did. He told the friends that Martin was in shock and that for everybody's safety he shouldn't drive or be in charge of anyone else for the next couple of hours. Martin thanked Jake and walked off dazed.

Shock is an experience that people, especially the young, often are unaware they are experiencing. It's possible to transition in and out of shock and a fight-or-flight state. The experience of different levels of shock over time gives people an ability to sympathise and empathise with others whom they see in a similar situation. People can tell when it's not possible for someone to think straight. When people are in minor shock, they can often talk and remember, but they're still preoccupied on a subconscious level with something else.

To determine how vulnerable people are and how safely they can carry out activities is important. A person in shock should not be handling heavy machinery. As mistakes are a common occurrence when people are in shock, they should not be put into a position where a mistake of theirs could harm anyone. Their minds are not fully on the job. Their minds wander off. It may not be possible for people to pay due care and attention when trying their best to do so. Typically, it's a bad idea that people drive whilst in shock.

No one is immune to shock. This innate mechanism inadvertently shows the limitations of conscious attention. It demonstrates how consciousness gets reduced when high levels of unconscious processing are needed. If people think they don't experience shock from time to time, it means they are unaware of the times when they do. It's an evolutionary safe guard – an everyday occurrence that many people understand from direct experience. Shock is one of those reactions that sheds light on the deeper intelligence at work in everyone. It may be called the soul, spirit, the unconscious or core, but there's definitely something substantial working below conscious awareness.

Stress Related

Shock

Old French. *Choquer* = strike against.
Middle French. *Choc* = violent attack.
Middle Dutch. *Schokken* = to push, jolt.

1. Military: the encounter of an armed force with the enemy in a charge or onset; also, the encounter of two mounted warriors or jousters charging one another.

2. A sudden and violent blow, impact, or collision, tending to overthrow or to produce internal oscillation in a body subjected to it; the disturbance of equilibrium or the internal oscillation resulting from this. Also, a sudden

large application of energy other than mechanical energy, esp. thermal shock; a shock wave.

3. A sudden and violent effect tending to impair the stability or permanence of something; a damaging blow (to a condition of things, a person's health or constitution, an institution, a belief, etc.).

4. A sudden and disturbing impression on the mind or feelings; usually, one produced by some unwelcome occurrence or perception, by pain, grief or violent emotion, and tending to occasion lasting depression or loss of composure; in a weaker sense, a thrill or start of surprise, or of suddenly excited feelings of any kind.

Spite

Spite is an expression of modest malice that most often refers to reactive expressions that stem from being irritated with someone. A spiteful remark is less serious than a planned malicious action.

The emotion is volatile. It's a little out of control and often stirred by the pettiest of issues. Spite is understood to be a punitive action with no real value to justice. It's neither deemed to be specifically just or unjust in its overall application, but spite has a distinctive petty and pathetic aspect.

It can be quite a shocking experience for both the person on the receiving end and, less noticeably, the person expressing the spite. When people receive spite, they will usually be left with the distinct impression of hostility and aggression. This is unsettling and creates an uncomfortable air that keeps people on edge and wondering what could come next.

A disrupted environment results. Spite's volatile and out of control nature taunts the mind to watch out and become anxious. The aim of the spiteful person is to make others feel pain or to deprive them of positive feelings. Spite can indicate resentment and envy smouldering below, and both of these emotions can fuel other negative emotions. Owing to these consistent connections, spite is often one of many negative emotions experienced around the same time: a symptom of darker underlying emotions.

Nevertheless, spite can be a temporary coping strategy. If people come into contact with others whom they perceive as unfair, spite may express the undercurrent of anger that's being experienced. Although not ideal, if people do not have a more constructive way to express themselves, it's better than suppressing anger and developing passive-aggressive* personality traits. As this would cause compulsive motivations – exceptionally strong impulses – to treat others with clandestine destructive behaviour, suppressing anger is worse than spiteful expressions, for the destructive anger is concealed and much more difficult to address.[1] Spite is an overt expression, so it's apparent and can be addressed.

Expressing spite constantly is unhealthy. Expressing spite frequently leaves people with an emotionally out of control, unpredictable and fazed demeanour. Defensive and aggressive attitudes change people's dispositions towards the fight side of the fight-or-flight[*] spectrum; it alters their metabolism[*] (chemical processes for sustaining life). For example, the suppression of the intestinal tract, suppression of organ functioning, increasing blood pressure, and prioritising blood flow to the muscles and heart.[2] When this happens continuously it interrupts the optimal metabolic balance for wellbeing, so it places accumulating stress on various systems. It contributes to an increased likelihood of suffering health conditions that stem from the body's state being inordinately occupied with defensive postures, such as those related to metabolic syndrome[*], heart disease and memory functioning (see Stress).[3]

As spite is often an outward expression of resentment (e.g. from a grudge), its intention is sometimes to get others to stop behaving in a specific manner. The idea is to rattle them, so they're scared or deterred from repeating the perceived offence. A problem occurs, however, because of the volatile way in which spite is expressed. The reasons behind spitefulness are often not related by its hasty interaction, so the cause remains overlooked. The people receiving the spite are then left feeling like they're being attacked. This then leads to a vicious cycle with both parties wanting to hurt one another, yet neither remembers how the mud-slinging started. Withholding the reason for the spite prolongs the experience. Explaining the reason often ends up defusing a situation or facilitating a more productive outcome.

Spite

Old French. *Spite* = action arising from, or displaying, hostile or malignant feeling; outrage, injury, harm; insult, reproach.

1. A malicious and usually petty desire to hurt, annoy or offend someone.

Stress

Stress is the experience of strain due to prolonged adverse circumstances. It regards attending to perceived threats that cannot sufficiently be dealt with. Over-stretching of bodily resources to meet some tasks forces the body to put other important activities on hold. This makes people feel under-par from attempts to cope with escalating demands and lack of rest. Stress always revolves around the limits of what can be managed – regardless of whether those boundaries are mental or physical. Although stress might not traditionally be considered an emotion, no account of emotions is complete without it.

To gain an up-to-date understanding of stress an appreciation is needed of how people psychologically, neuro-biologically and physically support good health. Homeostasis* is the original word used to describe a process of 'maintaining balance through change', but it's mainly used to refer to a limited number of bodily functions that are essential for life. The contemporary version of this concept is called *allostasis*.

Allostasis refers to how all systems – not just the ones essential for life – adjust the intensity of their activity while coping with perceived challenges and how those systems return to rest. Blood pressure, blood flow, catecholamine, and the secretion of cortisol are all involved in metabolic* (chemical processes that support life) efforts to maintain normal body functioning. Allostasis specifically defines how many bodily systems adaptively use limited resources to support health. Part of the reason the term 'allostasis' was coined was to distinguish a professional concept of stress for research. The concept gives considerable clarity to how the psychological and neuro-biological interactions are interwoven.

Allostatic-load refers to the wear and tear that's experienced due to the processes of allostasis. The 'load' refers to functional decline of internal organs and systems – especially the cardiovascular and endocrine – due to the arrangement of their work load. Internal constituents are stimulated thousands to millions of times to keep the body's chemical constitution balanced for a healthy life. Amazingly, the overall number of times a system performs its operations throughout a person's life is not the principal concern. Danger to health owes more to quantities of unsuitable and inapropriate responses. Serious problems are raised if one reaction is performed too much or too little. The body's resources become preoccupied and cannot do other duties. Inappropriate turning on and shutting off of these processes disrupts the body's ability to keep metabolic balance. When allostatic processes are overused or caused by maladaptive inaccurate perceptions, optimal balance cannot be maintained owing to complications from the added load.[1]

For example, especially over decades, excessive fight-or-flight* reactions are firmly believed to be important for the slow progression of primary hypertension* and metabolic syndrome* in humans.[2]

The stresses people meet in early life (neglect and abuse are extreme stressors) interact with innate behaviour (genetic and epigenetic* predisposition). These experiences are moulded into a unique set of psychological responses that can predispose people to overreact. Each disproportionate reaction is accompanied by an autonomic response. This includes the automatic secretion of hormones and neurotransmitters that prepare the body for the perceived threat. These over-the-top behaviours can become habitual ways of relating to perceived threats, particularly when learnt at a young age and repeated in adulthood.

Every time such an inappropriate defensive response is experienced it disrupts metabolic activity. Work *load* is added to the body's schedule to keep a healthy internal balance. The amount of rest needed by a system within the body is increased. Another overreaction around the same time will deprive the body of the rest it needed to recover, and it will keep the body living in a state of deficit. The list of scheduled things to do is increasing and neglected. Ongoing bodily operations are performed by systems that are progressively deprived of rest and not working properly. These systems contain an increasing probability of interconnected failure.

There is a cascading effect from over-reactive and maladaptive autonomic responses, onto overworked systems, which places the body in an endless state of catch-up.

For example, chronic mental stress includes overworking several brain regions that cascade troublesome reactions. One such symptom of chronic stress seems to be the over-production of a chemical called calcitonin gene-related peptide or CGRP. This mass manufacture of CGRP envelops the surface of the Langerhans cells and reduces their functionality. It inhibits the Langerhans cells from detecting infectious agents and bringing them to the attention of the immune system's white blood cells. Infections are then more likely to go undetected, compromise health, and create more work for the body while it has a reduced capacity to defend itself.[3]

Prolonged anxiety, sadness and despair can all suppress immune system functioning owing to similar cascades of neuro-biological processes. While depriving the body of much needed rest, excessive emotions interrupt and reduce the body's ability to keep a healthy internal constitution. Thoughts and emotions are immersed in the allostatic procedures of maintaining balance through change. They work according to such fatigue and rest cycles.

Research is showing that the neurological functions of positive emotions are biased towards the left-hemisphere, and the reverse is true for negative emotional functioning.[4] This structural definition is part of a larger psychological architecture that underpins thought and emotional processes.

Negative emotions cause thought processes to become slower. They redirect attention onto perceived problems. People are forced to respond to red-alerts. Instincts orientate the body's disposition with thought processes that best suit corrective behaviours.[5] Negative emotions induce effortful focused analysis and vigilant thought processes. This creates a mentality focused on external processing that's suited to solving problems, but it also keeps people in a tense mental, emotional and physiological state of alert. How long a person stays in a negatively affected state determines how stressed the systems involved in maintaining that state become.

Amygdalae, in the temporal lobes, receive perceptions from a wide range of cortical regions; they are a comprehensively interconnected part of brain functioning. When an event is perceived to be a potential threat – from any source of information, the amygdalae set in motion autonomic responses. People are then placed in a state of alert corresponding to a threat's intensity and temporal closeness. If this process is activated too much, inappropriately or not, the systems responsible for carrying out the functions will become strained. This includes structural strains as noted by several studies that associate enlargement of the right amygdala with depression.[6]

In contrast, research shows that positive emotions make thoughts quick and responsive. Attention can switch from one subject to the next effortlessly. When experiencing positive emotions, attention uses current knowledge bases (i.e. memory). At the same time, an instinctive tendency to push unneeded analytical searching thoughts out of mind is present. When in a good mood, people naturally shy away from thinking about negative experiences. Judgements are more superficial and easy going. Psychological, neurological and biological pathways are taxed less. Positive moods form more flexible thoughts, which include a wider range of focus points, as attention is not narrowed as when negatively affected.

All this evidence proves that people's ability to process social information changes according to what emotions are being experienced.[7]

The evidence-based theory, therefore, suggests that negative emotions direct attention towards a potential threat while adapting thought processes to accommodate searching for a solution to the problem. When the problem is solved, a positive emotion is experienced that induces thought processes towards current knowledge bases and away from external analytical thinking. The previously taxed right-hemisphere that was handling the negatively affective state releases the tension its systems were under, and they're allowed to rest. This natural functioning indicates an allostatic process of maintaining balance through change.

Good health is not maintained by maximising positive emotions and minimising negative ones; it requires both negative and positive emotions to be applied appropriately.[8] A mixture of fixing problems and resting needs to be respected. If not enough positive emotions are experienced, people might get stuck ruminating with analytical thought processes over problems that tax their systems, burdening them.

All living things support life by allostasis. The animals that are best at maintaining balance through change have organs, as part of a larger system, all dedicated to this process. Highly evolved animals sustain many body systems that themselves often encompass interconnected subsystems. The vast majority of all of these processes are instinctively carried out below conscious recognition.

Amassed over hundreds of millions of years, there's far too much information being processed and applied, every minute of every day, to control consciously. In an evolutionary sense, humans have only just recognised the allostatic processes that have been responsible for maintaining the lives of all their ancestors. Consciousness is the most recent product of evolution. It gives humans the ability to reflect intellectually on self with high definition, but its processing power is limited to focusing on a few things at a time.

Stress is a wide reaching term and encompasses a vast amount of issues. This is a general description of stress. Just like conscious thought, it should be considered the tip of a large iceberg. Stress commonly arises from being over worked or having insufficient rest. Nevertheless, the narrative often includes other emotions that have become overwhelming to a detrimental degree. For example, the effects of loss and expected failure, on a daily basis, cause sadness and anxiety. These two emotions naturally prepare the host for certain eventualities, yet it's possible for them to amass and have detrimental effects on the person in which they reside.

Emotions are good up to a point. They have to be an accurate reflection of circumstances to best help. Perception of an event is the defining factor. A looming failure, causing anxiety, could be real or unreal, yet if people believe a perception is true, they experience the associated emotion with its proper biological responses. Mistaken perceptions cause stress because people adapt their dispositions to them. As the real world also has to be dealt with, this introduces additional adaptations. Inaccurate perceptions increase allostatic-load.

A common form of stress is produced by having too many objectives to complete in a set amount of time. An example is when a person called Naive had forty-five hours in a week to get her scheduled work completed. She filled her weekly plan with forty-five hours of work and set appointments, but she forgot to include lunch breaks. A situation was created where she could not fulfil her commitments without injuring her health through lack of rest. She had a fifty hour timetable to do in forty-five hours. She would have to go the whole week with no lunch break to succeed. It would put strain on her life that could only be accommodated for a brief period. If it happened continuously, tension from prolonged activity, devoid of rest, would become too stressful, so it would lead progressively to ill-health.

Sometimes the term stress is used to place emphasis on negative emotions felt for a lengthy duration. People may fear negative things happening all the time. They can be sad about past losses whilst anxiously worrying about future injuries. Continuous negative emotions effectively drip-feed a cocktail of depressive neurotransmitters (onto nerves) and hormones (into the bloodstream) whilst keeping people constantly focused on their failures and fears. This affects their bio-chemical constitution (metabolism*). As sleep patterns often become interrupted, people's ability to recuperate is further decreased. The entire draining experience from these negative emotions and the inability to rest is termed stressful.

Feelings of lethargy can be incredibly debilitating for the unemployed, the depressed, the abused, and people living in constant fear and anxiety. Due to psychological elements such as anxiety, fear and sadness, this lethargic stress may be experienced without continuous physical activity, so it's more easily overlooked. When they say how stressed and tired they feel all the time, people who suffer from depressive stress are met with surprise and suspicion. Even their friends and family may question whether they're stressed at all – suspecting them of feigning their distress for sympathy. Thinking, 'They haven't got a busy work schedule or seem to do much of anything, so why should they be stressed?' rather than seeing it's the lethargy caused by stress that keeps them from doing things.

Similarly, people can stand in disbelief that such lethargic stress is related to tooth decay and dental health issues in general. In the sceptic's defence, the process is metabolic, so its progression does easily go unseen to the untrained eye. Nonetheless, the facts are compelling, and once learnt, they are irrefutable.

The process of dental decay is called 'caries'. Bacteria form a bio-film over the surface of teeth as they metabolise carbohydrate substrate. The bio-film is made up of micro-organism communities, such as streptococcus bacteria, particularly in parts of the mouth that have a low pH level. When the bacteria metabolise carbohydrate substrate (most significantly all sugars), plaque forms as a by-product and the mouth becomes more acidic.[9]

The more acidic the mouth is, the more the bio-film communities flourish in demineralising the surface of teeth, leaving plaque deposits in their wake. Micro-colonies establish themselves more aggressively at plaque sites because pH levels are low in those places; tooth decay accelerates. Saliva naturally neutralises this process by effectively diluting acid and carbohydrate substrate, so raising the pH levels of the mouth. Thus saliva plays an important role in managing pH levels and the formation of concentrated plaque producing micro-colonies.

When the bacteria feed off sucrose – refined sugars, the process is most rapid as the actual sugar content is massively more than that of any naturally occurring sugar.[10] This concentrated form of sugar is packed full of energy that the bio-film has evolved to exploit. The problem is that the unnatural doses mean that humans' evolved salivary defence is insufficient for dissolving the by-product, hence plaque deposits build.

Saliva flow is at its lowest during sleep when it nearly stops. What is more, distinct bacterial micro-colonies form in a four to twenty-four hour window.[11] When these two factors are considered together with refined sugar consumption, brushing teeth before sleeping is seen as vitally important to managing pH levels in the mouth. It is a hugely significant action in preventing tooth decay. This is why brushing twice a day and flossing is standard dental advice: it's about dislodging the bio-film; especially with normal fluoride toothpaste, for it's fluoridated at 1500 ppm, and fluoride at this harmless concentration makes it difficult for bacteria to demineralise teeth.[12]

Brushing before sleep disrupts the bacterial bio-film that's formed during the day and prevents it from taking hold in the low pH hours. Because brushing in the morning disrupts the bio-film that's developed whilst sleeping, the bacteria have to start over, and they only have a fourteen to sixteen hour window before their production is disrupted once again; thus bacteria are prevented from forming stubborn micro-colonies.

When this dental knowledge is applied to stress, significant problems are revealed. Lethargy of stress compels people to eat high energy foods – refined sugars – that take the least amount of energy to consume. As a result, pH levels in the mouth drastically drop, and streptococcus bacteria aggressively advance into distinct micro-colonies within twenty-four hours. At the same time, the lethargy of stress increases the likelihood of not brushing before sleep (the importance of the activity seems insignificant when compared to the stresses in mind), so bacteria formations are less likely to be disrupted before forming micro-colonies. As patches of plaque depositing micro-colonies remain intact for days, bacteria diversify. As bacteria's metabolic activity creates acid which lowers pH levels, tooth decay accelerates specifically in colony spots. Sites of bacteria that cannot be removed by brushing and can only be seen with a mouth mirror easily form under such circumstances. A bout of lethargy that lasts several months can lead to cavity formations that appear many months after the experience. Therefore, stress is easily overlooked as significantly contributing to tooth decay.

Several decades have passed with attachment theory (which has amassed over fifty years of evidence-based research)[13] persuading people to pay attention to the negative and positive emotions of children. The theory links with other approaches that discuss parenting styles that support emotional-coaching behaviours.[14] Emotionally dismissive parents are largely characterised by dismissing emotional expressions altogether or encouraging positive emotions whilst discouraging negative ones. Negative emotions are more commonly shunned and may even be punished. A child might grow learning that emotions such as sadness, fear, and anger are emotions that only the weak, cowardly or 'out of control' express. Given the evidence that suggests both negative and positive emotions are necessary for good health, it leads one to ask 'What are the detrimental effects of non-expression of negative emotions?'

Theoretically, because negative emotional experiences are so strongly associated with problem solving, it suggests that stress would occur due to neglecting perceived threats – problems – that build to become overwhelmingly stressful. This fits with findings that show cognitively avoidant people, who ignore the thought of their feared thing, are more confident than people who think about an eventuality they fear. That is until the cognitively avoidant people's feared event comes true. At which time, the cognitively avoidant become the most physiologically stressed, and they are more likely to experience psychological crisis (see Ignorance).[15]

Two of the ways problems build up and lead to crisis are as follows.

First, expressing negative emotions in social relationships is proven to give relief to those who express it, for it increases sympathy and empathy from those who care. It's shown to make people more likable and deepen social bonds. People are far more likely to actively participate in collaborative problem-solving when they see a family member or friend expressing negative emotion.

Second, over the past fifty years, it has been repeatedly suggested that expression of emotion is an important element in coping with stressful circumstances. This is proving true. Studies show that people who suppress (conscious) and repress (subconscious) their emotions are more at risk of cancer onset than people who do not.[16] Stress is also found to create high levels of cortisol and speed up disease progression.[17] Raised cortisol over sustained periods is associated with system dysfunction and contributes to manifestation of serious health complications.[18] Corticosteroids are also linked to tumours.[19] At the same time, studies show that cancer patients who express negative emotions, especially anger, live longer.[20] Bottling up emotion raises cortisol levels whilst reducing the natural communication that would lead to help from others.

Inexpression of negative emotions is a double whammy to regulating health, and this can be said with immovable conviction.

Although humans do not have a complete understanding of the inexpression of negative emotions, the accumulating evidence firmly associates it with the onset and progression of biological diseases. A scientific philosophical approach to emotional health is based on expression and not repression. It includes the social consequences of not expressing anger, such as letting abuses go unchallenged (see Anger). So it's sound advice. Children should not have their negative emotions shunned or belittled. Repression of such emotions, over long periods of time, is proven to manifest serious health conditions, especially those connected with high cortisol levels.

On the other hand, oxytocin releasing behaviours – such as breast-feeding and cuddling – are highly associated with a sense of touch, affection and feelings of security (see Gratitude). Oxytocin is a hormone and neurotransmitter that has potent anti-stress effects (e.g. reducing blood pressure, heart rate and cortisol levels for potentially weeks at a time).[21] It has been proven that the company of others can reduce cortisol levels.[22] In epidemiological circles (the science of health and disease in populations) it has long been known that socially isolated people are more likely to get sick and die younger than their peers who have the company of a partner, friends or family.

All the above should lead researchers, in social health, to place considerable attention on habitual relationship conflicts as risk factors for progressive mental and biological health problems.[23] Longitudinal research, over decades, shows that allostatic-load predicts incidents of cardiovascular disease, decline in physical functioning, and memory loss.[24]

Stress

Latin. *Strictus* = compressed, drawn tight.

1. Hardship, adversity, affliction.

2. Psychology and biology: an adverse circumstance that disturbs, or is likely to disturb, the normal physiological or psychological functioning of an individual; such circumstances collectively. Also, the disturbed state that results.

3. The overpowering pressure of some adverse force or influence: (a) force or pressure exercised on a person for the purpose of compulsion or extortion; to distress; (b) to do or make (a person) stress;; to press hardly upon; to oppress.

<u>Surprise</u>

Surprise is a reaction to suddenly perceiving something unexpected. Surprise creates moderate expressions which cause the features to move in a less pronounced way than astonishment, which is a more intense form of surprise.

The eyes and mouth open in coordination with each other, a fluid motion that raises the eyebrows and opens the mouth moderately. These motions are read instinctively by observers as an impression that something new has been realised. The heart rate increases a few beats a minute, and a little gasp of air is drawn and then held to aid hearing. These prepare the body in the mildest of fashions to move away if needed. This is an observably common emotion and its features can be witnessed in many animals.[1]

All the expressions are mild; the event is not seriously alarming in nature. The little gasp of air that's inhaled hardly inflates the lungs or increases posture. The breath is held to aid hearing and then released with a barely perceptible sound or quite frequently as a sigh of relief or chuckle. These are all soft moderate expressions.

The reaction itself is neutral and preparatory in nature. The sudden and unexpected perception instinctively causes the mind to wonder what is happening, so that the situation is assessed immediately. If the experience is perceived as positive, the expression morphs into amusement. If the experience is perceived as negative, the expression morphs into that of being scared, or relief when the scary thought is assessed as untrue. These processes would normally happen in milliseconds or seconds, and other emotions may be felt as a result of the appraisal. After the initial assessment, gladness or sadness may be felt at the same time as feeling amused or scared. Yet the wonder of people's surprise may not be completely satisfied and may continue to reappraise the situation if no solid conviction is reached. In these cases people would feel the amusement or scare of the situation taking up part of their conscious thought while they continue to feel other emotions at the same time.

Surprise

Latin. *Prehendere* = to grasp, seize, something unexpected.

1. To encounter suddenly or unexpectedly; take or catch unawares.

2. To attack or capture suddenly and without warning.

Sympathy

Sympathy is identifying with another person's feelings, especially emotions of distress, due to having experienced a similar situation. People identify what they have previously felt in a similar past situation and relate that to another person's experience, so they have greater insights into the other's subjective* reality. People share common ground.

Sympathy works through identification. If people felt deeply sad and disorientated after the loss of a loved one, they can feel sympathy for a person who has just lost a loved one. They had a similar experience, which they recall to memory, and use it to identify what types of feelings another could be having. It does not have to be the same loved one for people to appreciate the sense of loss, sadness, despair, lethargy and disorientation another is experiencing. People are able to plan for the behaviour of others they feel sympathy towards and make allowances that are appropriate.

Everyone uses sympathy as a key indicator to see if people are following a conversation, or to what depth someone has grasped what has been said. This happens in virtually all conversations, and, most of the time, people do it subconsciously. In the course of following a conversation, people have different feelings that relate to what has been said. People imagine the scenario and relate it to their experience and then express the similarities they have grasped.

Expressions are compared to see if they match. A match equals an expression of sympathy. Everyone does this. It's the most natural and common way of relating to people. An amazing amount can be gathered from expressions of sympathy. People learn how much they have in common: what types of emotional expressions to which people react negatively; what ones to which they react positively. This means people can adapt and fit responses that are tailored to an individual – informed from experience.

Sympathising is humanity's natural way of relating, and people do it without thinking. The more emotionally literate people become, the more the experience of sympathy filters into conscious awareness, so slowly becoming a process that is wielded and appreciated. This is a fundamental aspect of developing good interpersonal skills – which take years to learn.

To be proficient in sympathising gives people advantages in real-time interpersonal situations. To some degree, they have advantages that others are susceptible to because others are unaware of the information they are revealing. Every little expression of sympathy is a potential insight into the behaviour and experiences that a person has had. It is an insight into motive and orientation. It tells where people's interests lie, and what sort of convictions they have on the subjects expressed.

Sympathy is a very natural way of communicating, but it does rely on people having had similar emotions from similar situations. This can lead to strong emotions fazing people's perceptual framework that keeps them from depths of understanding they could otherwise achieve. This is because sympathising describes a state where emotions from the past are directly recalled to memory. People can become over involved. They can distort the communication they are receiving by intermingling it with their feelings and what they recalled from memory. This is the fundamental difference between sympathy and empathy. Empathy does not require people to remember a past event that is associated to their self (ego). Nevertheless, sympathy makes it possible to identify with someone and feel a much stronger bond of common ground than is achievable with empathy.

Sympathy and empathy are often used as if they mean the same thing. This is wrong. The definition of sympathy is a couple of thousand years old and works on having had similar experiences. The definition of empathy is less than a hundred years old and means 'to look as if through the eyes of another' and does not require people to have had similar experiences.

The sympathetic process is performed consciously, but also on a pre-semantic level* too, so sympathy instinctively compels people to respond in certain ways.

For example, when people see a sad face, evidence shows they instinctively sympathise with the owner of the distressed face.[1] Onlookers have physiological responses and expression to perceptions of distress, and these manifest as overt attempts to help from children (as early as eight months old) and adults.[2] The eyebrows and cheeks are what humans predominantly use to detect sadness.[3] There is a direct link between subconscious processing of such features and behaviour.

This can be seen as a useful evolutionary strategy that automatically selects a beneficail social response, and speedily enacts a bias (emotional and cognitive) towards choosing it. One can only imagine how easily fluent child-parent interactions would evolve on the back of such interactive instincts.

Nevertheless, this dynamic also allows people to have their instincts duped. Sympathy can be abused. For example, when people disproportionately create a sad face, or perception, they can manipulate others to engage in helping them. If the sympathiser is unaware of the deceit, they will feel inclined to aid whoever they perceive to be in distress. The more intense the perception, the less control the sympathiser will have over their response, for as emotions reach the limits of their intensity, they progressively assume control over behaviour.[4] The sympathiser will feel like they are doing a good thing, and act to protect the deceitful person.

Similarly, cuteness could be considered an evolutionary emotion that compels parents to overlook a child's inappropriate behaviour due to innocence. Are adults who do bad thing and then act cute exploiting this sympathetic path?

Sympathy

Latin. *Sympathia* = having a fellow feeling.

1. A (real or supposed) affinity between certain things, by virtue of which they are similar or correspondingly affected by the same influence.

Terror

Terror is an expression of extreme fear.

Generally, intense perceptions cause emotional expressions to become exaggerated and more erratic in nature. Terror is a prime example of such varying extremes of expression. Typical characteristics, such as dramatically raised eyebrows with a corresponding gaping mouth, of the emotion do exist, yet at the upper limit of terror continuity breaks down, and some motions are expressed while others are not.

Initially, terror is reached through shock at a negative thing. When a person is shocked, the instinctual reactions are a preparation for another emotion. The eyebrows are raised, as the eyes open, removing them from obstructing vision and letting more light onto the pupils. The posture becomes more erect as the lungs take a deep breath, and the body is poised to move away if any danger is present. The breath is held to reduce sound from being created and to aid hearing anything that would threaten one's health.

When the shocking event turns out to be negative, the expression morphs into terror or horror. Both have an element of extreme fear. These two emotional states are very similar in their expression. The eyes and mouth are opened instantly, in synchronicity, as wide as possible. The muscles become strained to their limit and are held twitching in this position. The forehead is corrugated from the extreme height of the eyebrows. The violent facial-muscle contractions pull the eyelids tight against their sockets – exposing white eyeballs.[1] The mouth gapes open to aid the lungs expanding instantaneously to maximum capacity. Then without delay the muscles that surround the lungs lock themselves tight to allow no air to pass the lips, so aiding hearing and reducing noise. The upper body is erected due to the lungs being fully inflated with the taut muscles that surround the lungs clinging solidly to the rib cage.

At this stage the heart's palpitations accelerate to maximum in a fraction of a second. The heart is wildly pumping blood around the circulatory system as some blood vessels shut (e.g. the digestive tract, kidneys) and other vessels open as much as they can to deliver blood to regions such as the heart, lungs and leg muscles. The exertion may be so great at this point that the heart fails. Otherwise, the blood flow of the skin, face and upper regions is redirected by closing capillaries and sent to the legs as they are prepared to run. This makes the skin on the hands and face cold and pale looking. The skin is cold, yet the body often produces sweat – to reduce the body's temperature – in expectation of the heat produced from the exertion of running away. This is referred to as cold sweat.

The person is typically frozen on the spot with the features described above still strained in every way. The voice might fail temporarily while the eyes become fixed on the object of terror. As if lightening the load for an oncoming escape, the sphincter muscle may relax and the contents of the intestines may breach the body. The hair stands erect, all over the skin, from alertly shivering muscles that can cause limbs to tremble; these are the hallmark expressions of terror.

The effects of ongoing fear from terrifying experiences should not be underestimated. Memories last a lifetime, and this is an extremely serious matter for people who suffer from post-traumatic stress disorder. As narratives to perceptions imbue people with a sense of control and security, the memories need to be addressed and resolved in some way. Sadly, at present there is not sufficient knowledge to treat satisfactorily such memories and their associated effects on a person's life. Unresolved memories can cause people to live with permanent sadness, anxiety and stress that can seem ingrained in their heads.

The over activation of the right amygdala and its many interconnected neighbouring systems is highly associated with heightened states of alertness and anxiety. The processes involved in memory are extremely complex, however, and beyond full understanding at present.

Post-traumatic stress disorder can affect people for decades after the initial trauma, and because it impairs people's ability to function socially, it causes them to develop habitual evasive behaviours.

Devastating memories are relived on a conscious and unconscious level. The memories seem vivid and powerful, yet they are difficult to describe. Behaviours are created that last long after the initial exposure that induced the terror. Sufferers report walking around whilst feeling the memory and associated fear burning a hole in their heads, and being continually stressed and unable to relax. This is, to a significant degree, most probably due to the sensation of the amygdalae which become enlarged or inflamed when over activated.[2]

There are neuro-biological tolls to many of the connections throughout the brain that are interconnected to the amygdalae, for they are also constantly activated without rest. Constantly experiencing negative emotions and having defensive responses turned on and turned off – repeatedly and inappropriately – makes the experience of post-traumatic stress disorder a serious threat to long-term health (see Stress).[3]

The problems of being made to feel terror in this modern civilised world are many. It is possible that terror triggers responses that are primal in nature. Responses that are more appropriate to an age long gone, yet stay with people throughout their lives. Although it was possible in the hunter-gatherer era for humans to live as long as they do today, people's lives are on average much longer than those in which instincts were originally applied. When considering that at a surface level human instincts developed as a hunter-gatherer species (over the past two million years with an average life expectancy of twenty to thirty-seven years of age), is human genetic code going to provide a perfectly accurate instinctual response to modern problems? Humans have doubled average life expectancy from forty, to eighty, within the last five hundred years, and it's increasing year on year.

Is it surprising that people react to extremely intense stimuli with instincts that have served them for hundreds of thousands of years and are more relevant to a different age? Maybe living in a continuously alerted state was not so unusual two hundred thousand years ago. Perhaps the volume of a single traumatic memory would have been drowned out from a hundred other more alarming things?

People can remain on high alert for decades after a terrifying event due to the vivid nature of their memory and its fidelity to survey for similar situations. In sudden and extremely threatening circumstances, people are instinctively induced to process the information they record to memory in a different way than they would do normally.

The term *weapon focus** refers to this perceptual processing that forcefully redirects attention in milliseconds onto the source of the threat whilst excluding other information from being processed. People's subsequent memories are then overwhelmingly biassed towards intensely threatening objects.

A clear demonstration of this *weapon focus* was provided by an experimental study that showed participants a videotape of a staged bank robbery. For half of the participants, towards the end of the violent crime, the escaping robbers shoot a small boy in the face. The other half of the participants watch the same robbery with only one difference – there was no shooting of a boy. Those who watched the gunshot showed impaired memory of events immediately preceding the graphic violence, yet their memory preserved vivid recall of the shot itself. Eye-tracking instinctively follows the intensity of perceived events. The more extreme a perception, the less consistent memory becomes around it – preceding and succeeding the apex of intensity.[4]

People innately orientate their behaviour towards the intensity of their perception. This automatic change in psychological, neuro-biological and physical disposition also prepares people in the same way for anticipated events. The instinctive orientation is strongest at the time people perceive an event is going to happen. What is astonishing is that the intensity of a perceived event outranks the probability of its happening.[5]

This can be viewed as an evolutionary adaptation that chooses biological preparedness over the potential stress of an inaccurately perceived threat. Because intense events would have related to very serious things in early human evolution, it would have been most important and a considerable advantage to have dispositions ready to encounter threats as and when they happened.

More intensity equals less conscious control. Automatic behaviour is significantly related to how intensely affected people become. The closer an emotion's intensity gets towards its limits, the more the emotion progressively assumes control over behaviour, so the more likely it becomes that people act from instinct.[6]

This has many advantages in a sudden and intensely threatening scenario as within milliseconds people are preparing to use evolutionary strategies to avoid harm. Nevertheless, this means that perceptions of extremely intense anticipated events are the most difficult to reason with in terms of their probability, for people have less conscious control over their behaviour as the anticipated time draws closer. The more intense an emotion becomes, the more instincts orientate behaviour. This means people can intellectually want to act in one way and find themselves behaving in an unwanted and radically different way.

Violent events can shock psychological networks deeply. They can brand an intense impression into implicit-memory* that's most difficult to alter. These memories are then referred to for a long time after on a conscious and unconscious level. Memories are used to prime responses to present events that resemble past experiences, and this happens at a pre-semantic* (subconscious) level. Evidence from neuro-imaging studies supports this pre-semantic detection of threats.[7] People do not have to recognise consciously a similar event for the responses to be engaged, for their subconscious is continually scanning for patterns and associating them to memory. If the search finds a match, it engages the appropriate bodily disposition. So people react to threats even if they have no meaning associated to the cause of their reaction.

Memories of intense events compel people's behaviour. Instinctively people may feel as though they need to avoid places or persons, but their day-to-day life dictates they visit those places and persons. A conflict is created on a viscerally* deep level. The subconscious creates feelings of dread that the conscious mind repeatedly stumbles into without understanding. Pervasive anxiety begins. The cost of being in such a conflicted situation can be neuro-biological stress that's typically felt as lethargy, for it's exhausting.

Memory is used to gauge the validity of possible threats. If anything resembles a violent memory, the subconscious throws biological responses to extreme danger into action. Heart rate increases, blood vessels expand and the lungs inflate. The brain shuts down unnecessary thinking to prime the body for physical exertion. The senses are heightened whilst the mind becomes suspicious and alert. Due to the intensity of the experience that's etched into memory, such changes can happen to people if they simply imagine an event that resembles the original terrifying experience. People can be transported from briefly hearing or seeing something that reminds them of a memory to finding themselves forced into a stricken state of emergency. People experience fight-or-flight* instincts that are massively disproportionate to the situation they are really in, and due to the automatic reactions to intense perceptions, people can be at the mercy of inappropriately activated instincts.

Terrifying events rarely are experienced and then dismissed because they remain in memory to evaluate ongoing events. Once terrible experiences are in memory, they are real possibilities. They cannot be ignored. They can only be updated with the use of narrative. The fact that autonomic responses prepare for the intensity of a perceived event – even an imaginary one – rather than its probability is difficult for most people to grasp. The lack of understanding around this concept means that experiencing such automatic fight-or-flight responses can be very worrying. People can feel pathetic, and find it difficult to come to terms with their weird behaviour, yet the responses are explainable. Consciously adding a narrative to the original experience helps the unconscious to distinguish if a present event is actually similar.

People are generally unaware of how deeply moved they become by intense perceptions. Whether they are negative or positive, the intense perceptions that humans experience are responsible for ordering their lives. Humans instinctively orientate their behaviour according to their hopes and terrors. Unconsciously, they react to intensity. Unwittingly, viscerally and neuro-biologically, interests and disinclinations are governed by the extremes of perception, for humans possess an innate ability that prepares them physically for the temporal ebb and flow of things.

Stress Related

Terror

Latin. *Terrorem* = great fear.

1.   Extreme fear.

2.   The use of such fear to intimidate people.

Trust

Trust is a 'credit slip' based on what people reckon the quality or consistency of someone or something is.

When people trust, they leave themselves vulnerable to the person they have bestowed trust in. It could be a physical item that a person is trusted to give back, or it could be advice on an important issue. Whatever the situation is, people who trust leave themselves vulnerable in some way.

When trust is broken, it's called betrayal. Being betrayed can leave people feeling many negative emotions (such as fear, jealousy, envy, resentment, sadness, despair and anger) whilst thinking that they were fools for being duped. Feelings of betrayal are usually intense, and behaviour becomes difficult to manage. The higher the intensity of an emotion, the more it progressively assumes control over behaviour, so the more actions are motivated by automatic instincts, which can seem impulsive.[1]

Although it leaves people vulnerable to potential betrayal, trust also creates peace. Trust upheld materialises peace, and this has relevance to people's psychological, biological and physical environments. When people trust they feel safe. They are not, on edge, reacting defensively. Thus trust reduces the energy people have to spend on biological defensive reactions, so it's an important contribution to good health as it reduces stress or *allostatic-load** (see Stress).

People live with the consequences of their actions, and talents of knowing who to trust are significant to this process. If people would like to disbelieve in the reality of trust, they would be instant social misfits. All lives revolve around trust. Human interaction is all about the degree of trust people have in their lives. The question is not whether trust is of consequence, but how well people perceive it to be of consequence. Trust undoubtedly plays a huge role within all lives.

Trust is also a cure for fear. Where there is fear, there is a lack of trust. Trust is at the heart of overcoming fear. Knowing who to trust can be the most dubious aspect of trusting, for it can often leave people feeling deeply insecure. When attempting to make such discernments, a sort of emotional paralysis can grip those who have been taken advantage of or abused before. People can believe that they're helpless to gauge personality. This helps to manifest a psychological crisis at the point of making a decision of where to place trust. Decisions are then skewed by panicky fear. So this leads to a greater chance of making a bad allocation of trust, and a bad outcome is more likely. A bad outcome then reinforces the belief that they're helpless to gauge which personalities to trust. It is an intensely frustrating experience that can lead to self-deprecating thoughts rapidly progressing towards self-loathing and even self-sabotage.

Judging consistency is the essence of gauging trust. It could be trust in science; trust in one's self; trust in a partner; trust in a friend; trust in the spiritual; or trust in an ability. Whatever the situation is, the results are the same. More trust equals less fear. Less fear equals less panicky decisions. Less panicky decisions equal more accurate decisions.

This is not promoting a purist view of the world and suggesting that everybody trust everybody else. The suggestion is that people specifically learn to use consistency to gauge trust, and to temper trust to specific and individual situations. Trust is the ability to judge consistency of behaviour. People are at different stages of development, and they see life in different ways, so it's only reasonable that trust is given according to what is deemed fit for each individual case, yet using consistency as a guide.

There is *no one size fits all*. To tailor trust to the individual situations and be willing to update judgements when new information is brought to light is the only reasonable course of action. Trusting is a continual process of updating. People evolve and grow on a personal level. Just as people find that they can trust themselves more with issues in time, they will find that they can do the same for others and vice versa. People trust some things more and some things less, and this is a continual process.

Consistency encompasses the essence of what trust is. Looking for patterns of consistency is a very simple way of looking at life. It also just so happens to be the most effective way to gauge where trust is appropriate. If people consider another's personality and behaviours in terms of consistency, it reveals aspects of the other's makeup in terms that relate exceedingly well for attributing trust. If people know how consistent or inconsistent different parts of a person's personality are, then it is much easier to attribute an appropriate amount of trust. Attributing different parts of a person's personality with different amounts of trust is the fairest and most reliable approach.

Feelings of betrayal can build up over frequent, yet minor, breaches of trust, and this can lead to an overall distrust of a person. If people do not trust someone, or trust someone less, for specific inconsistent personality traits, then they will not feel betrayed and disappointed when the person lives up to the inconsistent trait. In many cases, trust based in false expectations is what people feel betrayed over. Trust in false expectation most often leads to feelings of betrayal and disappointment. People can act indignant when their self-appointed false expectations are not met and even expect the other to feel guilty. Such narcissism is in no way fair.

Judging where to place trust with complex behaviour can be made straight forward when looking for consistencies. For example, a case of a person that people know has frequently borrowed money from others and not paid them back. The consistency of available perceptions says, 'If we lend the person money, we are unlikely to get it back.' The dilemma is that we fear for the person's health and sanity if we do not give the money. The person promises to pay us back because of the desperation of his or her circumstances. The issue is whether we trust the promise with which our sensory information is in conflict. Nevertheless, we lend the person the money anyway, as the sensory information about his or her welfare is a priority for us. Now it just so happens that we don't get the money back.

This situation can pan out, for us, in two very different ways. If we *trusted* or *believed* the promise that we would be paid back, then we will be disappointed and feel betrayed. If we were counting on the money to provide us with important necessities, we may even experience a bout of despair that increases feelings of hostility. All the negative feelings will be associated with the person, and we will feel demoralised as if our good will has been taken advantage of. These are hallmark feelings of the very unpleasant experience of broken trust, yet the situation has been brought about only because we believed in a promise. A promise that just so happened to be in conflict with our perceptions of the consistency of the person's behaviour around borrowing money. This makes us feel like fools too as we went against our better judgement.

On the other hand, if we lent the person the money while *distrusting* his or her promise, we would not feel betrayed. Instead of 'distrusted', we can put it another way. Say we 'trusted in our perceptions', based on the consistency of this person's behaviour around borrowing money, that we would not be paid back. In this situation, far from falling into feelings of betrayal and despair we are actually glad with the trust that we placed in our perceptions. We are not disappointed as we judged correctly that we would not be paid back. In fact, we feel good about our discernment and are self-assured.

This example shows how distrusting a person's promises (or trusting one's perception) can be the best course of action. The attribution of distrust is fair and appropriate in the example. It's not disrespectful.

If people look through the lens of consistency onto another's personality, it's far easier to gauge that person's natural tendencies. Accepting this information and attributing the appropriate level of trust per tendency is a most appropriate and thorough way to trust.

Nevertheless, although the process is simple to follow, perceptions can be difficult to accept when the consistencies of nature are found to be significantly different than what people wanted, or expected, them to be. It can be more comfortable to trust in one's inherited beliefs and associated expectations than to trust in the consistency of perceptions. Realising the consistency of their perceptions can unsettle people. It can lead them to distort their judgements as accepting reality is not always the most comfortable or agreeable choice. These altered, inaccurate perceptions create inappropriate emotions. As the consistency of perceptions has been tampered with, it's virtually impossible to attribute the correct amount of trust. In this respect, trusting is very much an art of life that concerns how honest people can be with themselves regarding the consistency of their perceptions.

Trust

Old Norse. *Traust* = rely on, strong and safe,
confidence in or reliance on some quality or attribute
of a person or thing, or the truth of a statement.

1. The firm belief in the reliability of truth, ability,
    strength, someone or something etc..

Vanity

Vanity is preoccupation with appearance. It is an obsessive-like frame of mind that's focused on how people appear to others, putting more effort into looks than substance. Overtime, this progressively leads to conceited, hollow personality traits.

Many aspects of life can be overlooked due to a continuous preoccupation with appearance. This is often represented by a person who has little interest in other people and their concerns. Except when the interest of others is associated to his or her appearance, and then large amounts of time may be spent focusing on intricate facades. Such bias of attention leads to a growing neglect of other issues, so an underdeveloped personality gradually takes root. It's the preoccupation that leads to the neglect of other aspects of life and not the interest in physical appearance alone. Vanity is the empty shell syndrome*. As there's too much focus upon the external shell, the vain person increasingly possesses an inner cavity. Lack of inward attention makes people empty. This of course is not what the external shell is made to represent. The outside world is denied such unflattering representation, so vanity is therefore a progressively dishonest condition. It is a frame of mind that becomes set on taking credit for the appearance of things.

The product of vanity when successful is attention and esteem from the approval of others. All the effort or cost of maintaining the physical appearances is to this attention-seeking aim. It's considered a bad investment, for it's like throwing money into a fruitless venture – a vanity project. Originally, the meaning of vanity only described fruitless behaviour, but now it has a distinct sense of narcissism (excessive interest or admiration for one's self).

Vanity's preoccupation with the external things in life can be motivated by different things, yet attracting the admiration of others is highly associated with the condition. Having an addiction to admiration is one way of viewing the experience for some people. This can be very crippling as time goes by. The mechanisms of physical appearance that were employed to gain the admiration of others are seen as a means to an end, and the admiration itself is taken as validation of greatness, so a conceited personality slowly manifests. The conceit can be very difficult to tackle as it's held in place by real perceptions of admiration from others. The quality of that admiration is highly questionable though, for the people who display it have bought in to the surface image that has been presented, and the vain know this in their heart. This gives the condition its notably subtle, yet self-delusive, impact on any psychological makeup. In this respect, vanity is concerned with receiving admiration for admirations sake. It may not matter how questionable the admiration is, only that it's received.

To be preoccupied with anything is to focus on that thing above and beyond other issues. This is a useful ability to have in the short-term when people are dealing with immediate issues. If it continues for any length of time, the preoccupation will be at the expense of other issues. This is true for any issue, and not only appearance.

If the problem is left to develop unchallenged, neglect to other aspects of their life is not the only problem. People can become absorbed into the preoccupation of their appearance as it becomes established as their way of receiving positive attention. This means the vain increasingly use skin-deep judgements, criticise, and discipline others according to their shallow field of vision, asserting their beliefs with convictions based on the approval they have received from others.

The main point is that it's the preoccupation that's the important focus. A healthy mentality cares about appearance as many aspects of reality show themselves in physical characteristics. To pay attention to appearance is important, but vanity's obsession does this at the cost of everything else.

Vanity

Latin. *Vanus* = fruitless, empty, to leave, abandon, give out.
Latin. *Vacare* = to be empty.

1. Given to or indulging in personal vanity; having an excessively high opinion of one's own appearance, attainments, qualities, possessions, etc.; delighting in, or desirous of attracting, the admiration of others; conceited.

2. Devoid of real value, worth, or significance; idle, unprofitable, useless, worthless; of no effect, force, or power; fruitless, futile, unavailing.

3. Of persons: devoid of sense or wisdom; foolish, silly, thoughtless; of an idle or futile nature or disposition.

<u>Glossary</u>

Acting-out

The term acting-out is used to describe behaviour that is an unconscious expression of impulses, thoughts or emotions. The reason why the impulses, thoughts and emotions are not in conscious control is typically because a person has ignored them or denied they exist. This fear of owning[*] experience is usually called suppression when the material is consciously pushed out of mind (cognitive-avoidance/ignorance) and repression when the process is unconscious. This denial of experience does not erase the perceptions that have caused the uncomfortable experiences. Instead the conscious mind ignores that the impulses, thoughts or emotions exist, leaving them to motivate behaviours without conscious control. Acting-out refers to behaviour that is affected by such suppressed emotions.

Affect-infusion

The term affect-infusion is used to describe the amount of influence – affect – that emotions and mood can have on people's judgement, usually without them knowing it. It has been found that people are more likely to take external suggestions into the consideration of their processing of information if they are in a sad or negative mood. Affect-infusion interplays with mood-congruent[*] processing and there are many variables to this complicated process. For a simple example, if people have experienced many positive emotions in the past week and are in a positive mood their mental processing of information will use a broad range of current knowledge from memory and be more creative, but in a shallow and effortless manner that is prone to stereotypes. On the other hand, if people have experienced many negative emotions in the past week and are in a negative mood their mental processing of information will be focused on solving problems by effortful searching for new information, externally driven. At the end of the week, when the two sets of people above react to the same situation their mental processing of information will be different.

Allostasis

The term allostasis (coined as an update of homeostasis[*]) describes how living organisms, especially humans, biologically adapt and 'maintain balance through change' to keep a metabolism[*] – chemical mixture – that supports life. These changes that maintain balance include behavioural changes such as defence responses or behaviours supported by different emotions. These holistic adaptations are instinctive responses to perceived events and engage the body in activity which has a metabolic cost, turning on and turning off biological processes. The difference between homeostasis and allostasis is that the former has traditionally been used to describe only changes that are vital for life while the latter is used to describe all of the 'maintain balance through change' processes – including those for optimal functioning that could be considered peripheral.

Allostatic-load

The term allostatic-load describes the detrimental effects of the turning on and turning off of neurobiological processes incurred by allostasis. These biological adaptations to external events are repeated throughout life and are the workload of the systems that execute them. Over decades such workloads lead to poor performance of a subsystem within biological interconnected systems, resulting in health complications. Allostatic-load also refers to the biological stresses caused by the body trying to adapt to too many perceptions, especially misperceptions. The body has only so many resources and can perform a limited amount of biological adaptations at any given time. If threats are perceived continuously the body's disposition will continuously be set in a state of alert in an attempt to best cope with the perceived situation, primed to survive. Nonetheless, the alert disposition will deprive the body of metabolic[*] resources to maintain normal functioning. At such times the body will be less able to fight infections and more susceptible to system malfunctions due to the overloaded metabolic schedule.

Attachment Theory

Attachment theory principally describes the innately bundled communicative behaviours that exist between mother and baby/toddler. The core aspects of attachment theory that John Bowlby, James and Joyce Robertson, Harry Harlow and Mary Ainsworth revealed are extremely robust and based on empirically based observable research. For example the 'Young Children in Brief Serparation' series made by James and Joyce Robertson. A series of five 30 minute documentaries following five toddlers who have been separated from their mothers. One of the most notable achievements of attachment theory is the understanding of The Strange Situation. A most basic, yet fascinating, example of the principles involved was given by Harry Harlow's surrogate mother experiments with Rhesus Macaque Monkeys (found on YouTube with the heading *'Harry Harlow's Monkey Love - Contact Comfort and The Strange Situaiton'*). Mary Ainsworth, however, developed a social science test to measure a 1 year old toddler's attachment to their mother, and it was called The Strange Situation (an example can be found on YouTube with the heading *'The Strange Situation - Reunion'*). It explains the experience of when a baby becomes a toddler and gains a limited amount of mobility. At this stage of development a toddler is acutely sensitive to the distance they maintain to their primary care giver – evolutionarily the mother – and becomes intensely distressed if the mother figure is out of sight. The sensitivity to distance and distress is amplified in a situation that is strange to the toddler: The Strange Situation. This behaviour continues until the child's perception of time and behaviour develops, and they know that their parent will return. Nonetheless, the way a parent reacts to their child's distress in the toddler stage has serious consequences for their mental development. Contact-comfort (i.e. a cuddle) is the instinctive way humans reassure their children in this distressed state and is associated to the anti-stress hormone oxytocin. The physical touch of a parent instinctively reduces the stress the toddler is experiencing and is the most effective way for them to relax and then continue to play. Attachment theory successfully proved that there is a biological component to childhood trauma. Therefore, in one swipe, proving Freud was right that many mental health problems originate in childhood whilst proving that he was wrong in asserting that this was due to fantasies and unrelated to biological behaviour.

Child of Rage

A thirty-minute documentary about the amazing and admirable transformation of a young girl, Beth, that can be found on YouTube with the title '*Child of Rage - Full Original Documentary*'.

Cognitive-avoidance

The term cognitive-avoidance describes the process of mentally ignoring experience, typically, because people fear what the experience represents. If people mentally avoid thinking about a feared experience, they will be less anxious or stressed than those who think about the feared event, but if the feared event is encountered the cognitively avoidant will become the most stressed and may even experience a mental crisis. Cognitive-avoidance is a balancing act that relies on judgement; if a feared event is a real possibility, it is sensible to think about it and prepare for its eventuality, so that crisis and helplessness are avoided. If a feared event is unreal, it pays to ignore it and remain unstressed.

Contact-comfort

The term contact-comfort describes the instinctive reduction in biological stress that is experienced from the physical touch of a significant other (e.g. a parent or lover). This biological reduction in stress is partly due to the release of the hormone oxytocin, which is stimulated by intimacy and trust. Oxytocin has potent anti-stress properties. The ability to control a toddler's stress revolves around contact comfort, and this was exemplified by Harry Harlow's contact comfort experiments (found on YouTube with the heading '*Harry Harlow's Monkey Love – Contact Comfort and The Strange Situaiton*'), and the dynamics were developed by Mary Ainsworth to help gauge a human 1 year old baby's attachment to their mother (an example can be found on YouTube with the heading '*The Strange Situation – Reunion*').

Defence-mechanism

The term defence-mechanism refers to sensory information that has been blocked from conscious view by the subconscious. Within the traditional definition of a defence-mechanism, this is done because, if the information were let into conscious view, anxiety would be felt. So the primary aim of a defence-mechanism is to manage anxiety levels relevant to an individual's ability to cope. An individual's psychological architecture determines how well they can cope.

Emotionally Competent Stimulus

The term emotionally competent stimulus describes a pattern of an object that is held in mind that fits a profile of an object stored in memory. When such a perceptual match happens it triggers a cascade of neurological and biological reactions that manifest as an emotion. This process adapts behaviour towards an object based on past experience, which is known as a dispositional response.

Epigenetic

Epigenetic studies focus on how genes are turned on and turned off, expressed, by influences other than DNA. Gene expressions are associated with a person's instinctive dispositional responses. Genes can be turned on and turned off within a lifetime, and there is some speculation as to how or if such activated or deactivated expressions are passed to offspring as a software update.

Explicit-memory and Implicit-memory

Memory is generally split into two types, implicit and explicit. A person is using explicit-memory when remembering an event, theory, story or name. Explicit-memory can be searched at will and the imagination can imbed additional information onto raw sensory experience, creating footnotes to experiential data. This makes explicit-memory very flexible and means it can be updated with idiosyncratic theories and even fantasies. Implicit-memory, which is sometimes referred to as procedural-memory, sits below conscious awareness and is not freely open to inspection. The easiest example of implicit-memory at work is the muscle coordination a person uses to breath, stand, walk, run and look. People do these activities without thinking about them and this is due to implicitly held memories. If a person does an activity over and over again, such as riding a bike, the process of how to do that activity is stored in implicit-memory. This eventually allows the person to do that activity whilst at the same time having his or her mind free to focus on potentially more important eventualities, making the activity safer and more productive.

Fight-or-flight

The term fight-or-flight describes the automatic biological responses that are initiated from the perception of dangerous situations. Both are considered defence responses and both release natural analgesia – painkillers – for the eventuality that injury will be incurred in either fighting or escaping. A fighting response will redirect blood from parts of the body that do not immediately need it, such as the digestive tract, to parts that do, such as the face and hands. A fleeing response will similarly redirect blood to the legs for running. The different biological responses will be accompanied by different mental processing of information. Importantly, these evolutionary responses are initiated by perception alone. Misperceptions of danger will activate specific defence responses as long as the misperceptions are believed. Because defence responses outrank other adaptations, such inappropriate turning on and turning off of biological activities costs the body energy and interrupts its metabolic* activity to adapt to real events, causing metabolic stress or allostatic-load*.

Homeostasis

The term homeostasis (often referred to as allostasis* now) describes how living organisms biologically adapt and 'maintain balance through change' to keep a metabolism* – chemical mixture – that supports life. These changes that maintain balance include behavioural changes such as defence responses or behaviours supported by different emotions. These holistic adaptations are instinctive responses to perceived events and engage the body in activity which has a metabolic cost, turning on and turning off biological processes

Hypertension / Hypertensive

Showing elevated blood pressure, implicit in defence emotions, and typified in the fight-or-flight* state.

Implicit-memory (see Explicit-memory and Implicit-memory)

Memes

A meme is literally the communication of any idea, object or thing to another person. In reality the word is predominantly used to refer to major concepts that are circulating in a culture. The concept of allostatic-load* is a meme that is conveyed in this book.

Metabolic Syndrome

People are classed as suffering from metabolic syndrome if they have at least three of the following five medical conditions: low high-density lipoprotein levels, elevated fasting plasma glucose, high serum triglycerides, abdominal obesity, and elevated blood pressure. Metabolic syndrome significantly increases the risk of cardiovascular disease and diabetes.

Metabolism

The metabolism regards the body's maintaining of a chemical constitution that supports life. This balance is sustained through processes of continuous change, and it's inextricably linked to homeostasis* or allostasis*.

Mirror Neurons

The term mirror neuron refers to interconnected parts of the brain that process the perception of other people's behaviour so that it can be understood immediately by the observer. The process happens in real-time and allows people to precisely imitate others with focus automatically being directed towards the intention of the other's actions. Mirror neurons endow us with the ability of comprehending intent by interpreting body language. If there is no perceived intention to the observed action, movement itself becomes the studied aim of the observer. The perceived intent then primes emotional and dispositional responses best suited for the situation. This is an incredibly complicated process that is not fully understood and is unconsciously processed, taking four-dimensional perceptions of behaviour and rotating them with the imagination into alignment with a concept of self, in real-time.

Mood-congruence

The term mood-congruence describes how specific emotions and moods can influence the memories and thoughts we are likely to recall and use. For instance, people who are found to be in an elated mood recall positive memories faster than they do negative memories. The reverse is true for people who are sad. It is generally accepted that this process makes it more difficult for depressed people to emerge from sad states.

Own

The term own refers to the mental process of holding an emotion, thought or behaviour in mind whilst associating it with oneself.

Passive-aggressive

The term passive-aggressive describes behaviour that is a destructive indirect expression of anger. Most passive-aggressive people have an above average IQ but a poor understanding of emotionally constructive behaviour. Passive-aggressive behaviour is created from a fear of expressing anger directly as and when it is felt, so resentment is kindled. A major problem with passive-aggressive behaviour is that the person does not direct the anger at the offending behaviour, so the offending behaviour continues. Instead the anger and resentment is indirectly expressed – to avoid accountability – by creating a situation that will cause the person who displayed the offensive behaviour misfortune or stress. Unfortunately this results in social disorder and is detrimental to relationships. Yet because of the craftsmanship that may have been used to create the situation and the satisfaction of relieved resentment, the passive-aggressive person may be secretly proud of his or her accomplishment.

Pavlovian Conditioning

The term conditioning refers to the process of introducing a habit into behaviour. Pavlovian conditioning describes a more manipulated form of this process by referring to Pavlov's experiment with a dog, food and bell. A dog was in a laboratory and every time a hand-bell was rung the dog was presented with food. After a short time whenever the bell was rung the dog would salivate in anticipation of eating food, even when no food was presented. This process exploits how the mind naturally uses association to prime adaptive behaviours.

Perception

To perceive means 'to grasp a meaning' or 'to comprehend'. To sense anything means that you have perceived that thing. Several senses about the same thing build a more accurate perception of what the thing is. Perception in addition to the sensing of something is also the meaning that is attributed to it. Everything that is sensed – subconsciously and consciously – in the outside world and deep within a person's body (viscerally[*]) can be used to inform a more detailed perception of what exists and is happening. A perception that is believed guides the biological responses and behaviour of the animal that holds the perception. Perception triggers emotions.

Pre-semantic

The term pre-semantic refers to the recall and cognition of memories and perceptions before any conscious meaning is recognised. Many aspects of the unconscious work at a pre-semantic level, and much of the information will not have any conscious meaning, but it can still affect conscious decisions. Even when there are conscious meanings associated with the information that's being handled pre-semantically, no conscious recognition exists until it's relayed to the conscious mind. In this way, the brain filters what perceptions are important for conscious recognition at any specific point in time. Thus perceptions that are deemed important press the conscious mind for recognition.

Projection

The term projection describes the process of feeling an underlying emotion or attitude that has been suppressed – usually through fear of owning[*] the experience – and then attributing that feeling onto someone else inappropriately. This happens because the emotion or attitude is experienced but disassociated with originating from one's self and then mistakenly attributed to another who somehow resembles the suppressed experience. This is predominantly an unconscious process of assuming another person believes or feels a certain way, because one is too scared of owning those beliefs or feelings.

Psychopathic/Sociopathic

The term psychopath and sociopath mean the same thing and are used interchangeably. Psychopaths usually have above average IQs and intellectual abilities, but they are internally disconnected from their emotions. Because they lack personal experience of emotions (such as sadness, despair, gladness and joy) they have a limited ability to sympathise and empathise with others. This results in psychopaths treating people in inhumane ways because they lack the instinctive understanding of what it must feel like to be in their victim's position. Emotions and feelings can seem illogical to psychopaths because they cannot account for them.

Somatic Markers

The term somatic markers describes the points (markers) in the body (soma) which are associated with memories. A part of any memory will have bodily information associated with it. For example, how much pain was being experienced when a specific memory was made and where that pain originated from. Implicit-memory* will record the position of the limbs when success is achieved or the feeling of the kidneys when a specific substance was drunk. Unknowingly to the conscious mind a record is maintained of the body's state relevant to ongoing events, visceral* implicit-memory. These memories are used by the subconscious to adapt the body's disposition to best suit anticipated events. This includes creating emotions, such as disgust, to bias judgement when one encounters something instinctively recalled as toxic.

Subjective

The word subjective means 'from a person's specific point of view'. A person's entire psychological architecture includes personal knowledge, skills, attitudes, opinions, interests and inclinations that give the individual a unique perspective – a subjective view.

Syndrome

A condition that is characterised by a set of associated symptoms.

Transference

The term transference refers to memories, typically of a person, from the past that are redirected onto an unrelated person in the present. For example, if people have strong feelings regarding a parent, and a mannerism of a person they just met reminds them of that parent, they may start transferring those strong feelings onto the unrelated person in the present. Thus people can have a strong feeling (e.g. love or hate) for a person because of a subconscious recognition of someone else.

Valence

Valence is a psychology term that refers to the inherent emotional attraction or aversion an object or event possesses. A situation that has a positive valence elicits a positive emotion. A situation that has a negative valence elicits a negative emotion. This relates to instinctive and learned dispositional reactions, which can be combined, and are ultimately created from subjective perceptions.

Visceral

The word visceral refers to deep inward feeling rather than to intellect. Medically it is used to describe bodily organs or the internal condition of the body as when referring to an incapacitating visceral pain. Nonetheless, it also refers to any deeply sensed experience and is used to emphasise unconsciously sensed information that affects feeling.

Weapon Focus

The term weapon focus refers to an effect on cognitive processing from terror while perceiving a violent event. In milliseconds, and usually without any conscious awareness of the shift, the unconscious forcefully redirects focus onto the source of the threat whilst excluding other information from being processed. Eye-tracking automatically and disproportionately shadows the intensity of perceived events. As a result of the shift in attention, memory of such a scene will be biassed towards the most intense objects within it. Memory immediately preceding and succeeding the apex of the scene's intensity will be less consistent, patchy or lost. The significance of processing peripheral information is virtually reduced to nothing, so as to decrease reaction time to a threat that's perceived as critically significant.

Notes

Admiration

1.   Charles Darwin, *The Expression of the Emotions in Man and Animals*, 1872.

Amazement

1.   Charles Darwin, *The Expression of the Emotions in Man and Animals*, 1872.

Amusement

1.   Charles Darwin, *The Expression of the Emotions in Man and Animals*, 1872.

Anger

1.   Jonathan Haidt, *Handbook of Affective Science*, Chapter 45: The moral emotions, page 856.

2.   Leonard Berkowitz, *Handbook of Affective Science*, Chapter 42: Affect, aggression and antisocial behaviour, page 818.

3.   Joseph P. Newman and Amanda R. Lorenz, *Handbook of Affective Science*, Chapter 49: Response modulation and emotional processing, page 923.

4.   Wilfred Janig, *Handbook of Affective Science*, Chapter 9: The autonomic nervous system and its coordination by the brain, page 171.

5.   Charles Darwin, *The Expression of the Emotions in Man and Animals*, 1872.

6.   Joseph P. Newman and Amanda R. Lorenz, *Handbook of Affective Science*, Chapter 49: Response modulation and emotional processing, page 923.

7.   Janine Giese-Davis and David Spiegel, *Handbook of Affective Science*, Chapter 56: Emotional expression and cancer progression, page 1075.

8.   J. Long, N. Long and S. Whitson, *The Angry Smile*, 2009.

9.   Phoebe C. Ellsworth and Klaus R. Scherer, *Handbook of Affective*

Science, Chapter 29: Appraisal processes in emotion, page 572.

10. Antonio Damasio, *Descartes' Error*, 1994, Chapters 2 and 3.

Anxiety

1. Susan Mineka, Eshkol Rafaeli and Iftah Yovel, *Handbook of Affective Science*, Chapter 52: Cognitive biases in emotional disorders, page 1000-1001.

2. Susan Mineka, Eshkol Rafaeli and Iftah Yovel, *Handbook of Affective Science*, Chapter 52: Cognitive biases in emotional disorders, page 999.

3. Douglas Derryberry and Marjorie A. Reed, *Handbook of Affective Science*, Chapter 35: Information processing approach to individual difference in emotional reactivity, page 692.

4. Arne Ohman and Stefan Wiens, *Handbook of Affective Science*, Chapter 13: On the automaticity of autonomic responses in emotion, page 261.

5. Joseph P. Forgas, *Handbook of Affective Science*, Chapter 30: Affective influences on attitudes and judgements, page 601.

6. Antonio Damasio, *Descartes' Error*, 1994.

7. Janine Giese-Davis and David Spiegel, *Handbook of Affective Science*, Chapter 56: Emotional expression and cancer progression, page 1093.

Arrogance

1. Joseph P. Newman and Amanda R. Lorenz, *Handbook of Affective Science*, Chapter 49: Response modulation and emotional processing, page 925.

2. Judy Dunn, *Handbook of Affective Science*, Chapter 18: Emotional development in early childhood, page 334-335.

3. Antonio Damasio, *Looking for Spinoza*, 2004.

Astonishment

1. Arne Ohman and Stefan Wiens, *Handbook of Affective Science*, Chapter 13: On the automaticity of autonomic responses in emotion, page 261.

2. Joseph P. Newman and Amanda R. Lorenz, *Handbook of Affective*

Science, Chapter 49: Response modulation and emotional processing, page 923.

3. Charles Darwin, *The Expression of the Emotions in Man and Animals*, 1872.

4. Laurie R. Santos and Venkat Lakshminarayanan, M. Keith Chen, *The Evolution of Decision-making Under Risk*, 2010.

Blushing

1. Alfons O. Hamm, Harald T. Schupp and Almut I. Weike, *Handbook of Affective Science*, Chapter 10: Motivational organisation of emotion, page 209

2. Arne Ohman and Stefan Wiens, *Handbook of Affective Science*, Chapter 13: On the automaticity of autonomic responses in emotion, page 258.

3. Wilfred Janig, *Handbook of Affective Science*, Chapter 9: The autonomic nervous system and its coordination by the brain, page 171.

4. Wilfred Janig, *Handbook of Affective Science*, Chapter 9: The autonomic nervous system and its coordination by the brain, page 169.

5. Charles Darwin, *The Expression of the Emotions in Man and Animals*, 1872.

Contempt

1. Charles Darwin, *The Expression of the Emotions in Man and Animals*, 1872.

Delight

1. Tim Dalgleish, *Handbook of Affective Science*, Chapter 33: Information processing approach to emotion, page 663.

2. Joseph P. Forgas, *Handbook of Affective Science*, Chapter 30: Affective influences on attitudes and judgements, page 604.

3. Joseph P. Forgas, *Handbook of Affective Science*, Chapter 30: Affective influences on attitudes and judgements, page 610.

4. Carol D. Ryff and Burton H. Singer, *Handbook of Affective Science*,

Chapter 57: The role of emotion on pathways to positive health, page 1093.

5.   Paul Rozin, *Handbook of Affective Science*, Chapter 44: Evolutionary and cultural perspectives of affect, page 843.

6.   Carol D. Ryff and Burton H. Singer, *Handbook of Affective Science*, Chapter 57: The role of emotion on pathways to positive health, page 1095.

7.   Carol D. Ryff and Burton H. Singer, *Handbook of Affective Science*, Chapter 57: The role of emotion on pathways to positive health, page 1098.

Despair

1.   Douglas Derryberry and Marjorie A. Reed, *Handbook of Affective Science*, Chapter 35: Information processing approach to individual difference in emotional reactivity, page 686.

2.   Charles Darwin, *The Expression of the Emotions in Man and Animals*, 1872.

3.   Joseph P. Forgas, *Handbook of Affective Science*, Chapter 30: Affective influences on attitudes and judgements, page 604.

4.   Antonio Damasio, *Descartes' Error*, 1994, page 120.

5.   Brenda Mallon, *Dying, Death and Grief*, 2008.

6.   Robert Karen, *Becoming Attached*, 1994.

7.   Susan Mineka, Eshkol Rafaeli and Iftah Yovel, *Handbook of Affective Science*, Chapter 52: Cognitive biases in emotional disorders, page 997.

8.   Bruce S. McEwen and Teresa Seeman, *Handbook of Affective Science*, Chapter 59: Stress and Effect: Applicability of the concept of allostasis and allostatic load, page 1129.

9.   Brenda Mallon, *Dying, Death and Grief*, 2008.

10. Susan Mineka, Eshkol Rafaeli and Iftah Yovel, *Handbook of Affective Science*, Chapter 52: Cognitive biases in emotional disorders, page 996.

Disappointment

1. Wilfred Janig, *Handbook of Affective Science*, Chapter 9: The autonomic nervous system and its coordination by the brain, page 169.

2. Joseph P. Forgas, *Handbook of Affective Science*, Chapter 30: Affective influences on attitudes and judgements, page 604.

Disgust

1. Charles Darwin, *The Expression of the Emotions in Man and Animals*, 1872.

2. Antonio Damasio, *Looking for Spinoza*, 2004.

3. Jonathan Haidt, *Handbook of Affective Science*, Chapter 45: The moral emotions, page 858.

Elation

1. Kevin N. Ochsner and Danil L. Schacter, *Handbook of Affective Science*, Chapter 32: Remembering emotional events: a social cognitive neuroscience approach, page 648.

2. Antonio R. Damasio and Ralph Adophs, H. Damasio, *Handbook of Affective Science*, Chapter 5: The contribution of the lesion method to the functional neuroatonomy of emotion, page 73.

3. Joseph P. Forgas, *Handbook of Affective Science*, Chapter 30: Affective influences on attitudes and judgements, page 604.

4. Joseph P. Forgas, *Handbook of Affective Science*, Chapter 30: Affective influences on attitudes and judgements, page 601.

5. Richard J. Davidson, Diego Pizzagalli, Jack B. Nitschke and Ned H. Kalin, *Handbook of Affective Science*, Chapter 2: Parsing the subcomponents of emotion and disorders of emotion: perspectives from affective neuroscience, page 15.

Empathy

1. Antonio Damasio, *Looking for Spinoza*, 2004.

2. George Loewenstein and Jennifer S. Lerner, *Handbook of Affective Science*, Chapter 31: The role of affect in decision making, page 628-629.

3. Kevin N. Ochsner and Danil L. Schacter, *Handbook of Affective Science*, Chapter 32: Remembering emotional events: a social cognitive neuroscience approach, page 648.

Evil

1. *Child of Rage: A Story of Abuse* (1990) directed by Gaby Monet [Documentary]. USA: HBO - America Undercover.

Fear

1. Charles Darwin, *The Expression of the Emotions in Man and Animals*, 1872.

2. Arne Ohman and Stefan Wiens, *Handbook of Affective Science*, Chapter 13: On the automaticity of autonomic responses in emotion, page 262.

3. Alfons O. Hamm, Harald T. Schupp and Almut I. Weike, *Handbook of Affective Science*, Chapter 10: Motivational organisation of emotion, page 203.

4. Arne Ohman and Stefan Wiens, *Handbook of Affective Science*, Chapter 13: On the automaticity of autonomic responses in emotion, page 258.

5. George Loewenstein and Jennifer S. Lerner, *Handbook of Affective Science*, Chapter 31: The role of affect in decision making, page 630.

6. George Loewenstein and Jennifer S. Lerner, *Handbook of Affective Science*, Chapter 31: The role of affect in decision making, page 633.

7. Arne Ohman and Stefan Wiens, *Handbook of Affective Science*, Chapter 13: On the automaticity of autonomic responses in emotion, page 270.

8. Antonio Damasio, *Descartes' Error*, 1994.

9. Antonio Damasio, *The Feeling of What Happens*, 2000.

10. Antonio Damasio, *Self Comes To Mind*, 2012.

11. Kevin N. Ochsner and Danil L. Schacter, *Handbook of Affective Science*, Chapter 32: Remembering emotional events: a social cognitive neuroscience approach, page 647.

12. Janine Giese-Davis and David Spiegel, *Handbook of Affective Science*,

Chapter 56: Emotional expression and cancer progression, page 1093.

13. Janine Giese-Davis and David Spiegel, *Handbook of Affective Science*, Chapter 56: Emotional expression and cancer progression, page 1073.

Ferocity

1. Wilfred Janig, *Handbook of Affective Science*, Chapter 9: The autonomic nervous system and its coordination by the brain, page 191.

Frustration

1. Bruce S. McEwen and Teresa Seeman, *Handbook of Affective Science*, Chapter 59: Stress and Effect: Applicability of the concept of allostasis and allostatic load, page 1120.

2. Antonio Damasio, *Descartes' Error*, 1994, page 120.

3. Leonard Berkowitz, *Handbook of Affective Science*, Chapter 42: Affect, aggression and antisocial behaviour, page 818.

4. Heinz W. Krohne, *Handbook of Affective Science*, Chapter 36: Individual differences in emotional reactions and coping, page 713.

Fury

1. Leonard Berkowitz, *Handbook of Affective Science*, Chapter 42: Affect, aggression and antisocial behaviour, page 818.

Gladness

1. Jonathan Haidt, *Handbook of Affective Science*, Chapter 45: The moral emotions, page 862.

2. Joseph P. Forgas, *Handbook of Affective Science*, Chapter 30: Affective influences on attitudes and judgements, page 602.

3. Joseph P. Forgas, *Handbook of Affective Science*, Chapter 30: Affective influences on attitudes and judgements, page 601.

4. Kent C. Berridge, *Handbook of Affective Science*, Chapter 3: Comparing the emotional brains of humans and other animals, page 31.

5. Carol D. Ryff and Burton H. Singer, *Handbook of Affective Science*, Chapter 57: The role of emotion on pathways to positive health, page 1095.

Gratitude

1. Joseph P. Forgas, *Handbook of Affective Science*, Chapter 30: Affective influences on attitudes and judgements, page 601.

2. Antonio Damasio, *Descartes' Error*, 1994, page 120.

3. Joseph P. Forgas, *Handbook of Affective Science*, Chapter 30: Affective influences on attitudes and judgements, page 604

4. Carol D. Ryff and Burton H. Singer, *Handbook of Affective Science*, Chapter 57: The role of emotion on pathways to positive health, page 1097.

Guilt

1. Antonio Damasio, *Descartes' Error*, 1994.

2. Robert Karen, *Becoming Attached*, 1994.

3. Judy Dunn, *Handbook of Affective Science*, Chapter 18: Emotional development in early childhood, page 334-335.

4. Nancy Eisenberg and Sandy Losoya, Tracy Spinrad, *Handbook of Affective Science*, Chapter 41: Affect and prosocial responding, page 792.

Helplessness

1. Tim Dalgleish, *Handbook of Affective Science*, Chapter 33: Information processing approach to emotion, page 689.

2. Susan Mineka, Eshkol Rafaeli and Iftah Yovel, *Handbook of Affective Science*, Chapter 52: Cognitive biases in emotional disorders, page 999.

Hope

1. Susan Mineka, Eshkol Rafaeli and Iftah Yovel, *Handbook of Affective Science*, Chapter 52: Cognitive biases in emotional disorders, page 990.

2. Joseph P. Forgas, *Handbook of Affective Science*, Chapter 30: Affective influences on attitudes and judgements, page 601.

3. Joseph P. Forgas, *Handbook of Affective Science*, Chapter 30: Affective influences on attitudes and judgements, page 611.

4. Joseph P. Forgas, *Handbook of Affective Science*, Chapter 30: Affective influences on attitudes and judgements, page 604

Horror

1. George Loewenstein and Jennifer S. Lerner, *Handbook of Affective Science*, Chapter 31: The role of affect in decision making, page 633.

2. Charles Darwin, *The Expression of the Emotions in Man and Animals*, 1872.

Humiliation

1. Leonard Berkowitz, *Handbook of Affective Science*, Chapter 42: Affect, aggression and antisocial behaviour, page 818.

Ignorance

1. Heinz W. Krohne, *Handbook of Affective Science*, Chapter 36: Individual differences in emotional reactions and coping, page 715.

2. Heinz W. Krohne, *Handbook of Affective Science*, Chapter 36: Individual differences in emotional reactions and coping, page 706-707.

3. Leonard Berkowitz, *Handbook of Affective Science*, Chapter 42: Affect, aggression and antisocial behaviour, page 817.

4. George Loewenstein and Jennifer S. Lerner, *Handbook of Affective Science*, Chapter 31: The role of affect in decision making, page 633.

5. Antonio Damasio, *The Feeling of What Happens*, 2000.

Jealousy

1. Jonathan Haidt, *Handbook of Affective Science*, Chapter 45: The moral emotions, page 853.

2. Antonio Damasio, *The Feeling of What Happens*, 2000.

Joy

1. Joseph P. Forgas, *Handbook of Affective Science*, Chapter 30: Affective influences on attitudes and judgements, page 604

2. Joseph P. Forgas, *Handbook of Affective Science*, Chapter 30: Affective influences on attitudes and judgements, page 601.

3. Jonathan Haidt, *Handbook of Affective Science*, Chapter 45: The moral emotions, page 862.

4. Joseph P. Forgas, *Handbook of Affective Science*, Chapter 30: Affective influences on attitudes and judgements, page 602.

5. John T. Cacioppo, *Handbook of Affective Science*, Chapter 55: Introduction: emotion and health, page 1050.

6. Antonio R. Damasio, Ralph Adophs and H. Damasio, *Handbook of Affective Science*, Chapter 5: The contribution of the lesion method to the functional neuroatonomy of emotion, page 73.

Malevolence

1. Jonathan Haidt, *Handbook of Affective Science*, Chapter 45: The moral emotions, page 853.

2. George Loewenstein and Jennifer S. Lerner, *Handbook of Affective Science*, Chapter 31: The role of affect in decision making, page 630.

3. Paul Rozin, *Handbook of Affective Science*, Chapter 44: Evolutionary and cultural perspectives on affect, page 843.

4. Joseph P. Newman and Amanda R. Lorenz, *Handbook of Affective Science*, Chapter 49: Response modulation and emotional processing, page 904.

5. Antonio Damasio, *Descartes' Error*, 1994, page 120.

6. Carol D. Ryff and Burton H. Singer, *Handbook of Affective Science*, Chapter 57: The role of emotion on pathways to positive health, page 1093.

Optimism

1. Voltaire, *Candide*, first published in 1759.

2. Joseph P. Forgas, *Handbook of Affective Science*, Chapter 30: Affective influences on attitudes and judgements, page 611.

3. Susan Mineka, Eshkol Rafaeli and Iftah Yovel, *Handbook of Affective Science*, Chapter 52: Cognitive biases in emotional disorders, page 999.

4. Heinz W. Krohne, *Handbook of Affective Science*, Chapter 36: Individual differences in emotional reactions and coping, page 715.

5. Robert Karen, *Becoming Attached*, 1994.

6. Heinz W. Krohne, *Handbook of Affective Science*, Chapter 36: Individual differences in emotional reactions and coping, page 706-707.

7. Carol D. Ryff and Burton H. Singer, *Handbook of Affective Science*,

Chapter 57: The role of emotion on pathways to positive health, page 1098.

8. Carol D. Ryff and Burton H. Singer, *Handbook of Affective Science*, Chapter 57: The role of emotion on pathways to positive health, page 1095.

Rage

1. Leonard Berkowitz, *Handbook of Affective Science*, Chapter 42: Affect, aggression and antisocial behaviour, page 817.

2. Douglas Derryberry and Marjorie A. Reed, *Handbook of Affective Science*, Chapter 35: Information processing approach to individual difference in emotional reactivity, page 692.

3. George Loewenstein and Jennifer S. Lerner, *Handbook of Affective Science*, Chapter 31: The role of affect in decision making, page 633.

4. Wilfred Janig, *Handbook of Affective Science*, Chapter 9: The autonomic nervous system and its coordination by the brain, page 171.

5. Antonio Damasio, *Descartes' Error*, 1994, page 120.

6. Wilfred Janig, *Handbook of Affective Science*, Chapter 9: The autonomic nervous system and its coordination by the brain, page 170.

7. Leonard Berkowitz, *Handbook of Affective Science*, Chapter 42: Affect, aggression and antisocial behaviour, page 818.

Regret

1. Joseph P. Forgas, *Handbook of Affective Science*, Chapter 30: Affective influences on attitudes and judgements, page 601.

2. Susan Mineka, Eshkol Rafaeli and Iftah Yovel, *Handbook of Affective Science*, Chapter 52: Cognitive biases in emotional disorders, page 999.

3. Susan Mineka, Eshkol Rafaeli and Iftah Yovel, *Handbook of Affective Science*, Chapter 52: Cognitive biases in emotional disorders, page 1001.

Relief

1. Arne Ohman and Stefan Wiens, *Handbook of Affective Science*, Chapter 13: On the automaticity of autonomic responses in emotion, page 262.

2. Joseph P. Newman and Amanda R. Lorenz, *Handbook of Affective Science*, Chapter 49: Response modulation and emotional processing, page 923.

3. George Loewenstein and Jennifer S. Lerner, *Handbook of Affective Science*, Chapter 31: The role of affect in decision making, page 633.

4. Paul Rozin, *Handbook of Affective Science*, Chapter 44: Evolutionary and cultural perspectives of affect, page 843.

5. Richard J. Davidson, Diego Pizzagalli, Jack B. Nitschke and Ned H. Kalin, *Handbook of Affective Science*, Chapter 2: Parsing the subcomponents of emotion and disorders of emotion: perspectives from affective neuroscience, page 18.

6. George Loewenstein and Jennifer S. Lerner, *Handbook of Affective Science*, Chapter 31: The role of affect in decision making, page 630.

7. Joseph P. Forgas, *Handbook of Affective Science*, Chapter 30: Affective influences on attitudes and judgements, page 601.

8. Antonio R. Damasio, Ralph Adophs and H. Damasio, *Handbook of Affective Science*, Chapter 5: The contribution of the lesion method to the functional neuroatonomy of emotion, page 73.

Remorse

1. Leonard Berkowitz, *Handbook of Affective Science*, Chapter 42: Affect, aggression and antisocial behaviour, page 817.

Resentment

1. Leonard Berkowitz, *Handbook of Affective Science*, Chapter 42: Affect, aggression and antisocial behaviour, page 817.

2. Leonard Berkowitz, *Handbook of Affective Science*, Chapter 42: Affect, aggression and antisocial behaviour, page 818.

3. Leonard Berkowitz, *Handbook of Affective Science*, Chapter 42: Affect, aggression and antisocial behaviour, page 818.

4. Joseph P. Forgas, *Handbook of Affective Science*, Chapter 30: Affective influences on attitudes and judgements, page 601.

5. Tim Dalgleish, *Handbook of Affective Science*, Chapter 33: Information processing approach to emotion, page 663.

6. Gary G. Berntson, John T. Cacioppo and Martin Sarter, *Handbook of Affective Science*, Chapter 58: Bottom-Up: Implications for neurobehavioural models of anxiety and autonomic regulation.

7. Tim Dalgleish, *Handbook of Affective Science*, Chapter 33: Information processing approach to emotion, page 663.

8. Joseph P. Newman and Amanda R. Lorenz, *Handbook of Affective Science*, Chapter 49: Response modulation and emotional processing, page 904.

9. Antonio Damasio, *Descartes' Error*, 1994, page 120.

10. Wilfred Janig, *Handbook of Affective Science*, Chapter 9: The autonomic nervous system and its coordination by the brain, page 167-169.

11. Wilfred Janig, *Handbook of Affective Science*, Chapter 9: The autonomic nervous system and its coordination by the brain, page 167-169.

12. Bruce S. McEwen and Teresa Seeman, *Handbook of Affective Science*, Chapter 59: Stress and Effect: Applicability of the concept of allostasis and allostatic load, page 1118.

13. Bruce S. McEwen and Teresa Seeman, *Handbook of Affective Science*, Chapter 59: Stress and Effect: Applicability of the concept of allostasis and allostatic load, page 1120.

14. George Loewenstein and Jennifer S. Lerner, *Handbook of Affective Science*, Chapter 31: The role of affect in decision making, page 628.

15. J. Long, N. Long and S. Whitson, *The Angry Smile*, 2009.

Sadness

1. Susan Mineka, Eshkol Rafaeli and Iftah Yovel, *Handbook of Affective Science*, Chapter 52: Cognitive biases in emotional disorders, page 999.

2. Susan Mineka, Eshkol Rafaeli and Iftah Yovel, *Handbook of Affective Science*, Chapter 52: Cognitive biases in emotional disorders, page 1001.

3. Joseph P. Forgas, *Handbook of Affective Science*, Chapter 30: Affective influences on attitudes and judgements, page 601.

4. Douglas Derryberry and Marjorie A. Reed, *Handbook of Affective Science*, Chapter 35: Information processing approach to individual difference in emotional reactivity, page 692.

5. Tim Dalgleish, *Handbook of Affective Science*, Chapter 33: Information processing approach to emotion, page 663.

6. Antonio Damasio, *Descartes' Error*, 1994.

7. Dacher Keltner, Paul Ekman, Gian C. Gonzaga and Jennifer Beer, *Handbook of Affective Science*, Chapter 22: Facial expression of emotion, page 424.

8. Dacher Keltner, Paul Ekman, Gian C. Gonzaga and Jennifer Beer, *Handbook of Affective Science*, Chapter 22: Facial expression of emotion, page 425.

9. Charles T. Snowdon, *Handbook of Affective Science*, Chapter 24: Expression of emotion in non-human animals, page 465.

10. Antonio Damasio, *Looking for Spinoza*, 2004, page 66-70.

11. Antonio Damasio, *The Feeling of What Happens*, 2000.

12. Wilfred Janig, *Handbook of Affective Science*, Chapter 9: The autonomic nervous system and its coordination by the brain, page 167-169.

13. Antonio Damasio, *Descartes' Error*, 1994, page 120.

Satisfaction

1. Joseph P. Forgas, *Handbook of Affective Science*, Chapter 30: Affective influences on attitudes and judgements, page 601.

2. Antonio R. Damasio, Ralph Adophs and H. Damasio, *Handbook of Affective Science*, Chapter 5: The contribution of the lesion method to the functional neuroatonomy of emotion, page 73.

3. Antonio Damasio, *Self Comes To Mind*, 2012.

Shame

1. Dacher Keltner, Paul Ekman, Gian C. Gonzaga and Jennifer Beer, *Handbook of Affective Science*, Chapter 22: Facial expression of emotion, page 424.

2. Dacher Keltner, Paul Ekman, Gian C. Gonzaga and Jennifer Beer, *Handbook of Affective Science*, Chapter 22: Facial expression of emotion, page 425.

3. Antonio Damasio, *Descartes' Error*, 1994.

Shock

1. George Loewenstein and Jennifer S. Lerner, *Handbook of Affective Science*, Chapter 31: The role of affect in decision making, page 630.

2. Douglas Derryberry and Marjorie A. Reed, *Handbook of Affective Science*, Chapter 35: Information processing approach to individual difference in emotional reactivity, page 686.

Spite

1. J. Long, N. Long and S. Whitson, *The Angry Smile*, 2009.

2. Wilfred Janig, *Handbook of Affective Science*, Chapter 9: The autonomic nervous system and its coordination by the brain, page 169.

3. Janine Giese-Davis and David Spiegel, *Handbook of Affective Science*, Chapter 56: Emotional expression and cancer progression, page 1093.

Stress

1. Bruce S. McEwen and Teresa Seeman, *Handbook of Affective Science*, Chapter 59: Stress and Effect: Applicability of the concept of allostasis and allostatic load, page 1118.

2. Wilfred Janig, *Handbook of Affective Science*, Chapter 9: The autonomic nervous system and its coordination by the brain, page 171.

3. Antonio Damasio, *Descartes' Error*, 1994, page 120.

4. Kent C. Berridge, *Handbook of Affective Science*, Chapter 3: Comparing the emotional brains of humans and other animals, page 31.

5. Jonathan Haidt, *Handbook of Affective Science*, Chapter 45: The moral emotions, page 862.

6. Richard J. Davidson, Diego Pizzagalli, Jack B. Nitschke and Ned H. Kalin, *Handbook of Affective Science*, Chapter 2: Parsing the subcomponents of emotion and disorders of emotion: perspectives from affective neuroscience, page 15-16.

7. Joseph P. Forgas, *Handbook of Affective Science*, Chapter 30: Affective influences on attitudes and judgements, page 601.

8. Carol D. Ryff and Burton H. Singer, *Handbook of Affective Science*, Chapter 57: The role of emotion on pathways to positive health, page 1095.

9. Edwina Kidd, *Essentials of Dental Caries*, 2005 third edition.

10. Edwina Kidd, *Essentials of Dental Caries*, 2005 third edition.

11. Edwina Kidd, *Essentials of Dental Caries*, 2005 third edition.

12. Edwina Kidd, *Essentials of Dental Caries*, 2005 third edition.

13. Robert Karen, *Becoming Attached*, 1994.

14. Carol D. Ryff and Burton H. Singer, *Handbook of Affective Science*, Chapter 57: The role of emotion on pathways to positive health, page 1098.

15. Heinz W. Krohne, *Handbook of Affective Science*, Chapter 36: Individual differences in emotional reactions and coping, page 706-707.

16. Janine Giese-Davis and David Spiegel, *Handbook of Affective Science*, Chapter 56: Emotional expression and cancer progression, page 1070.

17. Janine Giese-Davis and David Spiegel, *Handbook of Affective Science*, Chapter 56: Emotional expression and cancer progression, page 1073.

18. Bruce S. McEwen and Teresa Seeman, *Handbook of Affective Science*, Chapter 59: Stress and Effect: Applicability of the concept of allostasis and allostatic load, page 1124.

19. Carol D. Ryff and Burton H. Singer, *Handbook of Affective Science*, Chapter 57: The role of emotion on pathways to positive health, page 1087.

20. Janine Giese-Davis and David Spiegel, *Handbook of Affective Science*, Chapter 56: Emotional expression and cancer progression, page 1075.

21. Carol D. Ryff and Burton H. Singer, *Handbook of Affective Science*, Chapter 57: The role of emotion on pathways to positive health, page 1097.

22. Janine Giese-Davis and David Spiegel, *Handbook of Affective Science*, Chapter 56: Emotional expression and cancer progression, page 1074.

23. Carol D. Ryff and Burton H. Singer, *Handbook of Affective Science*, Chapter 57: The role of emotion on pathways to positive health, page 1097.

24. Carol D. Ryff and Burton H. Singer, *Handbook of Affective Science*, Chapter 57: The role of emotion on pathways to positive health, page 1093.

Surprise

1. Alfons O. Hamm, Harald T. Schupp and Almut I. Weike, *Handbook of Affective Science*, Chapter 10: Motivational organisation of emotion, page 199.

Sympathy

1. Dacher Keltner, Paul Ekman, Gian C. Gonzaga and Jennifer Beer, *Handbook of Affective Science*, Chapter 22: Facial expression of emotion, page 424.

2. Dacher Keltner, Paul Ekman, Gian C. Gonzaga and Jennifer Beer, *Handbook of Affective Science*, Chapter 22: Facial expression of emotion, page 425.

3. Charles T. Snowdon, *Handbook of Affective Science*, Chapter 24: Expression of emotion in non-human animals, page 465.

4. George Loewenstein and Jennifer S. Lerner, *Handbook of Affective Science*, Chapter 31: The role of affect in decision making, page 633.

Terror

1. Charles Darwin, *The Expression of the Emotions in Man and Animals*, 1872.

2. Richard J. Davidson, Diego Pizzagalli, Jack B. Nitschke and Ned

H. Kalin, *Handbook of Affective Science*, Chapter 2: Parsing the subcomponents of emotion and disorders of emotion: perspectives from affective neuroscience, page 15-16.

3. Bruce S. McEwen and Teresa Seeman, *Handbook of Affective Science*, Chapter 59: Stress and Effect: Applicability of the concept of allostasis and allostatic load, page 1118.

4. Kevin N. Ochsner and Danil L. Schacter, *Handbook of Affective Science*, Chapter 32: Remembering emotional events: a social cognitive neuroscience approach, page 649.

5. George Loewenstein and Jennifer S. Lerner, *Handbook of Affective Science*, Chapter 31: The role of affect in decision making, page 630.

6. George Loewenstein and Jennifer S. Lerner, *Handbook of Affective Science*, Chapter 31: The role of affect in decision making, page 633.

7. Kevin N. Ochsner and Danil L. Schacter, *Handbook of Affective Science*, Chapter 32: Remembering emotional events: a social cognitive neuroscience approach, page 647.

Trust

1. George Loewenstein and Jennifer S. Lerner, *Handbook of Affective Science*, Chapter 31: The role of affect in decision making, page 633.